D0266252

yt

Books of Related Interest

THE PHILOSOPHY OF UTOPIA
Editor: Barbara Goodwin, University of East Anglia

HUMAN RIGHTS AND GLOBAL DIVERSITY
Editors: Simon Caney and Peter Jones, University of Newcastle

FOUCAULT
Editor: Robert Nola, University of Auckland

PLURALISM AND LIBERAL NEUTRALITY
Editors: Richard Bellamy, Reading University and Martin Hollis, University of
East Anglia

FEMINISM, IDENTITY AND DIFFERENCE
Editor: Susan Hekman, University of Texas at Arlington

THE CHALLENGE TO FRIENDSHIP IN MODERNITY
Editors: Preston King, Lancaster University and Heather Devere, Auckland
Institute of Technology

THINKING PAST A PROBLEM
Preston King, Lancaster University

Associative Democracy:
The *Real* Third Way

Editors

PAUL HIRST and
VEIT BADER

CHESTER COLLEGE

ACC No. 01124114   DEPT

CLASS No. 321.8 HIR

LIBRARY

IS 21329

FRANK CASS
LONDON • PORTLAND, OR

First published in 2001 in Great Britain by
FRANK CASS PUBLISHERS
Crown House, 47 Chase Side, London N14 5BP

and in the United States of America by
FRANK CASS PUBLISHERS
c/o ISBS, 5824 N.E. Hassalo Street
Portland, Oregon 97213-3644

Website www.frankcass.com

Copyright © 2001 Frank Cass & Co. Ltd.

British Library Cataloguing in Publication Data

Associative democracy : the real third way
   1.Democracy 2.Associations, institutions, etc.
   I.Hirst, Paul Q. (Paul Quentin), 1946– II.Bader,
   Veit-Michael
   321.8

ISBN 0 7146 5171 0 (cloth)

Library of Congress Cataloging-in-Publication Data:

Associative democracy : the real third way / editors, Paul Hirst and
Veit Bader.
    p. cm.
   Includes bibliographical references and index.
   ISBN 0-7146-5171-0 (cloth)
   1.Democracy 2.Associations, institutions, etc. I. Hirst, Paul
Q. II. Bader, Veit-Michael.
   JC423 .A8174 2001
   321.8–dc21

2001002465

This group of studies first appeared in a special issue on
'Associative Democracy: The *Real* Third Way' of *Critical Review of International Social
and Political Philosophy* 4/1 (Spring 2001), ISSN 1369-8320
published by Frank Cass and Co. Ltd.

*All rights reserved. No part of this publication may be reproduced, stored in or
introduced into a retrieval system, or transmitted, in any form or by any means, electronic,
mechanical, photocopying, recording or otherwise, without the prior written permission
of the publisher of this book.*

Printed in Great Britain by Antony Rowe Ltd., Chippenham, Wiltshire

Contents

1

Introduction

VEIT BADER

Associative democracy is a political theory, the core proposition of which is that as many social activities as possible should be devolved to self-governing voluntary associations. It has an intellectual pedigree stretching back to the mid-nineteenth century, but it has recently been revived in a new form. Associationalism might be described as the original 'Third Way' between free-market individualism and centralised state control. Associationalists argue that *laissez-faire* leaves large areas of social life ungoverned. Most citizens cannot fully realise their goals by acting as isolated individuals, but only by banding together with those who share their objectives. On the other hand, centralised state control not only restricts individual liberty, but also relies on the premise that the state can effectively sum the differing goals and preferences in society into a single scheme of collective provision. State socialism was only a special and exaggerated case of such centralised control. Despite the collapse of state socialism, states continue to organise large areas of social life, to spend a high proportion of national income, and to offer standardised 'one size fits all' public services.

Associationalists argue that there are different versions of the good life in society and that different contents and styles of provision of public services go along with them. Services should be public and publicly funded, open to all, but non-state. Associations should be free to compete with one another for members for the services they provide, and members would bring public funds with them according to a common per capita formula. Thus, far from there being one welfare state, there would be as many as citizens wish to organise, catering for the different values of individuals, but based on common entitlements. Such organisations would be democratically self-governing. Some might be highly participatory, others minimalist, but all would have the basic right to elect the governing council and members periodically would have the option to exit if dissatisfied.

In such a system, associations, rather than the state or corporations, would control most welfare provision and a good deal of economic activity. The state and the market would both continue to exist, but they would be paralleled by an associative system of governance. Thus, the state and the market would be limited to the roles that they can most effectively perform, and where they were subject to democratic control and consumer sovereignty. Authority would be as decentralised and pluralised as possible, but with a core state to ensure public peace and the rule of law.

Associative democracy has developed once again as a new paradigm in political theory during the past two decades. This has been primarily as an answer to the collapse of the two intellectual and political traditions dominating the left during the twentieth century: first, Marxism-Leninism and the collapse of 'actually existing' state socialism; second, statist social democracy and the decline of Keynesian welfarism. As a *theoretical* strand it promises to present better, that is, more morally satisfying and more fitting and feasible, solutions to urgent problems of contemporary societies compared with its main rivals in recent political theory (section I). Its radical, democratic, institutionalist experimentalism promises to open new avenues of *political* change compared with the recently dominant, alternative policy paradigms: the different varieties of neo-liberalism and the timid 'Third Ways' of modern social democracy (section II). In its early years, associative democracy showed a distinctively Anglo-Saxon bias, unfortunately neglecting important theoretical traditions and practical experiments of associationalism in Continental Europe, particularly those of Austro-Marxism and of the widespread cooperative movement. The chapters in this volume try to address some of its theoretical problems and they make a start in correcting this Anglo-bias by drawing on the rich associational experiences of other countries such as the Netherlands and Denmark (section III).

I

Recent state-societies, under the condition of regime competition in a globalising arena, have been confronted with a number of well-known, but quite intractable, *structural problems*. How can poverty and deeply entrenched structural inequalities both globally and inside state-societies be fought? How can ecological disasters, wars and civil wars, ethnic cleansings and genocide be prevented? How can we respond in a morally defensible way to increasing migration pressures and to the incorporation of heterogeneous migrants into existing state-societies? How can the levelling down of welfare and social policies under the condition of regime competition be resisted successfully? How can we respond to the challenges of cultural diversity without losing minimally required political unity, trust and solidarity? How can we deal with the fact that government and state bureaucracies increasingly lack both effectiveness and democratic accountability?

The claim that the existing *institutional and policy repertoire* available to address these problems shows serious deficiencies is not much contested. The main reasons for this distressing fact are equally well known: a serious mismatch between increasingly global problems and an inadequate and undemocratic institutional structure at the supra-state level; the complete incapacity and unwillingness of weak peripheral states combined with the unwillingness and, increasingly, the lack of capability and power of strong states; and a serious lack of economic and social governance capabilities of governments relying on a limited set of mechanisms of political governance. Much more contested is our claim that *predominant political theories and policy paradigms* are unable to present morally legitimate and feasible ways out of these conundrums. In this introduction, for the sake of simplicity, we focus on the main theoretical bottlenecks, indicating only in passing which paradigms in political theory are particularly beset with them. We also reduce the complexity of existing paradigms and refer only to (neo-)liberalism, republicanism and civil society theories.

The main *theoretical bottlenecks*, in our view, are as follows.

1. The competing philosophies of political liberalism, republicanism, communitarianism, and civil society theories show a *lack of institutional concreteness* and are thus unable to inspire an institutionally saturated, imaginative political theory.

2. Most political philosophies and most predominant political theories have not really taken into account that we, increasingly, live in *multilevel polities*. Federalism has had some impact on liberalism and republicanism on the sub-state level, but on the supra-state level, both traditions show a lack of imagination, sticking to no-longer defensible notions of state sovereignty. On the sub-state level, liberalism and republicanism are characterised

by a one-sided *unitary institutional bias*, particularly when it comes to the integration of representatives of social and cultural groups in processes of decision-making and implementation. If multilevel polities are discussed at all, then it is mainly as threats and dangers (blurred competencies, joint-decision traps, lowest common denominator policies and so on), not as interesting and promising prospects. If group representation and institutionalised forms of social and cultural pluralism are discussed at all, they are mainly seen as threats to social, political and cultural unity, solidarity and trust, not as promises for the development of a culturally diverse and more even-handed democratic polity.

3. All predominant paradigms paint seriously flawed and *simplistic pictures of recent societies* governed by the state, or *the* market, or 'civil society'. In a descriptive perspective, they are unable to capture the fact that all recent societies are complex mixes of different mechanisms of coordination (state and organisational hierarchies, markets, associations and networks) and, in a normative perspective, they rely too much upon simplistic, exclusive recipes: neo-liberalism on privatisation and the market; republicanism on state hierarchy (democratic government); and communitarianism and civil society on associations.

4. In their focus on government both liberalism and republicanism fail to take into account that the *governance capabilities of governments* are seriously *threatened* by two developments: by the erosion of legal sovereignty and, more importantly, the increasing limitation of actual governance powers on the one hand; and, on the other hand, by the fact that state bureaucracies in modern societies (facing turbulent environments, new forms of flexibility, individualisation and cultural diversity) increasingly lack the required information, skills and relevant local knowledge for successful standard setting, implementation and control of policies. They expect too much from government and administration. Civil society theories, by contrast, expect too much from freely contracting and consenting associations and networks.

5. In their focus on political governance and political democracy, liberalism and republicanism *neglect the role and importance of economic governance and social governance*. Neo-liberal privatisation strategies have led to a serious re-entrenchment of democratically uncontested private economic power (capital and

management) and they have seriously diminished the possibilities of economic governance by political actors (municipalities, regions, states and supra-state institutions). Neo-republicans have recognised that serious economic and social inequalities pose inherent threats to political democracy, but they have failed to develop institutions of economic democracy and economic citizenship, of democratic corporate governance and so on.

6. The implicit (liberalism) or explicit (republicanism) unitary institutional bias, combined with the *ideology of the 'neutral' or 'difference-blind' state*, has effectively blocked the development of egalitarian institutions and policies which do not neglect, but recognise, differences of gender, ethnic and religious culture and are favourable to explicitly multicultural policies of incorporation of immigrants. Communitarianism (explicitly) as well as liberalism and republicanism (implicitly) have defended thick notions of national political cultures and 'communities' incompatible with a minimally fair politics of first admission in our age of (forced) migration.

II

In general, the predominant political theories are 'out of tune' with the reality of functionally and culturally differentiated state-societies in a global context: their pictures of society just do not fit and their political recommendations do not bite. They seem to become more and more a 'footloose' politics of symbolic action contributing to the prevalent negative view of politics as making no difference whatsoever. *Associative democracy* opens new perspectives of thinking and acting. Associative democracy is the most recent variety of a broader strand of institutional pluralism. Compared with earlier traditions of institutional pluralism it is explicitly liberal and democratic. Associative democracy should be clearly distinguished from feudal pluralism, pluralism of estates, the Ottoman Millets system, colonial and post-colonial 'plural societies', and fascist and catholic corporatism.

Associative democracy is critically linked to different theoretical strands of institutional pluralism in the nineteenth and twentieth centuries such as the German Historical School (see Gierke, Kern and partly Max Weber), French institutionalism in law and sociology (Duguit, Hauriou and Durkheim), and English pluralism (Maine, Maitland, Figgis, Cole and Laski) as well as drawing on contemporary theories of federalism and consociational democracy, critical legal pluralism and critical legal studies. Its main advantage compared with competing political philosophies and theories, however, lies in its links with recent bodies of social scientific research, for example, sociological studies of new forms of corporatism, the new political economy of different types of capitalism, flexible specialisation and other attempts to reconceptualise and reorganise work and organisations, and studies of corporate governance, negotiated governance and multilevel polities in the sociology of administration and in political science.

This intellectual background may help explain why associative democracy has better conceptual and theoretical tools in three respects. First, *conceptually*, it criticises simplistic, unitary, homogenous and static notions of the state, sovereignty, nationality, citizenship, culture, political identity and commitment, replacing them with more flexible, dynamic concepts including many layers and levels. Second, it is much richer in a *historical and comparative perspective*. Third, in a *normative perspective*, its critical concepts in combination with its knowledge of broad institutional variety form a better basis for a complex and informed practical evaluation of existing institutions as well as for the design of alternatives.

Associative democracy, in our view, is thus better equipped to tackle the urgent structural problems mentioned above.

1. It shifts the balance *from* the exclusive focus on moral and legal *principles* toward the broad historical and comparative variety of economic, social, political and legal *institutions* compatible with the principles of the democratic and social constitutional state. It ties in with the recent revival of institutionalism in the social sciences, criticising the false necessities of modernisation theories and deep structuralism. It stresses the institutional diversity, historical contingency and path dependency of developments and the precarious stability of nested structures. It opens up new ways of learning from best practices. It bridges the gap between evaluating existing institutional settings and designing new ones. This shift from principles to institutions and practices is a characteristic feature in all the contributions to this volume.

2. It not only criticises the unitary institutional bias of liberalism and republicanism, but it explicitly tries to design democratic multilevel polities on infra- and supra-state levels. This is particularly dealt with in the contributions by Hirst, Engelen, Hoekema and Bader.

3. It not only criticises the simplistic catch-all (one-formula-fits-all) recipes of neo-liberalism (privatise and deregulate), republicanism (strengthen democratic government) and civil society (let associations do the job), it also tries to design alternative arrangements of markets, hierarchies, networks and associations which flexibly take into account the different requirements of the huge diversity of goods and services in the different societal fields. No one formula fits all, but nor does anything go either. Hirst, Bader, Achterberg and Engelen try to elaborate different aspects of an intelligent mix of mechanisms of coordination in their contributions.

4. It tries to develop alternative forms of state, private-public and private administration and governance, which promises to tackle the overload, inefficiency and lack of democratic accountability of government by democratic decentralisation, by making space for a huge variety of voluntary associations in the provision of all kinds of services, by clearly distinguishing between the provision of services and their regulation, control and scrutiny, and, thus, by restricting the state to its essential core functions, making it both thinner and stronger (see Bader, Achterberg, Hirst and Hoekema).

5. It not only criticises the 'myth of globalisation', 'negative' or disembedded 'market integration' in the EU and the re-entrenchment of private hierarchies, it also tries to develop democratic models of local, regional, national and supranational economic governance together with models of democratic and efficient corporate governance (see particularly the contributions by Hirst and Engelen).

6. It not only criticises difference-blind conceptions and practices of state neutrality and restrictive versions of purely political pluralism, it also designs alternatives for the institutional integration of religious, ethnic and national minorities which respond more productively to the many tensions and policy dilemmas of really incorporating cultural diversity (see particularly the contributions by Hoekema and Bader).

III

These huge gains should stimulate more serious attention for associative democracy than it has hitherto received. This volume is motivated by the hope of stimulating just such a wider critical reception. Associative democracy offers many advantages compared with its main rivals, but it also has to solve serious theoretical problems and, obviously, serious practical political dilemmas. It cannot offer simple recipes and is not meant to present a panacea. It is clearly a work in progress. The chapters in this volume contribute in various ways to the development of associative democracy.

Paul Hirst argues that the comeback of associationalism provides the 'only political doctrine well adapted to cope with the problems of ensuring democratic accountability' in a culturally diverse, individualised, post-liberal society. Associative democracy provides alternatives to the predominant institutional mix of 'representative democracy and the free market' that better realise their own intrinsic claims of performance and democratic legitimacy under the changed conditions of 'organisational society'. He restates the reforms associative democracy would inspire in welfare and social insurance, in health and education, and in private corporate governance in order to demonstrate that associative democracy 'could restore the key features of a liberal system within the constraints of an organisational society', thus challenging 'political apathy and intense dissatisfaction' in recent western societies. 'In this sense, associationalism is a political supplement to liberalism ... It should not be presented as an alternative society – states, market and organisations will remain. It is certainly not a panacea: associative governance does not eliminate all social problems or conflicts.' The following chapters discuss some of the theoretical and practical problems 'intrinsic to this scheme of governance'.

Veit Bader tries to reopen the lively debate of the early 1990s about Cohen and Rogers' variety of associative democracy, pointing out that most controversial issues have not been adequately addressed by Cohen and Rogers themselves nor by other advocates of associative democracy. Associative democracy can be defended against generalised moral challenges that it undermines the sovereignty of the people, that the system of organised interest representation is undemocratic, that it is weak on political equality and even weaker on distributive equality, and that it would be prone to the mischief of faction. Such a defence requires fair evaluation, instead of the widespread comparison of ideal models with actual muddle. It should, however, not make advocates of associative democracy self-confident and blind toward largely unresolved theoretical and practical problems, the many difficult trade-offs and the difficult arts of balancing and designing institutions and policies. This perhaps is even truer regarding the many prudential and realist objections. To work out realist utopias for different countries or societal fields is still the major challenge confronting political theorists.

Piotr Perczynski discusses the relationship between associative democracy and deliberative democracy, which has recently gained more currency in post-Rawlsian political philosophy in the Anglo-Saxon countries. He claims that associative democracy is a 'system' or a 'structure' without a predefined 'democratic mechanism' or a 'procedure' of decision-making and confronts it with deliberative democracy understood as a democratic mechanism without a structure. He then tries to combine the 'two different parts of democracy', stating that such an 'associo-deliberative democracy' creates better opportunities for a wide range of qualitative participation.

Wouter Achterberg also discusses the interrelationship between associative democracy and deliberative democracy, though in a more substantive way by focusing on the ecological problematic in 'advanced capitalist countries' or 'late modern societies'. So far Hirst, as with many other defenders of associative democracy, has not said much about environmental concerns. Summarising earlier articles, Achterberg states that associative democracy can contribute to sustainable development by contributing to a higher level of social cooperation, to a more effective social embeddedness of the market, and to a more equal distribution of income. Its weak spots, however, have to do with a too heavy emphasis on the production side of the process, neglecting or underemphasising sustainable patterns of consumption and lifestyles that come with the extent of qualitative democratisation brought by associative reform (in which regard deliberative democracy may provide assistance), and with the conceptualisation of advanced societies, which, according to Achterberg, can be better grasped as late-capitalist or late-modern societies (in which regard Ulrich Beck's analysis of risk society, an increasingly popular idea among sociologists and political theorists, may provide assistance). The practical importance of deliberative democracy relates to the ways in which risk communication is organised and practised. Beck points, in an empirical perspective, to what he calls 'subpolitics', that is, politics outside the formal political institutions and channels of parliamentary democracy. In a normative perspective, he suggests an 'ecological extension' of democracy. Both proposals, however, remain rather hazy and practically meagre and could benefit a lot from the conceptions of deliberative and associative democracy. It seems urgent and 'prudentially and morally unavoidable to extend and enhance democracy beyond the level reached in present-day liberal democracies. Associative and deliberative reforms show the desired direction of fit. But associative democracy without deliberative content is blind, and deliberative democracy without embodiment in associative and other institutions soars like a powerless spirit above the turbulent waters of present-day risk society.'

Against the background of these more general discussions concerning whether associative democracy better fits developments in recent societies, the next chapters zoom in on more specific issues and countries. Lars Bo Kaspersen and Laila Ottesen try to correct the Anglo-Saxon bias of associative democracy a bit by showing that associationalism as a model of governance has been developed and implemented as a political practice in Denmark for more than 100 years, going back to the development of voluntary associations such as the 'Farm Household Society' from 1769 and many smaller associations and clubs, to religious movements and associations opposing the established 'national' church in the early nineteenth century. This led on to the development of Grundtvigism and its influence on free schools and folk high schools, and to the associationalism of small local banks and credit unions, cooperative stores, sick-benefit associations, and the cooperative movement in the agricultural sector. Focusing on primary and secondary education, they try to show that many associative principles outlined by Hirst can easily be detected in the Danish school model. The same is shown for associationalism in the social and cultural field. Kaspersen and Ottesen state that this associational tradition of the Danish 'model', which is far more social liberal and more decentralised than the other social-democratic and centralist Scandinavian welfare states, helps to explain why the Danish welfare state proved to be fairly adaptable under recent pressures and has not run into a severe legitimacy crisis.

Ewald Engelen also deals with recent pressures upon Keynesian welfare states in his analysis of multilevel governance in the European Union comparing (in a practical institution-designing perspective) the approaches of Paul Hirst and Grahame Thompson, Wolfgang Streeck and Fritz Scharpf. Engelen argues that criticising the 'myth of globalisation' by demonstrating that the lack of political governance is a result of politics and by showing that different states react differently to similar pressures is enough for criticising false necessities and thus making space for political projects of institutional change, but it is not enough to answer questions such as 'how to do that' or 'what the right political conditions' would be. Resort to political will and 'optimism' is rather powerless against institutional logics. Institutional logics, however, are more indeterminate than 'pessimistic' sociologists seem to assume. In the case of the European Works Council, Wolfgang Streeck has shown that a logic of convergence at the lowest common denominator has been at work, but he seems unduly to generalise such 'negative' integration effects, such 'market making' instead of 'market correcting' measures. Fritz Scharpf, by extending his analysis of joint-decision traps from the level of German federalism to the European Union, at first seemed to reinforce such a determinist structuralism. In his later studies, however, drawing on detailed criticisms by Arthur Benz, who has demonstrated that the European multilevel governance system (adding more levels, more actors and less clear hierarchies) creates opportunities to avoid joint-decision traps or the race to the bottom. 'Loose coupling' systems of coordination show many advantages compared with 'hierarchical coupling', and drawing on empirical studies by Vogel that demonstrate 'trading up' or a 'California effect' in the EU, Scharpf breaks through this supposed deterministic logic. Still, the logic and the different possibilities of multilevel governance systems are very much under-researched, but we know enough to criticise both voluntarism and determinism. Politics, indeed, matter, and the chances of market-correcting measures depend upon the specificities of goods and services, the number and kind of actors involved, their preferred strategies and the design of the system of coordination.

André Hoekema discusses empirical tendencies toward a more plural organisation of the state and more interactive and reflexive forms of governance in two widely divergent fields of research: reflexive institutions of governance, that is, those public-private inter-organisational networks that are less hierarchical, more flexible and less exclusively interest oriented than neo-corporatist institutions of governance in highly developed countries; and newly emerging multicultural institutions of state and law that are developing in order to incorporate immigrant groups, national minorities and indigenous peoples. Reflexive governance emerges particularly in cases of intractable policy controversies, when the issues at hand as well as problem definitions are highly contested and reflection of fairly incompatible frames of interpretation is required. Research in the Netherlands shows that these new networks thrive on communication, not hierarchy, market or community, and that they tend to produce fragile, but nevertheless remarkable, forms of trust as reciprocity. Protagonists slowly come to see each other's position, seeing and redefining their own interests and testing proposals that ask for sacrifices from all parties involved. Hoekema suggests that such a common morality of cooperation might be the cornerstone of any scheme of associative democracy. He highlights the fact that one of the most important conditions for working out effective solutions to intricate problems is sufficient autonomy for all participants involved in order to prevent corporatist closure and to give more consideration for the interests of unrepresented weak parties. His main worry is not that reflexive governance would be too slow or produce only weak compromises, but how to make or keep it accountable (rule of law) and democratically legitimate. A minimal requirement, according to Hoekema, is the need to keep formal structures transparent and accountable (the 'shadow of hierarchy').

The pluralisation of state and law as a response to the incorporation of distinct communities through forms of self-rule is discussed in the following cases. The Ethiopian Constitution of 1991 established an indirect consociationalism giving not only special legal protection for the use and development of specific languages, religions, social customs and cultures without explicitly specifying and naming these ethno-cultural communities, but also the recognition of distinct political and legal institutions, that is, broader powers of legislation, adjudication, administration and taxation to the nine regions or states. The difficult task of organising the peaceful coexistence of distinct communities, while at the same time nurturing a common plane of shared values and shared political and legal institutions, requires 'associative institutions of common governance, allowing for regional pluralism' in general and official legal pluralism in particular. Hoekema summarises two types of case that demonstrate the clash of rights and of frames of interpretation. The problem of how to reconcile collective with individual autonomy without generally sacrificing one set of principles and world-views for the other has been acutely felt by the Colombian Constitutional Court in cases of freedom of religion (proselytising by Protestant sects such as the New Tribes in native territories in Latin America) or complaints about torture. Simplistic formulas such as an automatic prevalence of 'the Constitution' or of human rights on the one hand, or of automatic immunity for cultural practices that violate these rights on the other hand, would effectively block the development of an intercultural dialogue. The James Bay and Northern Quebec Agreement as an example of co-management of natural resources shows that often the task of reflecting deeply different cognitive frames seems to be nearly a mission impossible given the unquestioned predominance of western styles of scientific knowledge and its methods. The prospects may be bleak given the huge asymmetries of power and the danger of tokenism (often the reforms have only a very restricted scope and force). 'Nevertheless, as an observer of recent trends in state renewal on many continents one cannot help being struck by the massive upsurge of "multicultural constitutionalism". Yes, it is professed on constitutional paper only, but to some extent it pervades political and social life too.'

Veit Bader also starts from the assumption that democratic institutional pluralism in general and associative democracy in particular provide the best chances for morally legitimate and realist incorporation of religious, ethnic and national minorities. Associative democracy, indeed, is 'not utopian at all', but 'can build on formidable trends already well under way', as Hoekema suggests. In order to achieve better, more elaborate answers to the many dilemmas confronting incorporation policies, Bader focuses on the following questions. Is the thin public morality of associative democracy strong enough to stimulate the loyalty and commitment needed for political projects aiming at fairly radical societal and political transformations? Conversely, is it thin enough in a radically culturally diverse setting? How does Hirst answer the intrinsic problem of all varieties of meaningful institutional pluralism: individual autonomy versus collective autonomy? How does the voluntariness of associations, so much stressed by Hirst, relate to ethno-national communities of fate? Is the fact that Hirst's version of associative democracy is comparatively 'weak on equality' not particularly disturbing in the case of ethno-national underclasses? Is his hope that the fragmenting tendencies of associationalism could be met by his design plausible? Which institutions and policies follow from the general outline of associative democracy for the incorporation of minorities in the case of education? A lot of work has to be done in answering these questions in a more convincing way, combining both theoretical clarification of policy dilemmas and comparative studies of different cases of pluralist incorporation.

Associative democracy remains a promising agenda for democratic reform and for the revitalisation of existing institutions. It claims that greater democracy and institutional efficiency are closely connected. Unlike most modern normative political theories, associationalism is closely tied to specific institutional changes and thus to the empirical question of whether they work or not. It thus has to be alert to concrete problems and to pay heed to research on institutional performance and outcomes. In this respect, it needs to build bridges to the new institutionalism in the social sciences. Associative principles cannot be divorced from the specific social and institutional contexts in which they are implemented, and need to address particular problems of institutional design in each specific case. Hence the theory is committed to an open research agenda and to rigorous questioning of the impact of its application in particular cases. The intense questioning of associationalist principles and institutional designs in this special issue should not be seen as negative or as a source of weakness in the basic ideas, but as a condition of continued progress.

2

Can Associationalism Come Back?

PAUL HIRST

In the early twentieth century, associationalism was a fashionable and increasingly popular political doctrine. In combination with the theory of the pluralist state, it proposed a radical, but non-authoritarian, redistribution of economic and political power. Indeed, it claimed to be a third way between free-market capitalism and state socialism. It was presented as such by Bertrand Russell in his widely read political primer of alternative doctrines, *Roads to Freedom*.[1] Yet, in the 1920s, it was rapidly and almost completely eclipsed. It certainly suffered from the political mistakes of some of its advocates, such as the Guild Socialists, who thought they could achieve major changes by action in civil society while bypassing the state. However, a doctrine that relied on the pluralisation and decentralisation of political power, on governance through civil society, and on the cooperation of labour and management could hardly prosper in a period of bitter national and class conflicts, the concentration of central state power and the dominance of large-scale, hierarchically organised mass production.

In the 1980s, associationalism began to come back as a political theory, albeit with a rather different political content and theoretical form. The main negative factors that had inhibited its appeal had begun to lose their force. Fordist standardised mass production was in decline as new and more flexible methods of production were introduced to cope with a more volatile economy and rapidly changing patterns of demand. Large scale, highly centralised firms were no longer the necessary form of industrial efficiency (Piore & Sabel 1984). Bigness was no longer undergirded by economies of scale in production. After the turbulence of the 1960s and 1970s, class conflict and class politics declined precipitously throughout the industrial world. The cold war thawed in the mid-1980s and then ended with the collapse of Soviet socialism. This reduced the military necessity for highly centralised state power.

Rodney Barker (1999) has recently questioned whether political pluralism, a central part of the associationalist doctrine, is a revenant or recessive trend, that is, whether it will be a sustained and genuine political renewal or a brittle intellectual revival. The question has merit, for the removal of the negative factors that killed off associationalism in the 1920s will not of itself make the doctrine relevant again. Surely, on the contrary, the new conjuncture that began in the late 1980s ensures the success not of associationalism, but of representative democracy and the free market. Is not the whole world endeavouring to adopt these institutions? The picture is very different if we look not at eastern Europe or Latin America, but at the advanced countries that have long had these institutions. We then notice something quite different: in politics, a mixture of political apathy and intense dissatisfaction with the performance of existing democratic institutions; in the economy, a mixture of growing affluence and growing inequality in many of the larger advanced industrial countries. Rising GDP is coupled with growing insecurity and uncertainty.

Existing political and economic institutions are fragile both in their performance and in their legitimation. They can no longer derive automatic support from the repeating of the cold-war claim, 'What else? Soviet-style dictatorship? The shortages of the command economy?' Now, there is no such 'else'. Hence, western institutions have to be measured against their own intrinsic claims. Does representative democracy currently deliver genuine accountability of government to the people? Is economic performance in market economies sustaining broad-based prosperity? Are the major corporations answerable to their key stakeholders and do they consistently act in the consumers' interests? To each of these questions the answer is 'manifestly not'. Thus the widespread feeling of dissatisfaction, but without a coherent alternative to mobilise and shape it. Part of the reason why there is no conception of an alternative is because the dominant perception across the political spectrum is that we live in a liberal society, that is, a social system with a limited government answerable through representative institutions and with a self-regulating civil society based on market competition and social cooperation by individuals and the companies and associations freely formed by them.

In fact, we live in a post-liberal society, that is, one where government is extensive and its scope not clearly defined and where society is not effectively self-regulating (Hirst 1997: Chs. 1&6). Post-liberalism means something quite different from the oft-feared threat to liberalism of a totalitarian state. The issue is not that a single, dictatorially led mass party controls the state and utilises the state to control society. Rather, the issue is that the architecture of a classic liberal society has been superseded by another. This is a social system in which the division of public and private spheres and the forms of accountability particular to each sphere have been gravely compromised. Governance is not clearly limited because its scope is difficult to determine. It is no longer confined to a clearly demarcated public sphere. In fact, both representative democracy and the free market are serious misdescriptions of our prevailing institutions. It is not that they do not exist, but that they function quite differently from how they are supposed to and in a context quite different from the one for which they were devised. Representative democratic institutions were devised for the supervision of small-scale government in a self-regulating society. The free market supposes strong competition and ease of entry, a world of relatively small firms each without substantial market or social power.

This is not the world that we face. We live in an organisational society in which large agglomerations of top-down power control the activities on both sides of the public-private divide. Big government and big business are, of course, not new. However, in the mid-twentieth century such institutions remained compatible with democratic political control. Big business organised standardised mass production. Big government strove to stabilise the macro-economic environment and to protect citizens against the vicissitudes of a market economy. Large companies acted in predictable ways that were relatively easy to regulate. They entered into a symbiotic relationship with government as 'national champions'. Mass welfare services were also standardised and were relatively easy to deliver by branches of local and central government under hierarchical control. Fordist mass society was dominated by big organisations in both the public and private sectors, but the way they operated made it possible for them to be controlled from the top by elected politicians and, therefore, for there to be a degree of accountability to the citizens. Bureaucracy and representative government could be combined. Corporations managed markets and governments regulated corporations, ensuring a combination of competition and managerial activity that outperformed command economies. Indeed, the mixture clearly performed better with large-scale operations than *laissez-faire* could have done.

Three major changes that have gained momentum since the end of the 1960s have made modern societies harder to govern in top-down ways. The first major change that undermined the bureaucratic, corporate and representative democratic mix was the changing nature of companies and government agencies. We still live in an organisational society, but the way organisations are structured and behave has changed. This makes top-down control more difficult. Most major firms in both manufacturing and services are involved in diversified, complex and rapidly changing activities that cannot be planned and predictably controlled in a bureaucratic manner. Top managements struggle to retain strategic control, but they can only respond to demand and to competitive pressures if they devolve a large part of decision-making to subsidiaries, to more junior managers and to frontline workers. Firms also increasingly enter into strategic alliances with other firms and join looser multi-firm networks. Both of these strategies are an attempt to stabilise the firm's environment, but they also have the effects of blurring its boundaries and cutting across its internal patterns of authority.

The public sector has also changed radically. States can make fewer credible promises to firms and workers because they are perceived to have less independent control over the macro-economic environment. Hence they find it harder to govern symbiotically. The result of the decline of centralised corporatism and of macro-economic activism has not been a diminution in the scale and scope of the state's activities. Instead, there has been a switch to legal and administrative regulation as governments attempt to cope with a wider range of market externalities. States seek to protect citizens against potential harms from big business by means of rules and norms. States have also privatised, ditching extensive portfolios of state-owned enterprises that were responses to business failure or attempts to control natural monopolies. Privatisation has seldom led to the abandonment of regulation, rather, once firms leave the public sector, they are subject to new and often more intense regulatory regimes. Within the remaining state sector public administration has been transformed, with hived-off agencies being run on commercial lines.

The result of these dual processes of privatisation and commercialisation is to blur the line between the public and the private sectors. Many privatised firms retain public powers, such as the utilities, and agencies are subject to commercial practice and disciplines. The result is that the clear divide between the two spheres, crucial to the architecture of a classical liberal society, has been undermined. On both sides of the public-private divide the citizen finds large commercially oriented organisations that operate in essentially similar ways and that are not subject to effective democratic control. What we are confronted with is a realm of *de facto* private governments, whether formally state or corporate, that are weakly accountable to the public in general and to their own stakeholders in particular.

Welfare services too have become complex and more difficult to deliver in a standardised way that can be subjected to central control. Public spending has not fallen. Indeed, throughout the advanced world it has risen above the levels of public expenditure to GDP of the 1960s. Citizens now demand far higher standards of environmental protection and extended public services. The health, education and welfare sectors have all grown and diversified. Medicine has become increasingly complex, higher education has expanded greatly and the care of the aged has become a major industry. These new services have been added to basic welfare services such as unemployment benefits or elementary education.

The outcome is a social system, public and private, too complex for effective democratic control by conventional elected governments. The external environment is too volatile and internal procedures too complex for either big government or big business to control what happens simply by top politicians and managers setting overall policy and receiving evidence of its implementation filtered up through the chain of command. The dominant responses by managers and politicians to this problem of control merely tend to make matters worse. Everywhere we see attempts to reassert hierarchical control. This seems to be possible because of the potential of information technology. However, this merely sharpens the old bureaucratic dilemma in a new guise. Central control can only be had if subordinate units conform to a detailed script of guidelines and rules designed to make their operations predictable and reportable in standardised forms. This generally fails on two counts. First, such control can only be won at the price of responsiveness and flexibility, the very assets needed to deliver complex activities in a changing environment. Second, such rules are usually sufficiently complex and contradictory that they cannot all be obeyed. This gives subordinates new forms of discretion and thus leads to unpredictability.

Another equally problematic response consists in attempts to simplify administration by contracting out services. Such practices, far from deregulating, usually lead to elaborate contractual specifications and the proliferation of norms governing service delivery. In the state sector, such practices merely switch the delivery of services from one organisation to another or lead to the legal relabelling of the organisation. Such contracted-out services, because they are no longer part of the public sphere, require formal legal control and detailed regulation rather than administrative supervision. Contingencies therefore have to be formally specified rather than dealt with by administrative action as they arise.

The result of the various attempts to respond to the problem of loss of control is the proliferation of laws and rules. Far from achieving greater certainty, conformity to norms and central control, the result is to weaken the rule of law. Rules become so complex that they cease to be guides to action, their role can only be interpreted *post hoc* by specialist lawyers. They interact and conflict in complex and unpredictable ways. Such complex rules often impose contradictory demands on those to whom they are addressed. Hence, they lead to discretion on the part of rule followers, not hierarchical control, and uncertainty as to which rule applies. The result is not to restore accountability, but to create a regime in which litigation proliferates and in which those who are penalised for rule infractions or acts of discretion that higher authority dislikes come to see law and rules as arbitrary and capricious.

The second major change that has undermined the delivery of standardised services is the growing pluralism of modern society. This has several sources. Value changes have led to new communities, such as the public acceptance of gay people for example. New religions and cults have proliferated. Most advanced countries have admitted substantial numbers of foreign workers and members of ethnic minority communities. The result is that most major western cities are now culturally heterogeneous. There are limits to this, of course. Most citizens accept representative democracy, the market and the rule of law as core values. They also want good public services. The problem is that they have different ideas as to what the content of those services should be and often different conceptions of the role of public authority in their provision.

The third major change is the extension of individuation. Widespread higher and universal secondary education, greater disposable incomes, and the relaxation of public and religious moral controls have led to a radical divergence of lifestyles. More people have the time, the cultural skills, the money and the personal freedom to choose to live how they wish. This was previously a privilege confined to the upper echelons of the middle class. Individuation has not merely reinforced value pluralism, it has also led to a new consumer consciousness in a large part of the public in relation to public services. The 'old' welfare services (elementary education, pensions and social insurance, basic medical care and workers' housing) were generally gratefully received when they were first introduced. Their target was a mass manual working class whose lives had previously been subject to great insecurity. Most recipients of mass welfare accepted what the public service bureaucracies gave them and were not troubled by the 'one size fits all' provision available. Since the 1960s, the scope and complexity of public services has changed greatly and so too has the public receiving them. Citizens now want services adapted to their specific needs and interests. They want providers willing to respond to their desire to craft packages of services suited to their circumstances and who will consult them. All of these expectations are incompatible with standardised services delivered by a uniform top-down bureaucratic administration.

Associative democracy is the only political doctrine well adapted to cope with the problems of ensuring democratic accountability in a culturally diverse organisational society. Traditional social democracy has fared badly both in defining new programmes of welfare-state reform and in devising new strategies for economic regulation. Indeed, social democratic parties have tended to retreat before the pressure to defend existing entitlements by citizens, the tax aversion of key social constituencies and pressure from business opinion for welfare cuts and deregulation. Even a moderniser such as Anthony Giddens, who argues in *The Third Way* (1998) that traditional bureaucratic social democracy needs renewal in response to the major social changes of recent decades, fails either to recognise or to tackle the problem of the organisational society. He emphasises changes leading to individuation and social fluidity, but ignores the prevailing social institutions. He argues that a central value in modern societies is that there should be no authority without democracy. Yet that is just what the organisational society is: government bureaucracies and corporate power beyond effective accountability to citizens. Existing political structures do not ensure this accountability, and so formally representative institutions are hollowed out by the unchecked autonomy of the very organisations that they are supposed to supervise.

The result is that either politicians lack the means to oversee organisations, caught in the contradictory roles of being responsible for providing services and of rendering providers to account, or they give up that conception of political accountability in favour of a managerial definition, that is, redefining their role as ensuring efficiency and controlling cost. Election in the latter case merely becomes a route to managerial authority, rather like being appointed to a board of directors. No wonder that such managerial politicians are indifferent to wider issues of organisational power. They see themselves as members of a common elite with business managers and leading public-sector bureaucrats. The assumption of managerialist politicians is that the public are consumers who want the greatest quantity of services at the lowest cost and are indifferent to how the job is done.

That, of course, is far from being the case. The public wants many contradictory things at once and is divided into many sub-publics with very different values and expectations. Increasingly, citizens seem to be politically apathetic. Party membership and voting participation have fallen substantially in many western democracies. Electorates tend less and less to identify strongly with a particular political party. Yet citizens do have strong expectations about public services and they expect to be protected from an ever-wider range of contingencies. They also have little intrinsic loyalty toward private corporations – they see their leaders as entirely self-interested. At the same time, the public demands high standards from business. The public thus gives little endorsement either to politicians and political parties or to corporate capitalism. This means that particular politicians and companies are very vulnerable to a dramatic withdrawal of support. Examples are the electoral punishment of the British and Canadian conservatives or the campaigns against Shell over the Brent Spa oil platform or Monsanto over GM foods.

The public is not indifferent: it will punish those who flagrantly violate its core values. At the same time, it lacks a coherent alternative as to how to remedy current institutions and thus opinion is evanescent and volatile. The hitherto dominant alternative, state socialism, has only recently been comprehensively discredited and its radical forms were never popular with more than a small minority. Few perceive the organisational society to be the source of our political problems. Associative democracy is thus an answer to a political question that most people have not asked. This necessarily limits its current appeal, but not its potential as a doctrine to organise reform. It provides a political model that can unite diverse concerns with the democratic performance of contemporary institutions and that can link up and, therefore, reinforce the effectiveness of many specific reform efforts and social experiments. It has the advantage, in a post-collectivist era, that it does not require a single social agent or 'carrier'. The doctrine can be adopted by different social groups with otherwise diverse objectives.

This also means that different groups can utilise the doctrine in different ways at the level of the particular organisation. Some will create highly participative small-scale organisations. Others will create an organisation adapted to the large scale and adapted to the needs of the lazy. In that case, limited participation will be available through formal representative structures and effective control will be centred on the right of members to choose between organisations and to exit if dissatisfied. The principles and practices of associative democracy have another advantage. Unlike many doctrines which demand a 'big bang' social change, they can be put into operation piecemeal and iteratively, providing an open-ended agenda for reform.

However, the political success of associative democracy does depend on a wider perception that the organisational society is a political problem, that hierarchical power subject to too little accountability and democratic sanction tends to produce bad decisions and is incompatible with core social values. The dominant values are strongly in favour of both individual choice and the consultation of affected publics. Hierarchical power tends directly to undermine democratic mores. It produces unaccountable elites who treat the public as something to be managed. Social mores may not favour economic redistribution to produce greater equality, but they do favour equality of manners. They are thus incompatible with the notion that elites know best. Hence, it should be possible to demonstrate that democratic modernisation can be furthered by associational self-governance.

To do this requires a dual strategy: on the one hand, concentrating politically on specific issues where associational reforms would make an immediate improvement and, on the other hand, showing theoretically how the principle is applicable to the widest range of objectives and social sectors. The obvious place to start campaigning for reforms is welfare and social insurance, both public and private. Here there are obvious dissatisfactions with bureaucratic state welfare, but also with equity and value for money in private provision. The aim of associative reform in the welfare state is to devolve public services to democratically self-governing voluntary organisations that compete for members and that receive public funds to provide services proportional to their membership. These funds would be available only for the provision of specified services according to a common capitation formula. Associations would only receive such funds if they were open to everyone, including those who only had public formula funding. Associationalism seeks to bridge the public-private divide in welfare, giving everybody the chance to choose suitable public service providers and to craft a package of services appropriate to their needs.

This combination of public funding and individual choice would tend to counter the tax aversion now well established in the UK and USA, but spreading to many other advanced countries. It enables all citizens to benefit from collective consumption, but encourages the better off to stay with common services. If they wish, the well-to-do are able to top up with their own money to pay for extended services above the publicly financed minimum. This would not eliminate inequality as such, but it would discourage the division of services into a state sector, which mainly the poor use, and a private sector. Because taxpayers then see the state sector as a pure deduction from their income, they seek the lowest possible taxation to pay for it and thus ensure exclusionary welfare for the poor.

Associative welfare is not simply another form of privatisation of public services. In fact, it transforms the public-private divide, installing democratic governance and effective individual choice on both sides. It thus does what markets and existing state institutions have failed to do. If anything, it is more of a 'publicisation' of the private sector. In the case of social insurance and pensions provision, a merger of the state and private systems would be beneficial. A few large mutual providers would dominate provision; they would be sufficiently numerous to ensure competition, but all would be large enough to pool risks and obliged by law to offer a minimum level of provision. Periodic transfers between them would be possible. Thus the considerable differences between contributors' rights and returns that characterise the present system of private provision would be reduced. Citizens would be protected against personal contingencies, such as sickness and old age, but without the added risks of extremely poor performance that characterise current private schemes. Undoubtedly, this scheme would eliminate a few super-performing funds, but the price of that lucky minority currently is the substantial number of providers that seriously underperform. Most citizens would top up their basic public entitlements, putting their own money into the schemes, and thus avoiding moral hazard on their part. Managers would be constrained to perform by the threat of defection by contributors and supervised to make prudent investments sufficient to meet minimum levels of provision by the state. Such a system would combine most of the best features of the current public and private systems.

Many countries are facing a crisis in pensions and social insurance. Countries such as Italy face a crisis in the public system in the next 20 years because there will be too few adults to meet the generous entitlements conceded by previous governments – pensions being paid from current employees' contributions. Britain faces a dual crisis: appalling basic state pensions that condemn those dependent upon them to poverty and the failure of many private schemes to provide adequate annuities. This is on top of the scandal of the misselling of privatised pensions to supplant the state scheme. Associative principles provide a way to rethink this crucial sector in a way that would meet many current objectives of reform.

In health and education, many consumers of public services would like to have more choice: both the option of quitting poorly performing providers and having the clout of bringing formula funds with them, and the possibility of using their voice to build services they really believe in. All would have greater control, but some would have the option of building real alternatives to the dominant style of provision. Such alternatives would have the effect of introducing further competition into the system, not just between providers of services for members, but between providers in the type of service offered. Such alternatives are necessary to reinvigorate public provision. At present real alternatives are available only to those with private money and in the UK, for example, the central state is trying to micro-manage the type of provision available in hospitals and schools. Without alternatives there can be neither genuine competition nor real evolution of services. Associative democracy would promote diversity and social learning. To those who claim that the result will be greater inequality in provision, I reply that the central state's attempts to enforce uniformity have so far not eliminated it and they continue to reproduce the root cause of inequality, which is disempowerment. The difference inherent in diverse provision should not be seen as inequality, but as a source of creativity and choice.

In time, it may prove possible to extend the concept of self-governing voluntarism to the private corporate sector. The aim would be to internalise affected interests within the governance structure of the company, through ownership rights and an institutionalised voice. The aim is to minimise externalities through the political mechanisms of the company, rather than through external state regulation and legal action. In associationalist doctrine, the dominant organisational form of the company would be mutual, with various interests represented, such as consumers, employees and local communities where the company has a significant presence, depending on the circumstances. Ownership rights would be primarily political: the company would be non-profit, would not pay dividends and ownership rights would not normally be traded, except to other stakeholders. Ownership and control would be closely linked. Companies would issue bonds, rather than shares, to raise capital. The shareholders would be the stakeholders, but the supervisory board would represent different interests, thus limiting cosiness and cronyism. Where possible an associationalist policy would encourage the deconcentration and decentralisation of companies, promoting medium-sized firms that can be effectively governed by democratic means. Alternatives to the large scale would be pursued, such as networks and inter-firm services. Many examples currently exist that enable firms of modest size to operate on a large scale, such as the Visa network, and e-commerce will make this even more of a possibility.

Many of the current pressures toward concentration are driven neither by production nor product markets, but by the capital market. The present hegemonic Anglo-Saxon model of the company is based on shareholder value as the primary objective of economic activity (Froud et al. 2000). The typical company has highly dispersed shareholdings and indifferent shareholders; the shareholders are primarily financial institutions that hold diversified portfolios and regularly trade the shares they hold on the markets. The company is controlled by a professional management, who are disciplined to perform not by an active shareholder voice, but by the stockmarket (Roe 1994). Shareholders typically make little use of their governance rights, while all other affected interests are excluded. The present structure devalues voice, giving it to those who do not use it. Shareholders are typically uninvolved in the firm and can sell quickly. Other affected interests have no easy exit option through the market, for example, communities affected by pollution or workers faced with mass unemployment in the case of a plant closure. The combination of ownership through involvement and political control by the owners of the management would make companies publicly answerable institutions rather than unaccountable private governments as at present.

The case in favour of mutual ownership in democratic theory is clear. The economic advantages of the present stockmarket-driven system are by no means overwhelming. Currently, however, the prospects for reform seem fanciful. In the UK, it is mutual financial institutions that are under threat as free riders seek to appropriate assets built up over a long period. The cooperative movement is inefficient and backward compared to conventional commercial firms. Citizens are still fearful of tampering with property rights, seeing this as socialism. Associationalism is quite different since it aims to disperse control, not concentrate it in the hands of the state or of a single interest such as the workers or the providers of capital. Changing governance rights would not expropriate current holders of capital: they would still hold marketable financial assets with a yield, but they would be bonds not shares. The modern company is a relatively recent creation and the rights and powers of corporate property were granted by legislation. Untrammelled managerial capitalism has high costs for society, and managements have little intrinsic legitimacy with the public. Arguing for radical reform in corporate governance will be a long haul. It may have to await the aftermath of a major stockmarket crash that delegitimates Anglo-Saxon institutions and their elites with the public. Without radical reform of the way companies are run our societies will remain very imperfect democracies. It makes little sense to give a high value to the right to vote if in doing so one has no influence over the means of earning one's livelihood. The exclusion of economic affairs from the direct scope of representative government made sense at a time when civil society was deemed to be largely self-regulating; it makes no sense in the era of large private governments that control much of social life (Dahl 1985; the Political Quarterly 69/4 1998).

The effect of the devolution of control over welfare services to their consumers, equipped with the powers both of voice and of exit, and of rendering the currently private governments of companies to those whom their decisions affect would be to bring the organisational society under democratic control. This control would be dispersed in the various organisations and exercised by those to whom the activities of those organisations were relevant. Citizens would gain the option to control the sources of policy in a complex society, where currently the detailed control of a mass of large organisations is no longer effective. This change would have a triple effect. First, it would limit the exercise of managerial power and establish the principle of no impact without representation. This would force managers to consult and thus to make decisions based on communication with those most directly affected. Second, it would oblige and enable politicians, state officials and managers to abandon attempts to reassert hierarchical control over complex and changing activities and services. As we have seen this process is self-defeating. It can only be successful if it makes the practice of the organisation conform to a rigid centrally determined script and thus lose the advantages of flexibility and choice. Third, local democratic control would reduce the tendency to rule proliferation. This attempt to compensate for undemocratic authority in organisations by subjecting organisations' procedures and outcomes to an ever-increasingly elaborate system of legal norms and regulatory rules is also self-defeating. As we have seen the sheer volume of rules and norms creates sources of uncertainty in and of itself. Of course, associational governance could not eliminate all rule proliferation. There are other sources, new contingencies, such as a heightened priority for environmental protection, and the fact that a highly individuated population has higher expectations of security and a higher consciousness of its rights. The tendency to rule proliferation is accelerated by the fact that there are no alternative voice- and exit-based methods for the prevention and relief of harms and because the power to manage, unrestrained, leads to an excessive degree of control from above, which relies on laying down rules of conduct for subordinates.

Associationalism is a political model that can be used to reform governance in an organisational society and to make it more compatible with the values and interests of a culturally diverse and individuated citizenry. A consequence of such democracy in and through associations would be that both representative democracy and the market could be made to function more effectively. Representative institutions could thus oversee a government that was more limited in scale and scope. The functions of government would be limited to setting overall policy and to supervising a now largely self-governing society of voluntary organisations. The market would be supplemented by the organisational voice options of consumers, communities and employees. Political power would thus deal with a large range of what otherwise would be market externalities within the governance procedures of the firm. Large companies would be more tolerable as actors in the wider society since they would be subject to the influence of involved citizens. They would thus have greater legitimacy in trying to influence public policy since they would be more like other associations; at present such influence is resented because it is exercised by managerial oligarchies. In this sense, associationalism could restore the key features of a liberal system within the constraints of an organisational society, that is, limited government and the dispersion of power in a self-regulating civil society.

In this sense, associationalism is a political supplement to liberalism, one that saves the central liberal institutions of representative democracy and the market from being undermined by the power of big organisations. It should not be presented as an alternative society – states, markets and organisations will remain. It is certainly not a panacea: associative governance does not eliminate all social problems or conflicts. Indeed, it will create problems and conflicts peculiar to itself. Firms that are internally democratic have more legitimacy if a large number of employees and consumers support a policy that the firm advocates to government, yet this does not stop them being self-interested. Associations may use the option of self-governance to withdraw from the wider community and seek to control their members through the services that they provide. This may well be the case with some religious and ethnic minority groups. An associationalist system will not in and of itself eliminate poverty or social exclusion. A society of self-governing associations not only creates scope for the success and failure of individuals, but also of the associations in which they are involved. Public power will remain to cope with the worst of such problems and abuses. Associationalism supplements, but does not replace, the liberal state. However, one must admit that such problems are intrinsic to a system that gives great scope for dispersed democratic control and local initiative.

I make no effort to hide the existence of problems intrinsic to this scheme of governance. Indeed, no scheme of governance is conceivable that does not create certain conflicts and problems by the very methods by which it operates. Many of the issues that critics raise are genuine problems, but most of them would exist in any decentralised society, associationalist or not. Positing a wise all-powerful state is hardly the answer to those problems either, since such an entity does not exist. I have frequently tried to address such problems and criticisms, trying to show how they could be overcome or why they do not vitiate the overall scheme of reform (Hirst 1994; 1996; 1999). In the end, the problem with responding in this way is that one does not deal with the true source of many of the criticisms, which is an ideal of good government, universal provision and equal conditions (Hirst 1996 on criticisms by Morgan and Stears). This ideal is at the core of traditional social democracy. It implies a level of social homogeneity and a degree of social standardisation and stability that is no longer available to us. We need to renew social democracy, but we must try to achieve the aims of extensive welfare suited to peoples' needs and a regulated market economy in a new social context. How does one govern a society divided into large organisations that are struggling to cope with complex activities and volatile conditions? The critics have to show not merely that there are difficulties with associationalism, but that another method of reforming governance is available and that it is sufficiently democratic.

NOTES

1.   Since its first publication by Allen and Unwin, London, in 1918, *Roads to Freedom* has been frequently reprinted, and is currently published by Routledge.

REFERENCES

Barker, R. 1999. 'Pluralism, revenant or recessive?' Hayward et al. 1999: 117–45.
Dahl, R.A. 1985. *A Preface to Economic Democracy*. Cambridge: Polity Press.
Froud, J., C. Haslam, J. Sukhder & K. Williams, eds. 2000. *Shareholder Value and the Political Economy of Late Capitalism*. *Economy and Society*, special issue, 29/1.
Giddens, A. 1998. *The Third Way*. Cambridge: Polity Press.
Hayward, J., B. Barry & A. Browing, eds. 1999. *The British Study of Politics in the Twentieth Century*. Oxford: British Academy and OUP.
Hirst, P. 1994. *Associative Democracy*. Cambridge: Polity Press.
      1996. 'Associative democracy – a comment on David Morgan'. *Australian and New Zealand Journal of Sociology*, 32/1, 20–26.
      1997. *From Statism to Pluralism*, Chs.1 and 6. London: UCL Press.
      1998. *Owners and Citizens. The Political Quarterly*, special issue, 69/4.
      1999. 'Associationalist welfare – a reply to Marc Stears'. *Economy and Society*, 28/4, 590–97.
Piore, M. & C. Sabel. 1984. *The Second Industrial Divide*. New York: Basic Books.
Roe, M.J. 1994. *Strong Managers, Weak Owners*. Princeton, NJ: Princeton University Press.
Russell, B. 1996 (1918). *Roads to Freedom*. London: Routledge.

3

Problems and Prospects of Associative Democracy: Cohen and Rogers Revisited

VEIT BADER

Theories of institutional pluralism in general, and of associative democracy in particular, seem to have received more attention in recent years. Criticism of false historical and structural necessities in the social sciences demonstrates the huge and persistent variety of institutional settings in modern societies and opens ways to think and experiment with alternative institutional designs. The recognition of moral pluralism and of moral disagreement in post-Rawlsian political philosophy paves the way for models of republican and of deliberative democracy. Promising as these developments are, the new opportunities still seem to be blocked by three facts. First, the cooperation between the social sciences and political philosophy is dominated by a fairly traditional division of labour. The social sciences not only, rightly, insist on a sober and detailed analysis of social conditions and constraints on alternative democratic designs, they often fall prey to a profound practical scepticism.[1] Many political philosophers, rightly, insist that futures are open, that realist utopias and action matter, and that we cannot tell in advance what is possible without trying – their deep optimism is often shielded against sober analysis of social constraints and unintended consequences. Second, for ten years or so, different varieties of associative democracy have been proposed by Mathews, Cohen, Rogers, Hirst, Sabel, Cooke, Morgan and others, but the vivid and critical debate of these proposals in the early 1990s seems to have lost momentum. Third, both the proposals themselves and the debate remain quite general, which, by itself, is somewhat strange for a theoretical and political strand stressing context sensitivity so much as associative democracy does. A continuing, serious discussion of specific issues, of specific solutions to hard dilemmas in specific contexts such as cities, regions or state-societies is still lacking.

In this article, I take up the debate of *Secondary Associations and Democratic Governance* by Joshua Cohen and Joel Rogers (1992; 1995) which, in my view, is still the best way to present the problems and prospects of associative democracy. I hope to contribute to a reopening of this debate, to stimulate an ongoing, collective endeavour, to spell out some of the important and highly contested issues and, last but not least, to present the many dilemmas inherent in any design of associative democracy. Such an analysis is required to develop the difficult art of balancing divergent normative criteria in order to find better institutional and policy alternatives for specific contexts without neglecting that often trade-offs are necessary and recognising that a specific institutional mix of market, hierarchy, civil society and association appropriate for a specific country may be inadequate for another one. My theoretical strategy is guided by the intuition that a sober theoretical and empirical discussion of the conditions and constraints of associative democracy does not corroborate practical scepticism.

In the first section, I briefly recapitulate the core ideas of associative democracy as set out by Cohen and Rogers in comparison with its main rivals: neo-liberalism, civic republicanism and egalitarian pluralism. A fair evaluation of existing or alternative institutions is a complex and tricky matter including moral, prudential and realist arguments. In the second section, I discuss some of the most pressing moral objections raised against associative democracy: that it undermines the sovereignty of the people, that the system of organised interest representation is undemocratic, that it is weak on political equality and even weaker on distributive equality, and that it does not develop civic consciousness but the mischief of faction. In the third section, I briefly indicate prudential objections that associative democracy is weak on efficiency and effectiveness of economic, political and administrative governance. In the fourth section, I address the most important realist objections.

The Core Ideas of Associative Democracy

Cohen and Rogers have introduced the project of associative democracy by comparing it with three alternative strategies to cope with secondary associations or organised group interests: neo-liberalism, civic republicanism and egalitarian pluralism. *Neo-liberal* constitutionalism sees secondary associations and private government mainly as a threat (rent-seeking coalitions or exploitation and domination of government by coalitions of organised interests) and proposes clear constitutional limits to the powers of the affirmative state. It rightly stresses individual choice and allocative efficiency as important values, but in its single-minded preoccupation with liberty and efficiency it neglects values of political equality and distributive equity. Its radical programme is not feasible and its treatment of factionalism completely neglects the possible positive contributions of secondary associations with regard to both enhancing democracy and efficiency (Cohen & Rogers 1992: 397–406; Cohen & Sabel 1997: 315f).

Civic republican strategies of insulation recognise that associations can and often do assist public deliberation. Republicans wish to separate public deliberation and state policies as far as possible from group influence because they are alert to the profoundly unequal character of existing group organisations and wary of the conditions that groups impose on policymakers. The mischief of faction and particularism has to be countered by a 'stronger and more sharply delineated state'. Four crucial weaknesses, however, make it unattractive: (i) the strategy of insulation seems unrealistic under present conditions of structural or background inequalities because politics is still largely a game of resources, not a forum of principles;[2] (ii) it remains wedded to an essentially zero-sum understanding of the relations between associations and the state, and neglects the distinctive capacities of groups to facilitate cooperation depending on qualitative differentiation between interest organisations; (iii) associations are taken as fixed and the core of the republican institutional design is thus 'to design around groups'; and (iv) its despairing or tragic acceptance of fractious pluralism and the selfish habits of interest organisations is mistaken 'for it is inattentive to the artifactual character of groups' (Cohen & Rogers 1992: 406–11).

Egalitarian pluralist strategies of accommodation recognise that organised groups will inevitably play a central role in mass democracy, that insulation is impossible and even undesirable. Organisations help to represent interests more effectively, strengthen the power to bargain and are indispensable for individuals and groups with fewer resources. Without organisation structural background inequalities inevitably lead to unacknowledged interests and underrepresentation of actually disenfranchised interests. Its programme focuses on reform of legislative and administrative processes in order to eliminate all obstacles to participation resulting from inequalities (including strategies of affirmative action), the promotion of significantly greater equality in the distribution of resources that are relevant to organisations and the enactment of more exacting judicial scrutiny in ethnically divided societies. However, its ideal of a fair bargaining procedure is too indeterminate and thin to generate determinate judgements and it remains 'as inattentive to the importance of qualitative variation as the neo-liberals and the civic republicans' (Cohen & Rogers 1992: 411–16).

The core idea of *associative democracy* is 'to encourage forms of group representation that stand less sharply in tension with the norms of democratic governance' (Cohen & Rogers 1992: 395) and 'to curb faction through a deliberate politics of associations while netting such group contributions to egalitarian democratic governance' (Cohen & Rogers 1992: 425). It recognises, on the one hand, that in recent mass democracies democratic norms are routinely frustrated. Unrepresentative, particularistic and powerful interest groups are factional threats in three areas: to political equality, to popular sovereignty and to agenda formation. On the other hand, group organisations can contribute substantially to an egalitarian democratic order through (i) information, (ii) equalising representation, (iii) citizen education and (iv) alternative governance (cooperation, formulation and implementation of policies, quasi-public functions, reduction of transaction costs, help to establish trust and so on).

Associative democracy declines to take only negative sum or zero-sum relationships between associations and the state into account; it stresses the 'non-naturalness' or 'artifactuality' of groups and organisations, and the qualitative variation of organisations and systems of associative interest representation. It proposes to use 'conventional policy tools', such as legal sanctions, taxes, subsidies and so on, to craft associations and steer the group system in order to achieve three main aims: (i) 'promoting the organized representation of presently excluded interests' in cases where manifest inequalities in political representation exist (*more equal political representation*); (ii) 'encouraging the organized to be more other-regarding in their actions' in cases where group particularism undermines popular sovereignty or democratic deliberation (*less factionalism*); and (iii) 'encouraging a more direct and formal governance role for groups' in cases where associations have greater competence than public authorities for achieving efficient and equitable outcomes (*more efficient governance*) (Cohen & Rogers 1992: 416–26).[3]

Simply stated, associative democracy is motivated by two types of criticism and it promises to contribute to the solution of two deep structural problems.[4] The first type of criticism compares existing institutional settings of the capitalist market economy and representative party democracy[5] with moral principles and legal norms enshrined in the constitutions of liberal democratic states. The second type of criticism addresses problems of economic efficiency and effectiveness as well as problems of limited efficiency and effectiveness of government. Associative democracy promises a set of alternative institutions which is morally at least as satisfying as the existing institutional arrangements and which is at least as efficient and effective with regard to economic and political governance or, more hopefully, which promises to overcome the serious 'mismatch' (Cohen & Sabel 1997: 323) between recent problems and the problem-solving capacity of existing institutions. The *objections* to its institutional proposals can be divided accordingly into (i) moral objections, (ii) prudential objections of efficiency and effectiveness, and (iii) realist objections.[6] It is important to note that these objections are not only articulated by proponents of the main rival political projects mentioned above, but also by advocates of other varieties of associative democracy. They indicate hard problems, not cheap rhetoric.

Moral Objections

For the sake of a clear evaluation, it is advisable to keep moral[7] and prudential criteria separate, to take the 'normative axis' first and bracket the 'functional axis' (Offe 1995). I follow the advice that it is best when considering the question of how associative democracy comports with the moral 'more constitutive features of democratic governance' (Cohen & Rogers 1992: 442) to suppose that it is at least as good or better than the existing institutional setting evaluated by criteria of economic performance or state efficiency. Claus Offe has summarised the main concerns from the democratic left in his 'negative normative quadrant': even liberal corporatism interferes with fair and egalitarian methods of territorial representation (elections, parties, parliament, legislation and division of powers), privileged, even monopolistic, decision-making roles discriminate against other collective actors; the set of groups is almost by definition incomplete (negative externalities of excluded third parties); and it invokes the 'bourgeois' rather than the '*citoyen*'.

Popular Sovereignty

Only in the ideal type of direct democracy does popular sovereignty need no further specification, because *the* people are supposed to be sovereign in agenda-setting, decision-making, implementation and control. All forms of indirect democracy, be they 'political'/territorial or 'social'/functional, are based on formal and actual *delegations* of these sovereign powers and the meaning of popular sovereignty has to be specified accordingly. The sovereignty of the people is limited and delegated ideally in the following steps: by the constitution, by elected parliamentary representatives, by responsible government, by accountable administrations, by judicial control, and by political parties (as intermediary political associations). Delegation of powers always implies problems of *control* and *accountability*. Delegation of powers to intermediary interest organisations, characteristic of all varieties of (neo-)corporatist and pluralist forms of group representation, is said to achieve three main gains and to contribute to a positive sum relationship between associative democracy and 'normal' political democracy (Scharpf 1999: 20f). It provides information and additional enforcement power, and it removes constraints on political debate such that a 'wider range of proposals can be discussed seriously' (Cohen & Rogers 1992: 443). If it does so, it may help to alleviate serious problems of democratic control and accountability caused by constraints on time, information and qualifications. In addition, associative democracy is said to widen the range and scope of democratic participation directly by adding 'social' democracy to political democracy, expecting a considerable spillover from social into political participation.

The main objections concern three problems: (i) associative democracy undermines the sovereignty of the people as expressed in the existing arrangements of political democracy; (ii) it is incompatible with freedoms of political communication and association; and (iii) the democratic character of the proposed system of interest organisations and of the interest organisations internally is questioned.

Does associative democracy undermine the sovereignty of the people?
Does associative democracy 'contribute to, or create problems for, the ultimate authority of the people in the formation of policy' (Cohen & Rogers 1992: 442) as not only liberals, but also the democratic left, according to Offe, think? The main response highlights the fact that associative, functional representation does *not replace*, but only supplements territorial political representation: 'Systems relying heavily on group-based representation should always be systems of dual, and juridically unequal powers. Final authority should reside in

encompassing territorial organization' (Cohen & Rogers 1992: 448, 443, 447; Cohen & Sabel 1997: 334; Hirst 1994).

This response bypasses some of the most important problems: which powers should be delegated, in what degree, in which policy fields and how ought legislative and judicial supervision to be organised? These questions have been central for any combination of 'political' and 'social' democracy since the first elaborate versions by Austrian social democrats such as Otto Bauer, Max Adler and others. It is well known from all of the delegation of powers that 'final authority' may be effectively weakened and become more and more 'formal' (without any real bite and effective supervision), particularly in cases in which those to be controlled have more time, better information and superior qualifications. It is, thus, urgent that mechanisms of external control and accountability by 'public' institutions be combined with internal democracy (see below).

Cohen and Rogers recognise this problem as one of three sources of serious concern (1992: 444, 447–50): the problem of 'increasing threats of improper delegation of vaguely circumscribed powers and consequent abuse of discretion'. Compared with legislation in 'liberal systems', however, they think that the objection is not damaging: 'Delegation of powers to arrangements of group bargaining does not itself pose a problem for popular sovereignty any more than the existence of specialized agencies of governance poses such a problem.' (Cohen & Rogers 1992: 443.) Only in the case of 'irrevocable delegation' would this be different. They recommend stronger legislative and judicial oversight and control and clear performance standards.

In my view, this response seriously underestimates the issue and the proposed remedies are much too vague and sloppy. Empirical research into forms of semi-public, semi-private and private government has created abundant evidence demonstrating serious strains with norms of the 'rule of law' and, particularly, huge problems of asymmetry of power among semi-private organisations themselves and among powerful private organisations and the state, which might actually be further weakened by such a pluralisation or 'administrative feudalization' (Cohen & Rogers 1992: 393). Without *die Rute im Fenster* of a strong state, and without functional equivalences for the 'rule of law' and for external democratic control inside organisations of private government, the threat of undermining popular control by systems of delegation of government is much more serious than the more traditional and well-known threats of uncontrollable public administrations.[8] What such alternatives should look like is one of the most pressing, open research questions.

Is associative democracy incompatible with freedoms of political association? The neo-liberal right objects to all forms of political representation of organised interests because they 'interfere with the free market and free competition' (Offe 1995: 121) and imply cartellisation or open monopolies. Neo-liberals reject 'any limits to associational liberties' (Cohen & Rogers 1992: 400ff) and all 'not wholly voluntary organizations'. Cohen and Rogers agree that 'individual choice' is an important value and point out that entry into and exit from membership of interest organisations in associative democracy is formally free. They argue that only cases of enforced membership and legalised monopolies would really pose a 'legal' problem. Short of such monopolies, of course, many different sorts of social pressures, and not only incentives and gains, actually make entry and exit much less 'free'. The different proposals for organised interest systems differ widely, but it is evident that the expected gains of neo-corporatist systems involve actual limitations to associational liberties and that such a 'trade off' has to be legitimated.[9]

Is the system of organised interest representation undemocratic? This objection concerns, first, the selectivity of interests, groups, organisations, issues and policy fields in associative democracy and, second, the way in which to institutionalise such a system. Both objections are raised by authors who favour an end to institutionalised pluralism and organised group representation.[10]

Which interests? Which groups? Which organisations? Which issues? Which policy fields? Immergut, Schmitter and Young criticise the 'traditional', 'European', 'neo-corporatist', class-based version of associative democracy of Cohen and Rogers which illegitimately excludes a wide variety of interests, groups, organisations and issues. Ordered systematically, the charge is that only organised capital and organised labour are included, that other so-called 'economic' interests, groups and organisations (for example, small business, professional and 'maverick' groups such as 'isolated and ruthless' agriculturists and consumers) are excluded, that ethnic and religious groups are excluded, that only so-called 'distributional' issues are included, all non-materialist, ideal issues are excluded, and that all cultural and identity issues (advanced by 'new social movements' and their organisations) are excluded.[11]

Cohen and Rogers (1995) acknowledge that the whole problem had been inadequately treated in 1992. They are at pains to distance associative democracy from the proposal of 'traditional corporatism for America' and from 'postmodern corporatism'. As I understand it, they try to mix 'neo-corporatist' forms with 'more pluralist' forms of group representation,[12] on the one hand, and to mix this amalgam with deliberative or neo-republican democracy by highlighting their version of deliberative arenas (see below) on the other hand. Even this revised proposal, however, has to face two serious objections.

First, such a less rigid, more open ('more choice' and 'easier exit') and more flexible system of 'weaker organizations and more transient arenas of democratic deliberation' (Cohen & Rogers 1995: 236) may have a moral appeal, but its functional appeal is dubious for many reasons. Among others, Immergut has pointed out that the gains of cooperation depend not only on ruling out vetoing policy outcomes unilaterally (lack of alternative arenas), but also on two other conditions: that the number of groups must be sufficient to allow groups to balance one another, yet not so large so as to produce a 'joint decision trap' (Scharpf 1988), and that negotiations must be ongoing and repeated (Immergut 1992: 483ff).[13] Simply stated, the more interests, the more groups, the more flexible and unstable the organisations, the more issues and the more policy fields are included in a system of organised interest representation, bargaining and semi-public-private government, the less plausible are the expected efficiency gains and the less plausible are the expected gains in transforming particularist preferences. Some vaguely circumscribed, but narrow, limits of the inclusion and the scope of issues is a condition of any functioning system. Systems of peak bargaining require 'the exclusion of some interests' (Cohen & Rogers 1992: 445). The 'requisite exclusion', the limits of feasible numbers of social partners, may be among the 'unsettled empirical issues' (Cohen & Rogers 1992: 450f) and a matter of institutional tinkering, but it is easy to see that the long lists of activities of NSMOs and single-issue 'causes' (Schmitter 1992) cannot all be included in workable systems. To find a reasonable trade-off between inclusion and workability is an important open issue of research.[14]

Second, the basic problem of (neo-)corporatism and associative democracy has not been incorporation and group representation of ethnic and religious minorities, but class relationships and problems of economic and political governance. Immergut has rightly remarked that 'ethnic minorities will not necessarily feel adequately represented' and that so-called cultural and identity issues and cleavages will 'pose an even greater challenge to associative democracy than distributive issues. Certainly, corporatist bargaining institutions do not attempt to span such divides.' (Immergut 1992: 485.) This, however, does not follow from the supposed 'fact' that identity issues would prohibit bargaining and compromise,[15] nor from the 'fact' that institutional pluralism would have nothing to contribute to workable arrangements, quite the contrary. It follows, rather, from the astonishing fact that the traditions of institutional pluralism which have dealt with problems of incorporation of ethnic and national minorities, mainly consociational democracy, federalism and group rights, have never been linked to the theoretical discussion about neo-corporatism and only very recently and tentatively to the discussion about associative democracy.[16]

The dubious democratic legitimacy and the 'sclerotic' character of Cohen and Rogers' system of interest organisations. Phil Schmitter strongly disagrees with Cohen and Rogers' proposal. He seriously questions the democratic legitimacy of necessary exclusions and he questions the capacity and the neutrality of the political process by which decisions would have to be made about 'what the appropriate interest system should be for each policy area'. The first problem is that not all interests, organisations and issues are 'likely to be represented on all issue arenas'. How can refusing them be justified? Can one apply 'the same evaluative criteria of "encompassingness", "scope of responsibility", "formality" and "integrative capacity" as in cases of class, profession and sectoral interests'? Schmitter fears that Cohen and Rogers try to ensure that capital and labour 'will continue to occupy a predominant role at the expense of more diversified sectoral and professional cleavages and against the rising tide of less "productively" defined interests'. He objects to this reification of 'a particular set of cleavages' and states that this would be 'incompatible with [a] democratic political process' unless it was 'freely chosen by its citizenry'.

     Cohen and Rogers respond by claiming that their proposal would be potentially as open as Schmitter's proposal and that it also 'would be determined by citizens choice'. Whereas Schmitter wants this choice to be institutionalised through a voucher system, that is, 'through a form of political market' (Cohen & Rogers 1992: note 64; 1995), they themselves prefer that decisions about which organisations should be accorded quasi-public status, subsidies, delegated powers and so on should be made under normal democratic conditions of 'authoritative popular political choice' (Cohen & Rogers 1992: 451). 'The group system is itself regulated by the traditional system' (Cohen & Rogers 1992: 443). This direct political mechanism of democratic deliberation and decision-making is, according to Cohen and Rogers, preferable because it 'allows for deliberation'.

The capacity and legitimacy of this 'normal' political decision-making is, according to Schmitter, questionable for two reasons: the 'sheer complexity of making such decisions would completely overload the legislature' (509), and it cannot possibly be made 'neutral' because it presumes an 'existing capacity for judicious consideration and neutral choice'. Immergut also stresses the latter point: 'as the party system (as well as Congress, Courts) is riddled with interest group influence, supervision of associational life by the party system may reinforce rather than provide a counterweight to the problems of faction' (1992: 483). Claus Offe detects a 'controversial logic' in Cohen and Rogers' 'state crafting of the associational system': government should be contingent on the empirical will of the people; the task of government is to design and implement institutions which will have a formative impact on the will of the people. It is, however, not its empirical will, 'but its refined, deliberated and "laundered" set of preferences which are brought about through appropriate institutional arrangements' (Offe 1995: 130). He concludes that their version of associative democracy is vulnerable to 'oligarchic' and 'paternalistic' threats. Offe seems to join Schmitter in that 'proposed arrangements would have to be of a strictly procedural and interest-neutral nature' (Offe 1995: 131).

Four remarks on this complex and open issue seem appropriate at this point.

1. Cohen and Rogers rightly claim that comparisons should be 'realistic' and the important question is whether their associative democracy would be less or more neutral, less or more biased compared with 'normal' pluralist interest politics and with neo-corporatist interest politics. In both regards, it seems obvious that it would do better. In both settings, the organisational strength and the mobilisation of political resources under their control determines whether interest groups can overcome the thresholds present to get their claims heard, recognised and represented, and associative democracy tries to tip the balance in favour of the less resourced and powerful ones.[17]

2. No 'strictly' neutral institutional mechanism is available in territorial or in functional representation, neither a substantive one nor a procedural one. This is, though hesitantly, also recognised by Katznelson: Cohen and Rogers' proposal 'would have the effect of both narrowing and privileging some forms of political identities over others ... because any system of interest representation – whether a non-hierarchical, non-compulsory pluralism or a hierarchical, compulsory corporatism, or the scheme of associative democracy they advance – necessarily privileges some groups and preferences over others and in part because the specific vehicles for interest representation they suggest demonstrate substantive, not just procedural preferences' (Katznelson 1995: 199). The comparison should therefore not be between the utopian ideal of a strictly neutral system and associative democracy, but between Cohen and Rogers' associative democracy and alternative proposals based on voucher systems (Hirst 1994).

3. Cohen and Rogers only claim that, but do not discuss whether, the mechanism of democratic deliberation and political decision-making is more appropriate than the 'political market' logic of vouchers. Schmitter's claims that his voucher system is 'open without discrimination to all existing and potential interests', that it is more democratic for the citizenry and less burdensome for the political process (1992: 512) seem more plausible, if understood gradually. Contrary to his claim, it too is not 'institutionally neutral', but it seems to be *more* neutral, less 'manifestly intended to benefit any interest or cause' and it would still give 'presently underrepresented groups a better chance at self-organization'.[18] It seems to be 'morally' more adequate, more voluntary, more flexible, more 'bottom up', but it would have to meet the serious 'functional' troubles mentioned above. Schmitter himself does not balance these contradictory claims.

4. Offe's paternalism charge is misguided, because it may be the 'empirical' political will, articulated in democratic political deliberation and decision-making, to redesign the system of group representation in such a way as to foster more long-term, less particularist, more 'other-regarding' definitions of interests and preferences if one acknowledges the impact of institutions on preferences. Charges of paternalism would be more to the point if Cohen and Rogers were to engage in undemocratic political institution-making to change the 'empirical' political will of 'the

people' taking into account that the normal political process in representative political party democracies also shapes empirical political preferences. But they do not.[19]

'All existing corporatisms, state and societal, have had to face serious difficulties with the *fixity* of their interest categories and the vestedness of their constituent organizations.' (Schmitter 1992: 509; Visser & Hemerijck 1997: 182.) Cohen and Rogers also signal this 'potential for *sclerosis*' as a danger for associative democracy: the initial organisation of group interests would become 'quasi-permanent' (1992: 444). This threat may become more serious because associative democracy endows independent groups with public status, subsidies and power, which these groups may use to freeze their position and so work to distort future debate and choice.[20] Cohen and Rogers hope to mitigate this danger by a proposal to review and evaluate organisations at regular intervals for renewal of grants and status (1992: 444, 450), stressing that the threat of withdrawal or amendment must be serious and credible in order to work and that the gains of accepting such scrutiny must be considerable. Both Schmitter and Immergut are, rightly, not satisfied with these remedies. Cohen and Rogers 'do nothing to allay my fears' regarding the 'powerful tendency toward "locking in" the solution. How would new claimants be processed? ... a new policy area declared? ... derelict arenas be closed down?' (Schmitter 1992: 509.)[21] In addition, his fear of strong, conservative, oligarchical influence in all these questions is shared by Immergut (1992: 483). The danger is more serious if one takes into account the well-known difficulties for such a demanding legislative or judicial supervision in terms of time, information and qualification, as already mentioned. How to best prevent sclerosis and oligarchy is one of the most pressing problems for all systems of group representation. It should rank high on the research agenda and it is obvious that no easy solutions can be expected.

Oligarchy and bureaucracy – lack of internal democracy? The 'disjunction of interests between leadership of groups and their members', the 'oligarchy issue', is one of the serious concerns regarding popular sovereignty mentioned by Cohen and Rogers. They rightly stress that there is 'always some disjunction'.[22] The important realistic comparative question thus is: 'does associative democracy worsen the problem?' According to them, the evidence is contested: 'no clear relation between opportunities for voice and exit, on the one hand, and centralization and encompassingness' (Cohen & Rogers 1992: 447), on the other, can be established.[23] As a remedy Cohen and Rogers propose fairly unspecified and general measures of internal democratisation. Associative democracy should not be compared with an illusionary 'pure' democracy. Organisation and leadership are not only, obviously, inevitable for modern 'territorial' and 'functional representation', they may (contrary to the negative sum relation between organisation and democracy in standard liberalism) also involve important normative gains. But one should also explicitly recognise that effective internal democratisation of complex organisations remains an extremely demanding task. If one takes into account how important internal democratisation and openness are in order to enable external control and accountability (Mansbridge 1992), it remains particularly astonishing that Cohen and Rogers do not pay more attention to the possibilities and limitations of strategies to democratise complex organisations.[24] One can only guess what their proposals would be to heighten accountability effectively, to advance democracy in encompassing, complete and centralised organisations.[25]

Cohen and Rogers are hasty in their conclusion that the threat of associative democracy to popular sovereignty and control can be mitigated by internal democracy and by legislative and judicial oversight. Even on a fairly general level and without going into institutional details, which would very much depend on specific contexts, situations and fields, much more could and should urgently be said.

Political Equality

American politics and political theory have been preoccupied with the group bias of politics, more specifically with the bias of an interest-group system that favours the wealthy (Cohen & Rogers 1992: 393; Schattschneider 1975). Compared with neo-liberalism and civic republicanism, both egalitarian pluralists such as Dahl and proponents of some form of group representation share the minimalist democratic aim of limiting the inevitable distortions of a fair and equal political process by structural background inequalities. They also agree that it is important to secure 'greater equality in the conditions of group organization and facilitating group access to legislative and administrative arenas'. Proponents of group representation more explicitly favour neo-corporatist or more plural group representation 'as a means to more equal power'. It 'advances democracy when it requires the contest for power among interest groups to take place in conditions that redress to some extent the imbalances of the *laissez-faire* war of all against all'.[26] Associative democracy is said to advance political equality in at least three respects. First, it improves the 'representation of workers and other less well-endowed citizens'; the 'capacity to influence political outcomes becomes less dependent on position in the distribution of material resources' (Cohen & Rogers 1992: 444). Second, the improved representation of the less well off provides support for programmes of distributive equity. Third, to the extent that this is effective, it reduces the 'concern about the capacity of powerful private interests to effectively veto public policies'.[27]

It is important to note that neither this aim nor the general means have been questioned in critical replies. The main concern centres on the question of whether associative democracy imposes 'limits of its own on achieving a genuinely fair representation of social interests' (Cohen & Rogers 1992: 444). How does associative democracy tackle the problem of the transmission or even multiplication of background inequalities by the organisational power of groups?[28] *Moderate* objections state that even the measures Cohen and Rogers propose cannot effectively counter the political mobilisation of the private power of resource-rich groups. They point to transformation paradoxes (Katznelson), to the actor paradox (Hirst; see the section below headed 'Realist Objections') and to the limited possibilities available to prevent the exit of 'the rich' (Streeck; see below). If these objections are not countered and accompanied by alternative institutional and strategic proposals, they lead to scepticism and promote objectional acquiescence. Stronger objections may be raised in two versions. First, the specific measures of associative democracy would favour the already resource-rich and powerful interest groups even compared with the conditions of the more unofficial, informal 'political pluralism of interest groups'. This would be damaging, but I agree with Cohen and Rogers that their proposals are 'eminently more inclusive and fair than under less group oriented systems'. Second, Cohen and Rogers' proposals are said to address the problem less effectively compared with other possible forms and ways to institutionalise pluralism. If correct, such objections should encourage Cohen and Rogers to adopt these other forms to institutionalise pluralism.

Distributive Equity

In Cohen and Rogers' proposal, problems of distributive equity are at stake only in their direct or indirect impact on political equality and

CHESTER COLLEGE LIBRARY

popular sovereignty. They hope that associative democracy will contribute, in two ways, to a more fair and equal distribution of economic and societal resources and rewards. First, they look to an expected spin-off of the increased political impact of negatively privileged groups, particularly by policies of affirmative action and of more equal income distribution. Cohen and Rogers themselves do not substantiate this expectation by discussing empirical evidence or theoretical plausibility. Second, they hope that associative democracy will help to create 'a social base of support for the advance of egalitarian democratic ideals' (Cohen & Rogers 1995: 238ff). In 1995, they promise to address 'egalitarianism and democracy' more directly, to present a synthesis of social democracy and radical democracy. Here, their main claim is that the 'devolution to associational arenas of civil society' will strengthen democratic deliberation and, in this way, create 'responsible associations', which will 'support democratic political consensus' in general and egalitarian policies in particular.

The only relevant objection they indicate is that functional representation systems in general are 'ill-designed to cope with *regional inequalities*'. Regional inequalities are 'important but not intractable', however, and they claim that associative democracy is 'not less responsible to territorial inequality'. In particular, they hope that 'traditional territorial representation' will provide a sufficient counterbalance. Associative democracy 'should encourage group organization in regions'.[29]

For four reasons, their whole treatment of questions of distributive equity is disappointing.

1. They do not address the issues of ascriptive inequalities, particularly of ethnic and national inequalities, at all. Like its prototype, neo-corporatist representation, associative democracy is not only ill-suited to address regional inequalities, but even more so to address structural inequalities among ethnic and national groups.

2. They do not even signal a well-known, burning problem: you need a *fairly strong and fairly centralised state* in order to correct structural inequalities, be it class or 'functional' inequalities, regional inequalities or ethnic and national inequalities.[30] Strong centres are required to overcome the entrenched powers of the 'rich' and organised, the rich states in a federation or rich regions in a state, and dominant ethnic and national majorities.[31] Proposals to institutionalise pluralism are very vulnerable because they entrust

powers to associations in civil society which, on the one hand, may strengthen already resource-rich and powerful collective actors and, on the other hand, may weaken strong centres. If you attack, for good reasons, social democratic statism, you should take into account the historical and structural reasons of its existence: to correct extreme asymmetries of power in the 'private' sphere and in the sphere of 'civil society'. The old and vibrant 'associationalism' of socialism and social democracy has never been strong enough.[32] Neo-liberal strategies of decentralisation, deregulation and privatisation, obviously, redress the balance of power in favour of entrenched powers (be they capital or whatever). If you favour territorial decentralisation and regional autonomy, you have to take into account that only stronger centres are able to counterbalance and correct huge regional inequalities (or inequalities among states in the EU). Associative democracy promises to be different from neo-liberal privatisation (by public-private governance), deregulation (by exacting scrutiny) and decentralisation, and also different from the Christian Democratic *middenveld* (middle ground) and subsidiarity, but it has to spell out more clearly how the noble aims of both more equality and more decentralisation, will be achieved, particularly if one accepts markets, hierarchies and group bargaining, and the limitations imposed by these mechanisms of coordination upon 'overambitious versions' of radical democracy. The repetition of old formulas that 'a more radical democratization of traditional egalitarian practice' will do this job amounts to wishful thinking.

3. It has to face the central *transformational paradox* of 'equality and pluralism', that it may be necessary to deploy more and more central power in order to break the strongholds of the entrenched powers and that this same central power may effectively block the wide variety of institutional pluralism aimed at.[33] In addition, it has to face the central *dilemma of agency*: how to get this strong and central state to favour more egalitarian basic structures and policies.

4. Cohen and Rogers cannot legitimise their obvious weakness on equality by referring to a tricky act of moral balancing between the principles of *equalities and 'freedoms'* or 'pluralism'[34] or between equalities and *innovation or human emancipation*[35] because their project is more outspokenly egalitarian and less 'pluralist' than other projects to institutionalise pluralism.

Civic Consciousness

Two issues are raised under the heading of this fourth moral criterion: the famous problem of particularism or the 'mischief of faction' and the problem of minimal common identity and commitment as a precondition for accepting common obligations.

Mischief of faction? This has been the main charge from both neo-republicans and neo-liberals, originally by classical republicans and liberals, directed against all intermediary associations existing between individual citizens and the state, including political parties. Cohen and Rogers discuss the following 'three dangers' of associative democracy. First, there is the danger that associative democracy may contribute to the 'erosion of public authority' by exaggerating the tendency to devolve public authority to less politically encompassing organisations, placing a public imprimatur on it. Second, they discuss the danger that the centrality of successful organisations can undermine respect for more encompassing organisations. Third, the danger exists that some narrowness in group representation remains in such a system, which may encourage 'forms of group consciousness that compete with and may take precedence over civic sensibilities' (Cohen & Rogers 1992: 446f).

Yet they insist, rightly, that associative democracy should be compared with existing pluralist systems, and that it does better in all three regards. They hope that these dangers can be mitigated by stressing the 'supremacy of traditional representation'. Associative democracy is not more dangerous than the disease it aims to cure if it is able to use public power to encourage less factionalising forms of secondary associations by 'altering the terms, conditions, and public status of groups' (Cohen & Rogers 1992: 395), to 'steer the group system' (Cohen & Rogers 1992: 429). Whether it is possible to keep the risk of faction under control depends on seven qualitative features of groups and the group system which can be influenced by conventional policy tools (Cohen & Rogers 1992: 406).[36] These features are as follows: the accountability of group leaders; the centralisation of authority in group decision-making; the encompassingness or completeness of group membership relative to affected populations; the scope of responsibilities assumed or assigned; the relation to the state (from mere toleration to active state promotion); the characteristic mode of interaction with other groups (competition, competitive cooperation or cooperation); and background equality of the distribution of powers across groups.

If these characteristics are favourable, Cohen and Rogers expect a positive contribution by associative democracy to civic consciousness, social and political solidarity, empathy and public responsibility. This hope is based on theoretical considerations and empirical evidence from neo-corporatist experience. First, these arrangements lead to the cooperation and coordination of interests and to less narrow group programmes. Second, continued bargaining and compromise stimulate awareness of interdependence. Third, acting under these conditions induces long-term perspectives and less steep rates of time discount (Cohen & Rogers 1992: 446f).[37] Summarising the positive functions of neo-corporatism (Cohen & Sabel 1997: 333f), Cohen and Rogers hope that associative democracy increases these beneficial effects of interest intermediation (compared with mere interest aggregation) by exposing initial interest definitions to intergroup and intragroup deliberation, sorting out errant definitions, ensuring predictable and cooperative behaviour, stabilising the expectations of interlocutor groups, and building up trust and at least more public-regarding behaviour. Systems of semi-public-private government, in particular, are expected to 'educate' individuals and imply 'a call to look beyond the immediate concerns' of groups.[38] Compared with the older neo-corporatism debate and with the recent debate on private government, Cohen and Rogers put much more weight on deliberative arenas. They stress the role of democratic deliberation inside organisations and among associations as well as in 'territorial' politics.[39]

Jane Mansbridge also sees neo-corporatism as a means to better persuasion (1992: 497ff). Social corporatism, according to her, injects greater consideration of the public interest into the negotiations. In opposition to the 'transmission-belt mode' of interest aggregation, predominant in the USA's adversary political culture and pluralist political theory (which is a zero-sum 'transfer model' only aggregating existing preferences and downplaying the potential for preference change), she advocates a positive sum 'productivity model' developing in 'more recent deliberative models of corporatist representation' (Streeck & Schmitter 1985). Here, interest groups 'function to change preferences as well as to aggregate them' and new information and innovation can be gained. Corporate deliberation includes 'negotiation which stands between pure power and pure reason' (Mansbridge 1992: 500).[40] Whereas traditional models of corporatism expect these moderating and civilising effects from 'external negotiations' among elites, more recent ones add internal negotiations between elites and the rank and file. However, according to Mansbridge, 'few have asked how [the] rank and file can deliberate to reach new understandings' (1992: 501). In my view, Cohen and Rogers would agree to her normative claim 'that elite deliberation must be supplemented with deliberation among the rank and file' (Mansbridge 1992: 502). 'Only citizens themselves can know what outcomes they want.'

This newly developing strand of 'deliberative democracy', in its more neo-republican versions (the paradigmatic example of which is Barber), its more 'egalitarian liberal' versions (Gutmann & Thompson, and Jeremy Waldron), and its more pluralist versions (Cohen & Sabel 1997; Cohen & Rogers 1992) has to meet two, well-known critical objections.

1. Even if one rejects, as I do, the reduction of reasons and motives of (individual and collective) actors to strategic particularism typical for rational choice approaches, one should elaborate in more detail the 'strategic' gains inherent in neo-corporatist or associative democratic arrangements. This has been the main advantage of sober sociological thinking in recent years. Only in this way, does one not have to expect too much from the effects of the 'appeal to public values' (Mansbridge) or from the 'public use of reason'.[41] 'Public deliberation' may then be able to fulfil such a modest and restricted role more efficiently. This may help avoid the wrong, enforced choice between sober sociological scepticism ('interests') and old-fashioned normative wishful thinking ('reasons') looming large in political philosophy.[42]

2. Public democratic deliberation under the conditions of a Habermasian *'herrschaftsfreier Diskurs'* (domination free discourse) or Rawlsian fair basic structures is very different from actual deliberation and discourse under conditions of gross inequality (both background and political).[43] In a defence of associative democracy, it is of no great help to assume 'fair conditions of discussion' (Cohen & Rogers 1995: 260)[44] because its hard task is to make plausible the way in which actual discussions, talks and deliberations under the actual conditions of background inequalities and political inequalities may help to correct particularism and to keep the risk of faction under control. If they are unable to make this plausible (at least as a possibility), associative democracy will remain wishful thinking often accompanied by black pessimism: 'Today, few interest associations

in the US or Europe institutionalize any formal deliberative process among their membership, let alone deliberative processes designed to promote identification with the public good.' (Mansbridge 1992: 503.) This sounds very much like Claus Offe's 'deeply pessimistic tone', which he shares with the 'overwhelming majority of political theorists' (1995: 132). In my view, the only way to escape from this trap of oscillating between normate wishful thinking and pessimism masked as sober sociological analysis consists in a more detailed analysis of the open question of whether, and if so, to what degree, secondary associations actually do contribute to 'civic consciousness', and if not, which conditions could be realistically changed to achieve this at all, or to achieve it to a higher degree.[45] Cohen and Rogers did not take up this challenge in their response. The question lies at the heart of all new approaches of deliberative democracy and should rank high on the research agenda.

Unity, commitment and obligations. Surprisingly, the main neo-republican objection that all versions of institutional pluralism will inevitably threaten minimally required social and political unity (Bader 1999d; 1999e) has not been dealt with by Cohen and Rogers or any of their critics. The debate has focused on the issue of whether associative democracy may help to create new types of purely political identities, commitments, solidarities and obligations. Perhaps even more astonishingly, Cohen and Rogers did not respond to one of the most serious charges against the possibility of associative democracy under recent conditions, raised by Streeck. Streeck focuses on the problem of the 'creation and enforcement of collective obligations to and within a community' in order to make claims to loyalty and resource effectiveness. Factions in associative democracy 'are cajoled into accepting collective obligations by institutional arrangements which serve their particularist interest and transform them in the process as a result of carefully designed constraints for participating groups to expose their initial interest definition to inter- and intra-group deliberation' (Streeck 1992: 513). This works only on condition that groups are both able and willing to do so, and accept the constraints. Cohen and Rogers are less attentive to the question of groups being willing (514). Some groups may be unwilling to accept the 'laundry process';[46] they may 'refuse to identify with the community'. Then the big question of 'exit from collective citizenship [arises] where the matter is not rights lost, but obligations avoided' (514).

'Some groups (e.g. capital) find it easier than others (e.g. labour) to exit and do without collective voice.' 'In order to have associative democracy at all, exit from collective citizenship must be foreclosed in particular for groups commanding resources that are crucial for building a successful community.' 'Associative democracy presupposes boundaries around the society and powerful groups must have reasons to perceive themselves as members of a "community of fate" that they cannot leave and that they must improve.'[47] 'Democratic inclusion ... may require an effective prohibition on voluntary self-exclusion.'[48]

But how can this be enforced and legitimated? In addition, what is the relevant 'community or society'? Cohen & Rogers' answer is remarkably conventional: the nation-state. Streeck shows that boundaries cannot themselves be drawn democratically[49] and that corporatist welfare states presuppose a 'citizenry that is territorially and functionally captive'. Examples from Europe show that democracy has not convincingly answered the question: 'How can groups of citizens be required to organize and bargain in good faith even though exit or non-entry may offer them higher pay-offs?' (516). Under conditions of increasingly permeable national boundaries, governments of nation-states have lost a lot of governance capacity to prevent crucial groups from exiting from the national domain and jurisdiction (capital flight, runaway investment, taxation tricks, regime competition and increasingly deregulated and globalised financial markets). This is seen to be one of the reasons for the demise of the system of political exchange, of neo-corporatist **concertation** and of Keynesian labour-inclusive macro-economic management. 'How can one, in the face of this, be other than deeply pessimistic on the prospects of a move toward an associative version of democracy?' (519; Crouch & Streeck 1997; Streeck 1998; Offe 1998a). Some authors seem less pessimistic (Scharpf 1999), others much more optimistic (Hirst & Thompson 2000), but they fail to develop detailed institutional alternatives and policy proposals (see criticism by Engelen in this volume).

Prudential Objections

Many of these burning moral questions have to be answered in detail before we can evaluate the arguments and objections and balance competing moral requirements. That cannot be attempted here. Yet it still seems likely, at the end of the day, that associative democracy would compare well with the existing informally pluralist representative democracies. To evaluate prudential gains and losses, it is not necessary to defend a strong moral claim. It is enough to assume that associative democracy does some good, or at least no harm, from a moral perspective or, to be more precise, putting the 'moral axis' (for now) to one side.

Cohen and Rogers state that associative democracy would lead to important gains in three areas: in the formulation of national policy, in coordinating economic activity in the shadow of national policy, and in the enforcement and administration of policy by local and intra-firm organisations (1992: 430–32). Like many others, they hope that associative democracy will lead to better economic, political and administrative governance. Compared with other versions of associative democracy, however, or with closely related approaches, their hope is much less substantiated by theoretical arguments and detailed empirical research.[50] This is the reason why this article seeks to do no more than indicate, in a fairly general way, some urgent problems and open questions.

All varieties of associative democratic *economic* governance share a certain optimism: associative institutions and policies (in theory and practical experiments) are, at least in principle, superior compared with the existing economic institutions and neo-liberal or neo-Keynesian economic policies when measured by criteria such as flexibility, adaptability, innovativity, productivity and competitive performance. Because I myself believe in this superiority, I would like to underscore that two critical questions have not yet been properly addressed.

1. How can we explain and soberly discuss the apparent 'perverse outcome' of recent neo-liberal globalisation politics that 'the less well-performing Anglo-American model of capitalism' seems to outcompete 'the better performing Rhine model'?[51] In particular, how can we judge what is due to unfavourable changes in the environment of systems of neo-corporatist or developing associative democratic governance and beyond their impact or control and what may be due to immanent deficiencies in these developing systems? How can we be realistic and sober enough not to overestimate and misjudge 'emerging tendencies'?[52]

2. All designs of economic governance in associative democracy contain many overlapping levels and inherent difficulties in allocating and clearly delineating competences among a limited set

of actors with widely divergent interests. How is it possible to avoid lock-in effects and, particularly, 'joint decision traps' in multilevel polities with their doubly dysfunctional outcomes: grossly suboptimal policies and institutional rigidity?[53]

Markets and traditional state *administration* are increasingly unable to solve four kinds of regulatory problems because the setting and enforcement of standards of performance by the state is complex, not straightforward (Cohen & Rogers 1992: 425ff; 1995: 249f): (i) monitoring problems (non-market public standards on behaviour are needed but the objects of regulation are so diverse or unstable that it is not possible for the government to specify, or the objects are sufficiently numerous or dispersed to preclude serious government monitoring of compliance (Cohen & Sabel 1997: 331; Scharpf 1999: 20); (ii) lack of the most appropriate means at particular sites (administration lacks local knowledge of heterogeneous circumstances); (iii) uniform public standards are needed, but it lies beyond the government's or the market's ability to specify and secure them, that is, each 'cannot set appropriate ends itself'; and (iv) problems crossing conventional policy domains. Associative democrats and proponents of 'negotiating government' or some other form of public-private governance (in theory and practical experiments) are convinced that these new institutions are better able to solve these problems in an efficient and effective way.[54] A sober evaluation of the empirical performance of different forms of negotiating government and, particularly, of private government may at least temper these expectations. In addition, one should not forget that they pose new challenges to the rule of law as well as to democratic accountability and control, referred to above, which have not been appropriately theorised yet, let alone practically addressed.[55]

Realist Objections

Associative democracy may be morally preferable and it may promise important prudential gains. It still may not be possible. Realist objections try to show this. They can be grouped into three broad classes: arguments questioning its feasibility; arguments trying to demonstrate the incompatibility of proposed institutional mixes or their counterproductive consequences; and arguments focusing on the costs and paradoxes of transformation, of agency and of strategy.

Feasibility?

The most broadly discussed objection has been the 'impossibility charge' challenging Cohen and Rogers' specific version of the *artifactuality* of groups, associations and institutions: it is not possible to create a favourable associative environment through politics because groups are either a product of nature, or of culture, or of some other unalterable substrate of a country's political life which lies 'beyond politics' (1992: 426ff). In their first response, Cohen and Rogers claim that the objection 'exaggerates the fixity of the associative environment'. Yet groups, associations and institutions 'reflect structural features of the political economy' (Cohen & Rogers 1992: 427); they are 'in part a product of opportunities and incentives that are induced by the structure of political institutions'. They can thus be changed by politics, for example, by policies to change the background distribution of wealth and income, to shift the locus of public decision-making, to increase the availability of information and to assign public functions. Artifactuality does not mean 'to suggest that they are simply political creations'; the thesis only protests against the empirical and normative mistake of treating 'the extent and forms of group organization as a scheme of private ordering to which politics must simply adapt' (Cohen & Rogers 1992: 428).

Their original artifactuality thesis shows many weak points.

1. In my view, the models of contrast used by Cohen and Rogers are misleading: apart from socio-biologists and ethnocentric fundamentalists, 'nature' is quite uninteresting; 'culture' may be more to the point.[56] But even if groups, associations and institutions were only 'in part' (Cohen & Rogers 1992: 427, 428) to 'reflect structural features of the political economy', this structure may be very hard to change.

2. The general idea of artifactuality may be a welcome protest against 'false necessities', to use Unger's phrase. Some (long) time ago, it may have been 'all politics', the result of collective political action, but now it is 'structure' (nested, path-dependent lock-ins).

3. Of course, in principle, it is possible to change the economic, social, political, legal and even, eventually, the cultural 'substrate' of group formation, organisations and politics by politics. Yet, in theory and in practice, this is not possible in all situations. Even if the distinction between 'hot' and 'cold' is not as strict as is often thought, it refers to important differences in situations. It is not

possible to do so by 'normal' public policy. Even if there is no Chinese wall separating revolutionary politics from reformist tinkering, and radical reforms can change deep structures eventually, the distinction refers to important differences in politics. It is not possible to do it all the time or 'at once' (it takes time, is asynchronous and so on).

4. To be able to change the 'structural substrate' of politics you need a lot of power, including strong central state power, to hold in check the effective countervailing powers of entrenched, privileged interest groups, which otherwise are able to block all attempts in this direction.

In their responses to the charges of 'impossibility' or 'futility' in 1993, 1994 and 1995, Cohen and Rogers attempt to clarify 'the conditions under which associational artifaction is appropriate' and promise to close the gap in their original presentation. Yet, in my view, they do not address important arguments such as the abuse of organisational power by locked-in groups: the project of associative democracy cannot get started because it reaches far beyond 'deliberative' politics and thus will not work. They do not directly respond to Offe's objection that institutions are not 'alterable at any point in time' and only in 'exceptional cases' (1995: 124f) nor do they elaborate on different forms and tempos of institutional change.[57] They do not discuss the limitations of the structuration of groups, organisations and institutions by the political opportunity structure.[58] Nevertheless, they elaborate on two important aspects of artifactuality.

First, they discuss new forms of political identity, loyalty and commitment. The futility objection states that 'associations must be rooted in common pre-political identities which our "artificial" associations by definition lack' (Cohen & Rogers 1995: 238, 253). For Cohen and Rogers in 1995 the many deliberative arenas and identities or solidarities of associative democracy differ from 'workplace democracy' and traditional European social democracy with its 'organic', 'natural', 'particularist', 'densely culturally textured', 'common pre-political identities' that are 'rooted in common culture and life circumstance' (1995: 238, 251ff) as well as from the 'political' identities and 'solidarities of citizenship' (1995: 256), corresponding to the 'formal political arena' which, on the one hand, is also 'fabricated', 'deliberate', 'intentional', rooted in 'common concern, purposes, discussions' and 'less particularistic', but on the other hand, is still too particularistic and not cosmopolitan enough. Their hope is that new democratic associations and social movements in international civil society will foster 'more cosmopolitan but thinner solidarities': 'An ample supply of this new kind of solidarity ... at least hints at a way through the present morass of social democratic distemper and increasingly barren exchanges between radical, participatory democrats and statist egalitarians.' (Cohen & Rogers 1995: 252.) 'It is true that we are promoting what once marched under the banner of "citizenship". But the fact that it no longer marches indicates the utility of the project ... Practices within civil society come to look more like the state, even as they are given more autonomy from the state and are assigned a proportionately greater role in governance. Radical democracy and egalitarianism are joined through a state that stakes deeper social roots in a more cosmopolitan civil society.' (Cohen & Rogers 1995: 263.)[59]

Second, they elaborate and expand their criticism of Putnam's thesis of a strong cultural determination of politics, which seems to imply the view: 'if your associative environment is not good, your only option is to "get a history"' (Cohen & Rogers 1995: 266).[60] Implicitly, they thereby address also Offe's doubts about the 'transnational transferability' of institutions. Offe starts from a skilful misunderstanding of the project of 'artfully designing institutions', assuming that Cohen and Rogers would treat institutions 'as if they were organizations' (Offe 1995: 123). Organisations are understood as 'authoritatively imposed and relatively easily changed rules' and opposed to institutions understood as 'cultures' which 'cannot be treated like organizations'. They 'do not serve an external purpose', but are 'intrinsically valuable', 'expressive' and not 'designable'. Institutional change, thus, is 'slow, evolutionary, quasi-biological' (Offe 1995: 124). Offe's discretion on institutional design provokes some critical remarks.

1. While everyone may have his or her concept of 'institution', fairness requires that projects of institutional design do not (necessarily) compound 'organisation' with institutions in the sense of cultures. True, there is a lot of terminological ambiguity in Cohen and Rogers with regard to concepts of 'group', 'association', 'organisation' and 'institution', which has to be criticised, but this does not invalidate their or any notion of institutional design.

2. Pro-theoretical differentiation is urgently required. Instead of opposing 'rules' and 'culture', one should distinguish principles (operative or institutionalised principles), cultures (habits and virtues) and practices.[61] Such a framework enables more detailed

questions. It also introduces more possibilities for asynchronous change and for design. Change of cultures, habits and virtues, and practices takes more time than change of 'rules', and cultures are more resistant with design, which, by the way, should not be equated to 'engineering and manipulation'. This, however, does not mean that cultures, habits and practices would only change in a speed comparable to biological evolution, that they would be beyond design and beyond any attempts of political and even strategic influence.[62]

3. The design (and the implementation) of alternative structures for organisations is easier than that for institutional arrangements, let alone for cultures, habits and practices (which may or may not change as a direct or indirect consequence), but it is evident that actual organisational change is confronted with quite similar problems because it has not only to change the 'rules', but also the 'operative rules' and, of course, organisational culture, the habits of personnel and 'bad' practices.

4. Projects of institutional design try to prevent the famous 'dialectics of institutions and motivations' getting stuck in vicious circles and deadlock: you need motivated people to be able to imagine, design and implement new institutions and you need new, more participatory institutions to motivate people.[63] Happily, democratic projects can start at both ends at the same time because some people are actually motivated and most institutions actually allow for some change. But there are good theoretical and empirical reasons to focus on changing the 'rules of the game' and, particularly, of the organisational and institutional environments in the hope of changing cultures, habits and practices more indirectly, instead of focusing on 'cultural revolutions' and moral 'pedagogics' in order to change them directly.

Incompatibility and Unintended, Counterproductive Consequences?

Two forceful realist arguments can be mobilised against all varieties of associative democracy. First, one can object that all those nice things associative democracy intentionally wants to combine are incompatible: more democracy and more efficiency (higher economic performance and state performance), more equality and more efficiency, more efficiency and more accountability and legal security, and so on. Realists, rightly, press proponents of associative democracy to face the fact that these principles point in different directions and that hard trade-offs have to be made. Yet, they dogmatically presuppose that alternative institutional arrangements do not allow better trade-offs. A similar argument holds for the institutional mix of 'state', 'market', 'hierarchy', 'civil society' and 'association' proposed, in one way or another, by all varieties of associative democracy in order to save the 'best things' of these mechanisms of coordination.[64] Even if we can show that these mechanisms are not incompatible, and that they are actually mixed in existing orders, one should clearly recognise that their 'logics' point in divergent directions and that alternative institutional mixes are far from easy, full of tensions and never in some harmonious equilibrium.

Second, many of the morally preferable institutional options may have unintended, counterproductive, but recognisable and known consequences. If it is correct that systems of group representation lose many of the promised efficiency gains, the more 'flexible, open, fluid, pluralist' they become; it is urgent to find new ways to counter this dilemma, for example, by combining a system of 'vouchers' (Scharpf 1999: 152f), which may better guarantee that the distribution of money among established and new organisations changes with the actual changing preferences and considered judgements of the citizenry, with a system of 'thresholds' which may guarantee that the number of organisations involved (in more formalised systems of group representation in decision-making and implementation in different policy fields) is not too great in order to assure that the minimum of stability or institutional fixity can be achieved that is necessary to allow long-term efficient services, administration and minimal job security in organisations.[65]

Paradoxes of Transformation, of Agency and of Strategy

Most critics agree that Cohen and Rogers' presentation of associative democracy suffers from a severe lack in this regard. I deliberately neglect paradoxes of transformation[66] and of strategy[67] and focus only on one aspect of *agency*. If one distinguishes roughly between two types of institutional pluralism, *state* pluralism versus *societal* pluralism (Schmitter 1992: 529), Cohen and Rogers' version of associative democracy underscores the important role the state has to play both as an organiser and facilitator of the new institutional arrangements as well as within an established associative democracy. On this question, Cohen and Rogers are joined by Streeck, whereas Hirst and Schmitter would approach the 'societal' pole. Cohen and Rogers, accordingly, defend a 'more optimistic view on problems of state capacity' and of the state as a 'first organizer of social capacities to the solution of social problems' (1995: 236).

Critical questions regarding state capacity have been asked by Schmitter and Hirst most prominently. Schmitter objects that Cohen and Rogers' proposal not only presumes 'an existing capacity for judicious consideration and neutral choice for which there is no evidence in the United States..., but the sheer complexity of making such decisions boggles the mind'. It would 'completely overload the legislature' (Schmitter 1992: 509). Cohen and Rogers 'do not address the critical agency questions' (note 2). Hirst also recognises that the state is the agency of group transformation in Cohen and Rogers' proposal to use public power in order to alter the terms, conditions and public status of groups (Hirst 1992: 473). 'How can state agencies acquire the competence, neutrality, legitimacy to perform crafting?' In his view, the only plausible answer would be to downgrade the thesis of artifactuality while accepting that associations are political constructs. Crafting 'can only work if there are existing (pre-existing) foci of group solidarity to work on' and 'if the strong and exclusively established parties and interest groups accept the need for reform' (Hirst 1992: 477). Without such a 'New Deal', without such a consensus, it would remain a 'reform from above' doomed to failure. Therefore he adds three suggestions: rebuild associations from below, work on the regional level and include 'voluntarist and libertarian' elements. In my view, state and societal pluralism need not be completely opposed: it need not be 'either' using public power 'or' developing associations from below, either 'central' or 'regional and local', or either libertarian or regulated by the state. However, opposing misleading dichotomies is the easy part, the difficult, and still largely unaddressed, part (Hirst 1997: 110) is their skilful combination in a transformative perspective and in the perspective of the design of workable institutions on the basis of an established associative democracy.[68]

Conclusion

Revisiting the problems and prospects of associative democracy today shows that many of the problems raised during the first and second round of the debate are still as burning as they are unanswered. It remains disappointing that Cohen and Rogers themselves did not try to respond more directly and systematically to the questions raised by their critics and, more importantly, that they did not try to do so in the meantime. The most disappointing fact is that the debate seems to have lost momentum since 1995. Many social scientists and political theorists try to elaborate their respective models of associative democracy, but do not engage in critical and comparative debates with their colleagues across the borders of disciplines. It has not been my aim to evaluate these proposals or the practical experiments of associationalism in different fields and countries. Instead, I have tried to show that the 'old' problems are as pressing as ever and, by doing this, I hope to make a modest contribution to reopening the debate.

If the twenty-first century is to be the century of associative democracy, the prospects of associative democracy, in my view, depend on three intellectual tasks. First, there is a need for a clear recognition of the many tensions between moral principles themselves and between moral, prudential and realist requirements. Even if the trade-offs are not as big, 'tragic' and unworkable as many believe, even if they may be resolved into many smaller trade-offs, they are real. To neglect them or to promote premature solutions, spells intellectual dishonesty and political disaster. There are no easy answers, and to insist otherwise may have a paralysing effect on those who seek solutions to the problems of complex societies. For all others, it should be an invitation to engage in research and debate.

Second, all institutional pluralists know that there cannot be context-free solutions or optimal institutional models applicable in all countries, policy fields and situations. The prospects of associative democracy depend upon our capacity to design workable solutions for specific contexts and to engage in democratic experimentalism to develop existing institutions in the direction of such concrete or realistic utopias.

Third, we need to develop a new type of thinking. We have to criticise the normate optimism typical of many political philosophers, even those who, like Thomas Pogge, engage in matters of institutional design. In addition, we have to criticise the grim scepticism of many sociologists erecting insurmountable barriers for radical democratic experimentalism. Here lies a task for good political theory. Obviously, politics is still 'das geduldige Bohren dicker Bretter', but without trying we certainly will achieve less than is possible. To work out realist utopias may help our attempts.

NOTES

1. See Offe (1995; 1998a: 99, 111, 118f, 133f) and Streeck (1998: 16f, 32).
2. See below for a restatement of this criticism against deliberative democracy and against associative democracy.
3. See Cohen and Sabel (1997: 323). See also Paul Hirst's summary of the core of his version of associative democracy in the present volume.
4. See Offe (1995) for these two axes. See Scharpf (1999: 7–21): 'democratic' and 'efficient'.
5. These two core institutions of recent societies should not be melted into neat formulas of 'capitalist democracy' (Dryzek 1996). For tensions between 'capitalism' and 'democracy', see Macpherson (1973), Bader et al. (1976), Cunningham (1987) and Scharpf (1999).
6. It is remarkable that no strictly 'ethical' objections (in the Habermasian sense of the term) can be found. This may be understood as an indication that associative democracy may offer much more chance of institutional and cultural pluralism to all different kinds of groups, cultures, lifestyles and varieties of the 'good life' than its rivals, though this aspect of associative democracy is not well developed by Cohen and Rogers. See my critical discussion of Hirst's proposals in the present volume.
7. I take it that Cohen and Rogers' first four criteria of evaluation are moral principles of democracy: popular sovereignty, political equality, distributive equity, and civic consciousness. For the sake of simplicity, I follow Cohen and Rogers in their interpretation of these principles. Each principle is complex and it is no easy task to present the main moral objections in a systematic way. This lack of clarity may be one reason why Cohen and Rogers (1995) refrain from any detailed response to the broad variety of replies in this regard. I include both 'legal security' or the rule of law and 'accountability' under 'popular sovereignty' (opposing a long (Marxist) tradition to treat them as 'functional norms'). For tensions between the norms of efficient and effective government and administration, on the one hand, and security and accountability, on the other, see Hoekema et al. (1998: 277ff). The specification of criteria of democracy by Beetham (1994) is more sophisticated than Cohen and Rogers' and could serve as a better frame. Two basic general principles, popular control and political equality, are specified as four criteria by Beetham: (i) free and fair elections (roughly corresponding to popular sovereignty and parts of political equality in Cohen and Rogers); (ii) open and accountable government (lacking in Cohen and Rogers); (iii) civil and political rights (mostly lacking in Cohen and Rogers); and (iv) democratic society (roughly corresponding with parts of political equality and distributive equity in Cohen and Rogers).
8. See Mayntz (1995; 1998) and Hoekema et al. (1998). See also Mathews (1989) and Streeck and Schmitter (1985). See Hoekema in the present volume.
9. Cohen and Rogers do not reflect upon the 'dialectics of institutionalization' (see (1992: 438f) for enforcement and administration of policy by local or intrafirm organisations). They seem to ignore the dangerous consequences of the inclusion of social movement organisations into state policies and do not discuss strategies to deal with them (see Bader (1991a: 241ff; and 1999ff) for minority religions).
10. Rightly chosen by Schmitter (1992: 508) as the 'Archimedian point' to leverage change for normative and for instrumental reasons. See Young (1992: 533) and Offe (1995: 121f).
11. See Immergut (1992: 483–6), Schmitter (1992: 509–12) and Young (1992: 530ff). See also Hirst (1990; 1997) for a very simplistic criticism of corporatism. It is remarkable how sloppily central concepts such as 'groups', 'associations' and 'organisations' are used in all contributions to the debate.
12. See Young (1992: 533) who states that 'a "more plural understanding"' and 'rough

equality of representation for any associations ... call for a mechanism of different resource allocation and organizing capacity to associations arising from the oppressed and disadvantaged social groups'. See Mansbridge (1992): a neo-corporatist approach to the USA would not duplicate that in Europe.

13. The conditions for positive gains through neo-corporatist arrangements are more fully spelled out by Schmitter, Lehmbruch, Streeck and others.

14. See the balanced proposal by Engelen (2000: 124–9) for 'ondernemingsbestuur'.

15. This is an assumption made by Offe (1998: 119ff) and many others. See Parekh (1998) and Bauman (1996) for many examples of compromise and bargaining in 'fundamental' cultural and religious matters.

16. The Dutch system of 'pillarisation' is an extremely interesting case to study in terms of the intersections of 'class pluralism', 'religious pluralism' and regional pluralism (for the latter relationship, see Toonen (1996)).

17. The catchy phrase that Cohen and Rogers would 'legislate the centrality of class conflict' is quite misleading: (i) you cannot 'legislate away' the centrality of class conflict or the impact of private power on politics (Cohen and Rogers rightly criticise neo-liberals and civic republicans for this); (ii) if one 'legislates' systems of group representation (there are other, less 'visible', more 'flexible' forms of administrative recognition and 'Einbeziehung'), one does not legislate the 'centrality' of conflicts, but regulates on the matter of which organisations should have which powers in which policy areas.

18. Schmitter, Cohen and Rogers, and Offe agree on the most important point that, opposed to standard-liberal and neo-liberal dogma, one has to start from the 'plain fact that organization is a *sine qua non* of popular sovereignty. People have voice only by merging political resources.' Unorganised interests, initiatives and opinions are 'mere noise'.

19. See Bader (1991a: 147–53) versus undifferentiated charges of paternalism.

20. Frankly, I do not see any difference between this 'Frankenstein-issue', which is treated as the second source of serious concerns with regard to popular sovereignty, and the potential for sclerosis, which is treated as the first bad news for political equality. It is the same issue. In fact, both dangers to political equality depend upon the specific way in which systems of representation of interest organisations are designed.

21. See Cooke and Morgan (1998: 111) for functional, cognitive and political lock-in.

22. The 'logic of representation' and the 'logic of influence' point in different directions (see Streeck (1994: 13–15) and Czada (1994: 47–52)).

23. Paul Hirst seems to trust more on exit than on voice and participation in his recent presentations of associative democracy (see colloquium in Amsterdam, November 1998).

24. Only Cohen and Rogers' first three qualitative characteristics of 'groups' refer to internal democracy: (i) accountability of group leaders, (ii) centralisation of authority in group decision-making, and (iii) encompassingness or completeness of group membership relative to affected populations. See more extensively Bader (1991a: 243–56). See also Naschold (1970). Hirst (1997: 133) seriously underestimates the problem.

25. See for divergent criteria and tricky questions of balance Bader (1991a: 249ff) and Naschold's critical evaluation of the LOM project (1992: 45ff).

26. Mansbridge (1992: 495). See also both Offe and Young, as well as Bader (1998a; 1998b; 1999b).

27. See Cohen and Rogers (1992: 451f). Associative democracy is more equitable than classically pluralist systems: by organising and mobilising 'workers and other citizens whose "natural" level of welfare is lower; by gaining representation and power at the national level; by reducing the cost of making a welfare-effort (more solidaristic and generic wage policies and social welfare policies).

28. Cohen and Rogers' first concern regarding distributive equity, actually, is a concern with regard to political equality: 'less well-organized interests are also the interests of the less well off' (1992: 445f) and it is remarkable that no remedies are discussed to address this threat (1992: 451). This is the rationale behind Levine's (1992) simplistic assertion that the institutions of associative democracy cannot be implemented without socialism, which only reproduces old, radicalist versions of a Chinese wall separating capitalism from socialism, reform from revolution and so on.
29. See Streeck's critical remarks (1998: 30, 54). See Bader (1998a; 1998b).
30. See the weakness of the five replies to the problem in Cohen and Sabel (1997: 336ff). Even reply (v) does not address the problem.
31. These dangers of federalism and 'localism' are vividly demonstrated by Nancy Rosenblum (1998: 140ff). This is the reason why republicans, such as Unger, criticise federalism, the separation of powers and so on. See my criticism (Bader 1991b). For regions, see Cooke and Morgan (1998: 87).
32. See Novy (1983). Mathews (1989: 181f) and also Hirst very much underrate mutualism and democratic associationalism in the socialist labour movement in their biased attempts to distance associative democracy from 'Marxism'.
33. See Bader (1998a: 202f).
34. See, for example, Hirst (1994: 39, 61, 169, 196), and (1997: 147) for 'empowerment' versus 'equality of outcomes'.
35. See, for example, Unger (1998: 163ff).
36. See also Cohen and Rogers' response to the 'undesirability charge' (1992: 427ff).
37. See also Offe's summary of the two great advantages of organised groups over individual action: they pool resources (scale effects) and 'affect the ends of action itself in desirable ways' by discovering 'true' preferences. In addition, they engage in bargaining which has, compared with commanding and voting, advantages regarding 'future' and 'rationality': retrospective approval or non-regret because it filters out passions, introduces more qualitative variation and flexibility in time and space, and because long-term consideration can easily emerge (time-span capacity is greater, that is, common institutional memory of past behaviour and relative stability lengthens the 'shadow of the future'). Besides 'future-regardingness', bargaining has, according to Offe, two other advantages: fact-regardingness and other-regardingness. See, for a more extensive discussion, Streeck and Schmitter (1985; 1996).
38. For evidence they refer to Jaffe's *Law Making by Private Groups, Harvard Law Review* 51 (1937), 202–53.
39. See Cohen and Rogers (1995: 251ff) for the role of deliberative arenas and the hope that solidarity arises in civil society. See Cohen and Rogers (1995: 265, note 28) regarding positions for and against Schmitter's reply that pathologies of particularism will abound even if the pathologies of inequalities are partly remedied. Cohen and Rogers stress the role of associative democracy in building up social support for equality itself (see above) and the need for 'popular regulatory capacity'.
40. See her productive criticism of Habermas, Rawls and others in this regard. For similar positions, see Gutmann and Thompson (1996) and Bader (1999d).
41. Jeremy Waldron has rightly criticised John Rawls's constraints on the content of public reason (1993a: 837ff; Bader 1999a: 618ff). His own insistence on 'reasons' is somewhat ambiguous: to the extent that he criticises elitist, rationalist and cognitivistic approaches, his appeal to reasons does not exclude much. If so, why not directly focus on 'an open, challenging, and indeterminate form of public deliberation in which nothing is taken for granted'? (Waldron 1993a: 848.) See also Waldron (2000).
42. Something which is still predominant in Cohen and Sabel (1997: 320f).
43. See Elster (1997; 1998) and Bohman (1997).
44. See Cohen and Sabel (1997: 321, 328) where they refer to a 'well-ordered deliberative

body'; Waldron's counterfactual construction of a 'Rousseauian democracy' (1993b: 413–16) also suffers from such neglect of structurally unequal chances in actual public deliberation in which 'good faith disagreement' (2000: 166) cannot simply be presumed.

45. Nancy Rosenblum (1998) has criticised the predominant (liberal, communitarian and deliberative democratic) approaches in political theory for their undifferentiated assumptions about the effects of associational life on the moral dispositions of members personally and the consequences for liberal democracy. Neither optimistic 'liberal expectancy' about associations as schools of civic virtues and simplistic 'transmission belt' models of civil society nor the widespread pessimism about associations as a dangerous threat to liberal democracy and a seedbed of particularist vices are theoretically plausible or empirically corroborated. Rosenblum shows convincingly that the 'moral valence of group life is indeterminate' and that 'no general theory of the moral uses of pluralism' (1998: 17) can be expected. In practical terms, she rightly warns against the 'liberal democratic logic of congruence' (Rosenblum 1998: 36ff), particularly by legal enforcement, as if the prime purpose of associations would be to produce virtuous citizens (and this warning is also directed against Cohen and Rogers' design (Rosenblum 1998: 41)); and she highlights that associations indifferent or patently adverse to liberal public culture actually have beneficial moral effects: they help to contain vices, functioning as a kind of safety valve, and help to develop more general virtues (not specific for liberal democratic culture) such as self-control, cooperation, trust, generosity and civility, which are much more important for the democracy of everyday life than predominant theories assume.

46. They may do this by making intelligent use of their strategic strength arising from the organisational weakness of employers or define their interests in a way that extends beyond their territorial or functional domain.

47. As regards boundaries, see the conclusion (520): 'Without stable borders – which by itself it will find hard to supply – associative democracy cannot be stable.' See for further elaboration Streeck (1998: 18–25). See also Offe (1998a: 105ff) and Scharpf (1988: 261).

48. See also Scharpf (1988: 261).

49. For this double tension between democracy and exit, and between democracy and entry, see Cohen and Rogers (1992: 519) on immigration, restrictive entry and privileges. More extensively, see Bauböck (1994), Bader (1997b; 1999a) for critical remarks on the presupposed big trade-off between inclusiveness and motivation.

50. For economic governance in terms of the organisation of work, regarding flexible specialisation see Sabel, Hirst and Zeitlin, regarding DQP see Streeck (1992), regarding new concepts of production see Kern and Schuhmann (1984), and regarding socio-technical systems theory see de Sitter (1994). For models of the democratisation of organisations, regarding co-determination see Rogers and Streeck (1994); see also the excellent treatment of the different approaches to the democratisation of work, governance of firms, co-determination as well as market rights by Ewald Engelen (2000). For regional associational democracy see Cooke and Morgan (1998) and for economic governance by states, the EU and international organisations see Scharpf (1999) and Hirst and Thompson (2000).

51. See Streeck (1995), Crouch and Streeck (1997), Cooke and Morgan (1998) and Scharpf (1999). See also many of the contributions in Hollingsworth and Boyer (1997) and in Kitschelt et al. (1999).

52. The tendency not only, rightly, to object to the strong theses of an absolute incompatibility of democracy and efficiency and so on, but also to the weak theses of strain and tension can often be found in recent literature on 'diversified quality production', on NPCs (most markedly in Kern and Schuhmann (1984), but also in de

Sitter (1994) and many others), and on local and regional associational governance (Cooke and Morgan (1998)). It should be criticised in order to stress the crucial distinction between wishful thinking ('utopias') and 'realist' alternatives.

53. See Scharpf (1988) for German federalism and the EU, with indications that all forms of 'functional representation', particularly neo-corporatist arrangements, could be plagued by the same mechanism (272f). For an excellent criticism, see Benz (1998). Scharpf (1999) is more careful.

54. See Offe (1995), who mentions two of the three widely shared arguments in the favourable functional quadrant: (i) contracting out policymaking functions to voluntary, encompassing associations enhances the efficiency and effectiveness of government, and (ii) facilitates enforcement of policies.

55. See Bader (1999c: 166ff) for a short indication of accountability and control in multilevel polities and administration.

56. See below for their response to Putnam (and, as I may add, to Offe's reply).

57. Implicitly, they oppose the deterministic tendencies often inherent in institutionalist approaches as well as the revolutionary image of institutional change which restricts the possibilities of institutional change to hot, exceptional situations, but they do not show that Offe's 'tension between principles and structure and of the coexistence of multiple but potentially inconsistent principles within one institution' are not restricted to 'exceptional cases'. As Unger, Sabel and others have shown, they are inherent in all 'normal' organisations, institutions and practices, and this fact is the basis of democratic experimentalism, of incremental institutional change, which, if pushed through, in the end changes institutions quite radically.

58. See Bader (1991a: 299ff) versus the one-sidedness of the political opportunity structure approach. All seven objections by Claus Offe against the 'conventional answer' to the question of what makes for the existence of groups and their 'substance' (1995: 126–32) are thoroughly analysed in Bader (1991a).

59. See also Hirst (1994) and Bader (1999e).

60. See similar criticisms by Tarrow (1996) and Grew (1996).

61. See Cooke and Morgan (1998: 71). See Bader (1997c) and Parekh for 'operative principles'.

62. See Bader (1991a: 122ff). See excellent examples, regarding Wales, of relatively fast cultural change as a result of changes in the structure of institutional arrangements in Cooke and Morgan (1998: 65).

63. In this regard, the task of 'institutional design' seems as 'paradoxical' as the task of 'education for autonomy'. Nevertheless, this 'impossible profession' actually exists (Christis 1998: Part I, Ch.6).

64. See, recently, Hollingsworth and Boyer (1997: 12).

65. As an existing example one could discuss the German system of party financing which combines openness of financing (depending on percentages of actual votes in elections) with the five per cent hurdle. Compare Hirst's discussion of a voucher system in education: see 'as far as practicable' (1997: 126) and 'to a limited number of publicly registered associations of their choice (say 5)' (1997: 151). See Scharpf (1999: 152f).

66. See Katznelson (1995: 199). How do Cohen and Rogers expect that the transitional leap toward radical redistribution 'could be accomplished by democratic means'?

67. See the many accusations that Cohen and Rogers attempted to introduce social democratic European corporatism into the USA by the back door (by Schmitter, Katznelson, Mansbridge and Young among others) and their response that associative democracy is 'less an amendment to traditional social democratic strategies than … a synthesis of social democracy and radical democracy' (Cohen & Rogers 1995: 236). See also the debate about whether associative democracy is 'merely a strategy' or 'a new form of constitutional order' (Cohen & Rogers 1995: 236, 240, 252): a matter of degree, with no attempt to design a 'full range of appropriate new institutions and

organizations' (Cohen & Rogers 1992: 434).
68. The design of a 'societal' model of associative democracy, such as Hirst's, has to answer hard questions some of which are raised by Ash Amin (1996) directly and many more indirectly by Streeck.

REFERENCES

Amin, A. 1996. 'Beyond associative democracy'. New Political Economy, 1/3, 305–33.
Bader, V.M. 1989. Ungleichheiten. Protheorie sozialer Ungleichheit und kollektiven Handelns. Teil I. Opladen.
1991a. Kollektives Handeln. Protheorie sozialer Ungleichheit und kollektiven Handelns. Teil II. Opladen.
1991b. 'The constitution of empowered democracy: dream or nightmare?' de Lange & Raes 1991: 118–34.
1997. Citizenship and Exclusion. Houndsmills: MacMillan.
1997a. 'The arts of forecasting and policy making'. Bader 1997: 153–72.
1997b. 'Fairly open borders'. Bader 1997: 28–62.
1997c. 'The cultural conditions of trans-national citizenship'. Political Theory, 25/6, 771–813.
1998a. 'Dilemmas of ethnic affirmative action. Benign state-neutrality or relational ethnic neutrality'. Citizenship Studies, 2/3, 435–73.
1998b. 'Egalitarian multiculturalism: institutional separation and cultural pluralism'. Bauböck & Rundell 1998: Ch.7, 185–222.
1999a. 'For love of country'. Political Theory, 27/3, 379–97.
1999b. 'Religious pluralism. Secularism or priority for democracy?' Political Theory, 27/5, 597–633.
1999c. 'Citizenship of the European Union. Human rights, rights of citizens of the Union and of Member States'. Ratio Juris, 12/2, 153–81.
1999d. 'Unity and stability in modern societies and in recent political philosophy'. Harskamp & Musschenga 1999.
1999e. 'Institutions, culture and identity of trans-national citizenship: how much integration and "communal spirit" is needed?' Crouch & Eder 1999.
1999f. 'How to institutionalize religious pluralism?' Unpublished manuscript.
Bader, V. M., J. Berger, H. Janssman and J. V. Knesebeck, 1976. Einführungindie Gesellschaftstheorie. Frankfurt, New York: Campus.
Bauböck, R. 1994. Transnational Citizenship. Aldershot: Elgar.
Baumann, J. 1996. Contesting Culture. Cambridge: CUP.
Beetham, D., ed. 1994. 'Introduction' and 'Key principles and indices for a democratic audit'. Beetham, Defining and Measuring Democracy, 1–5, 25–43. London: Sage.
Benz, A. 1985. Föderalismus als dynamisches System. Opladen: Westdeutscher Verlag.
1998. 'Politikverflechtung ohne Politikverflechtungsfalle'. PVS, 3/1998, 558–89.
Bohman, J. 1997. 'Deliberative democracy and effective social freedom'. Bohman & Rehg 1997: 321–48.
Bohman, J. & W. Rehg, eds. 1997. Deliberative Democracy. Cambridge, MA: MIT Press.
Boyer, R. & D. Drache, eds. 1996a. States Against Markets. London: Routledge.
1996b. 'State and market: a new engagement for the twenty-first century'. Boyer & Drache 1996a: 84–116.
Christis, J. 1998. Arbeid, Organisatie en Stress. Amsterdam: Het Spinhuis.
Cohen, J. 1997. 'Procedure and substance in deliberative democracy'. Bohman & Rehg 1997: 407–38.
1998. 'Democracy and liberty'. Elster 1998: 185–231.
1993. 'Associations and democracy'. Social Philosophy and Policy, 50, 282–312.

1994. 'My utopia or yours?'. *Politics and Society, Comments on Roemer's: A Future for Socialism,* 507–21.

1995. 'Solidarity, democracy, association'. Wright 1995: 236–67. Also Streeck 1994: 136ff.

1998. 'Can egalitarianism survive internationalization?' Streeck 1998: 175–95.

Cohen, J. & J. Rogers. 1992. 'Secondary associations and democratic governance'. *Politics and Society,* 20/4, 391–472. The article is reprinted in Wright 1995.

Cohen, J. & C. Sabel. 1997. 'Directly- Deliberative Polyarchy'. *European Law Journal,* 3/4, 313–42

Cooke, P. & K. Morgan. 1998. *The Associational Economy. Firms, Regions, and Innovation.* Oxford: OUP.

Crouch, C. & W. Streeck, eds. 1997. 'Introduction. The future of capitalist diversity'. Crouch & Streeck *Political Economy of Modern Capitalism. Mapping Convergence and Diversity,* 1–19. London: Sage.

Cunningham, F. 1987. *Democracy and Socialism.* Cambridge: CUP.

Czada, R. 1994. 'Konjunkturen des Korporatismus'. Streeck 1994: 37–64.

Dryzek, J. 1996. *Democracy in Capitalist Times.* New York: OUP.

Ebbinghausen, B. & J. Visser. 1994. 'Barrieren und Wege "grenzenloser" Solidarität'. Streeck 1994: 223–55.

Eder, K., ed. 1999. *Citizenship, Markets, and the State.* Oxford: OUP.

Elster, J. 1997. 'The market and the forum'. Bohman & Rehg 1997: 3–34.

1998. 'Deliberation and constitution making'. *Deliberative Democracy,* 97–122. Cambridge: CUP.

Engelen, E. 2000. 'Economisch Burgerschap in de Onderneming'. Ph.D. thesis, University of Amsterdam.

Goodin, R., ed. 1998. *The Theory of Institutional Design.* Cambridge: CUP.

Grew, R. 1996. 'Paradoxes of Italy's 19th century political culture'. Paper EUI, Firenze, March.

Gutmann, A. & D. Thompson. 1996. *Democracy and Deliberation.* Cambridge, MA: Belknap Press of Harvard University Press.

Harskamp, A.V. & A.A. Musschenga, eds. 1999. *The Many Faces of Individualism.* Leuven: Peeters.

Hesse, J.J. & A. Benz. 1988. 'Staatliche Institutionenpolitik im Internationalen Vergleich'. *Speyerer Arbeitshefte,* 89.

Hirst, P. 1989. *The Pluralist Theory of the State.* London, New York: Routledge.

1990. *Representative Democracy and its Limits.* Cambridge: Polity Press.

1992. 'Comments on "Secondary Associations and Democratic Governance"'. *Politics and Society,* 20/4, 473–80.

1994. *Associative Democracy.* Cambridge: Polity Press.

1997. *From Statism to Pluralism.* London: UCL Press.

Hirst, P. & S. Khilnani, eds. 1996. *Reinventing Democracy.* Oxford: Blackwell.

Hirst, P. & Thompson. 2000. *Globalisation in Question.* Cambridge: Polity.

Hoekema, A.J., N.F. Manen, G.M.A. Heijden, I.C. Vlies, & B. de Vroom. 1998. *Integraal bestuur. De behoorlijkheid, effectiviteit en legitimiteit van onderhandelend bestuur.* Amsterdam: Amsterdam University Press.

Hollingsworth, J.R. & R. Boyer. 1997. 'Coordination of economic actors and social systems of production'. Hollingsworth & Boyer. *Contemporary Capitalism. The Embeddedness of Institutions.* Cambridge: CUP.

Immergut, E.M. 1992. 'An institutional critique of associative democracy'. *Politics and Society,* 20/4, 481–6.

Katznelson, I. 1995. 'On architectural syncretism'. Wright 1995: 193–9.

Kern, H. & H. Schuhman. 1984. *Das Ende der Arbeitsteilung?* München: Beck.

Kitschelt, H., P. Lange, G. Marks & J. Stephens, eds. 1999. *Continuity and Change in Contemporary Capitalism.* Cambridge: CUP.

Kymlicha, W. & W. Norman, eds. 1999. *Citizenship in Diverse Societies*. Oxford: OUP.

Lange, R. de & K. Raes, eds. 1991. *Plural Legalities. Critical Legal Studies in Europe*. Nijmegen: Ars Aequi Libri.

Lehmbruch, G. 1967. *Proporzdemokratie*. Tübingen: Mohr.

1979. 'Consociational democracy, class conflict and the new corporatism' and 'Concluding remarks: problems for future research on corporatist intermediation and policy making'. Schmitter & Lehmbruch 1979: 53–62, 299–310.

1982. 'Introduction. Neo-corporatism in comparative perspective'. Lehmbruch & Schmitter 1982: 1–28.

1996. 'Der Beitrag der Korporatismusforschung zur Entwicklung der Steuerungstheorie'. *PVS*, 37/4, 735–51.

Lehmbruch, G. & P. Schmitter, eds. 1982. *Patterns of Corporatist Policy-Making*. Beverly Hills: Sage.

Levine, A. 1992. 'Soft on capitalism'. *Politics and Society*, 20/4, 487–93.

Lijphart, A. 1968. *The Politics of Accommodation: Pluralism and Democracy in the Netherlands*. Berkeley: University of California Press.

1984. *Democracies. Patterns of Majoritarian and Consensus Government in Twenty-One Countries*. New Haven, London: Yale University Press.

Macpherson, C.B. 1973. *Democratic Theory*. Oxford: Clarendon.

Mansbridge, J. 1992. 'A deliberative perspective on neocorporatism'. *Politics and Society*, 20/4, 493–506.

Mathews, J. 1989. *Age of Democracy*. Melbourne, Oxford: OUP.

Matzner, E & W. Streeck, eds. 1991. *Beyond Keynesianism*. Aldershot: Edward Elgar.

Mayntz, R. 1995. 'Politische Stuerung'. *PVS*, 148–68. Sonderheft 26, Opladen.

1998. 'Private governance'. Public Lecture, Amsterdam, 8 May 1998.

Miller, P. 1996. 'Dilemmas of accountability: the limits of accounting'. Hirst & Khulnani 1996: 57–69.

Naschold, F. 1970. *Organisation und Demokratie*. Stuttgart, Berlin.

1992. *Den Wandel organisieren*. Berlin: Edition Sigma.

Novy, K. 1983. *Genossenschaftsbewegung*. Berlin: Transit.

Offe, C. 1995. 'Some sceptical considerations on the malleability of representative institutions'. Wright 1995: 114–32.

1998. '"Homoigeneity" and Constitutional Democracy'. *Journal of Political Philosophy*, 6/2, 113–41.

1998a. 'Designing institutions in east European transitions'. Goodin 1998: 199–226.

1998b. 'Demokratie und Wohlfahrtsstaat'. Streeck 1994: 99–136.

Parekh, B. 1998. 'Equality in a multicultural society'. *Citizenship Studies*, 2/3, 397–412.

Putnam, R. 1993. *Making Democracy Work*. Princeton: Princeton University Press.

Raufer, T. 1998. *Koordinationsprobleme politischer Steuerung*. IfS Werkstatt 3. Institut für Staatswissenschaften, Universität München.

Rogers, J. & W. Streeck, eds. 1994. 'The study of works councils: concepts and problems'. Roger and Streeck. *Works Councils*, 3–26. Chicago, London: University of Chicago Press.

Rosenblum, N. 1998. *Membership and Morals. The Personal Uses of Pluralism in America*. Princeton: Princeton University Press.

Sabel, C.F. 1993. 'Studied trust: building new forms of cooperation in a volatile economy'. Swedberg 1993.

1995. 'Bootstrapping reform: rebuilding firms, the welfare state, and unions'. *Politics and Society*, 23/1, 5–48.

Zeitlin, J., eds. 1997. 'Stories, strategies, structures: rethinking historical alternatives to mass production'. Zeitlin. *World of Possibilities. Flexibility and Mass Production in Western Industrialization*, 1–36. Cambridge: CUP.

Sitter, U. de. 1994. *Synergetisch Produceren*. Assen: v. Gorcum.

Szasz, A. 1992. 'Progress through mischief'. *Politics and Society*, 20/4, 521–8.
Scharpf, F.W. 1988. 'The joint-decision trap: lessons from German federalism and European integration'. *Public Administration*, 66, 239–78.
1998. 'Demokratie in der transnationalen Politik'. Streeck 1998: 151–74.
1999. *Governing in Europe. Effective and Democratic?* Oxford: OUP.
Schattschneider, E. 1975. *The Semisovereign People*. Hinsdale: Dryden Press.
Schmitter, P. 1979. 'Introduction. Still the century of corporatism?' and 'Modes of interest intermediation and models of societal change in western Europe'. Schmitter & Lehmbruch 1979: 1–6, 7–52, 63–94.
1982. 'Reflections on where the theory of neo-corporatism has gone and where the praxis of neo-corporatism may be going'. Lehmbruch & Schmitter 1982: 259–80.
1992. 'The irony of modern democracy and efforts to improve its practice. *Politics and Society*, 20/4, 507–12.
1994. 'Interests, associations and intermediation in a reformed, post-liberal democracy'. Streeck 1994: 160–74.
Lehmbruch, G., eds. 1979. *Trends Toward Corporatist Intermediation*. London: Sage.
Grote, J. 1997. 'Der korporatistische Sisyphus: Vergangenheit, Gegenwart und Zukunft'. *PVS*, 38/3, 530–54.
Streeck, W. 1991. 'On the institutional conditions of diversified quality production'. Matzner & Streeck 1991: 21–61.
1992. 'Inclusion and secession: questions on the boundaries of associative democracy'. *Politics and Society*, 20/40, 513–20.
1994. Introduction, 'Staat und Verbände: Neue Fragen, Neue Antworten?' *Staat und Verbände*, 7–36. PVS Sonderheft 2: Westdeutscher Verlag.
1995. 'Works councils in western Europe: from consultation to participation'. Rogers & Streeck 1995: 313–50.
1997. 'The efficiency of democracy'. Unpublished manuscript.
1998. Introduction, 'Internationale Wirtschaft, nationale Demokratie?' *Internationale Wirtschaft, nationale Demokratie*, 11–58. Frankfurt: Campus.
Streeck, W. & P. Schmitter. 1985. 'Community, market, state – and associations? The prospective contribution of interest governance to social order'. *Private Interest Government: Beyond Market and State*, 1–29. London, Beverly Hills: Sage.
Swedberg, R., ed. 1993. *Explorations in Economic Sociology*. New York: Russel Sage Foundation.
Tarrow, S. 1996. 'Making social science work across space and time'. *APSR*, June.
Toonen, T. 1996. 'On the administrative condition of politics. Administrative transformation in the Netherlands'. *West European Politics*, 19/3, 609–32.
Unger, R.M. 1987. *Politics*. 3 Vols. Cambridge: CUP.
1996. *What Should Legal Analysis Become?* London, New York: Verso.
1998. *Democracy Realized*. London, New York: Verso.
Visser, J. & A. Hemerijck. 1997. *A Dutch Miracle*. Amsterdam: Amsterdam University Press.
Waldron, J. 1993a. 'Religious contributions in public deliberation'. *San Diego Law Review*, 30, 817–48.
1993b. 'Rights and majorities: Rousseau revisited'. *Liberal Rights*, 392–421. Cambridge: CUP.
1999. 'Cultural identity and civic responsibility'. Kymlicha & Norman 1999: 155–74.
Wright, E.O., ed. 1995. Preface, 'The real utopias project', ix–xiv. Introduction, 1–3. Wright ed. *Associations and Democracy*. London, New York: Verso.
Young, I.M. 1992. 'Social groups in associative democracy'. *Politics and Society*, 20/4, 529–35.

4

Associo-Deliberative Democracy and Qualitative Participation

PIOTR PERCZYNSKI

The famous intellectual war within democratic theory between 'elitists' and 'participatory democrats' seems to have quieted down some time ago. The former were perhaps too pessimistic about the dangers of extensive participation and the latter too optimistic about its prospects and advantages. The debate was driven by their respective fear and support for the (possibly incompetent) people reaching for complete power. However, in the meantime, the reality of democracy in the western world, where most people turn out to have little interest in politics and where the level of participation is decreasing, has given rise to the common acknowledgement of the danger of people not even exercising the power they already have. Therefore, we now hear a general call for enriching democracy with a higher level of participation, and the debate focuses more on *what kind* of participation would be the most suitable.

Of the many modes of participation present within modern democracy, special attention is usually given to voting. At the beginning of the twenty-first century, there is great concern about low electoral turnouts manifesting the lack of interest of the people toward the democratic process. But voting for representatives is not the only form of participation that could be looked for to increase. Direct democracy, which usually appears in the form of referendums, and which to many is a synonym of participatory democracy (Held 1993b: 15), could be another option. However, it introduces more voting, and does not at all guarantee increased turnout, and hence an increased participation. It is, in fact, a form of *quantitative* participation, to which Anthony Downs' argument of 'rational ignorance' applies. Just like during (local or national) parliamentary or presidential elections, for voters, the 'time and effort required to overcome it do not represent a reasonable investment' (Fishkin 1995: 22).

Apart from the above-mentioned quantitative forms of participation, I also distinguish *qualitative* forms.[1] In the former, the participants are restricted to voting: a mere saying 'yes' or 'no' to subjects (or people) that they often do not know much about. The latter requires a deeper form of activity on the part of the participants, which connects to their interests and abilities, and it is that form that I will focus on in this article. Examples of qualitative participation are the contacting (or consulting) of representatives by the represented electorate and the organising and signing of petitions, or more radical forms such as political strikes or protest marches. However, these forms are, in western democracies, usually at a much lower level than voting, and are not expected to be easily increased; hence, they are not likely to compensate for the lack of participation elsewhere (Parry & Moyser 1994: 47).

Other forms of qualitative participation that are mentioned in the democratic theoretical debate are, on the one hand, activities within workplace groups (so-called workplace democracy) and in voluntary associations, and on the other hand, different types of democratic deliberation. In the past decade, two innovative democratic theories based on these forms of participation have got a lot of attention: associative democracy and deliberative democracy. Furthermore, in the light of the mentioned call for 'improving democracy' by stimulating participation, an interesting aspect of both of them is that they can provide a form of democratic participation which could be compatible with the existing representative (parliamentary, territorial and so on) democracy. Yet, so far, little has been done to study the connection between the two variants. In this article, I will try to analyse this relation between associative and deliberative democracy.

To begin, I propose a terminology for different types of democracy and for the ways in which those types can be combined. I make a distinction between types that describe a democratic system (structure) on the one hand, and types that refer to democratic mechanisms, or decision procedures, on the other. In this sense, for example, representative democracy is understood as a system that requires an intermediate level of representatives, who are elected by the represented, and they in turn take all the decisions that have to be taken. Although in most practical cases, the decision procedures are taken as a fixed part of representative democracy (namely, voting, both for the representatives and (by the representatives) for decisions), I do not consider this as a necessary part of representative democracy. Representatives could also be chosen by other means (for example, by argumentation or even by lot), and the same holds for the decisions that those representatives take.

Direct democracy is another example of a system, which, just like representative democracy, usually has the mechanism presupposed (voting), but again, at least in theory, it could also have other mechanisms (for example, deliberation). As a system, it is considered as the opposite of representative democracy: where representative democracy requires at least one intermediate level of representation, direct democracy requires that there is no intermediation. In this article, I will show that associative democracy is understood as a system as well, whereas deliberative democracy is understood as a mere decision procedure (mechanism), which obviously assumes a democratic system to be present, but does not specify *which* system it is exactly involved in. In the last part of this article, I will explore the possibility of these two models of democracy 'joining forces'.

Deliberative Democracy as a Mechanism

The term deliberative democracy was first mentioned by Joseph Bessette in 1980 and it was used in the debate between elitist and participatory democrats, where it was applied on the side of the latter (Bohman & Rehg 1997b). Therefore, we can say that deliberative democracy had the call for more (qualitative) participation already present at its roots. Along with the popularity of the debate on deliberative democracy, the depth of its theoretic-analytical research reached a high level in the second half of the 1990s. Deliberative democracy was developed from a fundamental democratic concern pointing to the fact that democracy should not only be about aggregation of voices, but also about their transformation as an outcome of free deliberation. In other words, a passive counting of votes is 'not enough', as that is only the measuring of opinions. Within deliberative democracy, greater importance is given to opinion *forming* as the outcome of a debate, after listening to arguments of others. In fact, this refers to the idea that before making a decision, one should take into account as much information as possible – and what better way of getting information than being exposed to the opinions of others in a face-to-face discussion? Within deliberative democracy the outcome of a deliberation should, however, not only be the *exchange* of ideas and information, but also a concrete agreement (compromise), based on the assumption that a group of people confronted with each other's ideas should come to a certain consensus built on the shared knowledge they have after the exchange. The fact that people change their views after deliberation was proven empirically in the deliberative poll experiments of James Fishkin (1995: 178–81).

As Elster points out, deliberation does not guarantee achievement of consensus, therefore, there must be at least one other mechanism kept in reserve in cases where the deliberation does not work. He writes that, in practice, deliberative democracy is 'always supplemented by voting or bargaining or both, because of time constraints as well as for other reasons' (1998b: 14). It is good to keep in mind that deliberative democracy does not cover all possibilities. In fact, even a precisely defined mechanism such as voting does not do that: there are cases (although much more rare) in which an even split causes deadlock.

A significant aspect of deliberative democracy concerns education. Apart from actually extending one's knowledge on the subject matter through the exchange of information, deliberation also may teach people empathy, because of contacts with people who have different points of view. Understanding them means putting yourself in the place of the other person. That may lead to a greater form of self-reflection and self-knowledge. On top of this, one could assume that exercising deliberation teaches people to look at the advantages of reaching for consensus, and makes them apply this principle even in their daily life. Elster underlines another interesting aspect of deliberative democracy in his analysis. He claims that deliberation has a certain predominance over other forms of democratic mechanisms, as he states that deliberation *precedes* them: 'the first decision to decide by voting is reached by arguing' (1998b: 10).[2]

Public deliberation by citizens could be applied in various circumstances. However, even though the scale of the democratic 'enterprise' is not mentioned explicitly, it is understood that deliberation on a large scale (that is, within a large group of people) is *not* feasible, since we are talking here about a 'face-to-face' mechanism. In our terminology of types of democracy, deliberative democracy should be put in the category of democratic mechanisms, rather than systems. The reason is that it only describes how decisions should be reached, but does not specify on which level or in which structure they take place. It is definitely focused on *democratic* systems, as all theorists underline; they mention, for example, that *all* those who will be affected by the decision or their representatives should take part in the deliberation. Elster even splits the 'democratic' and 'deliberative' parts of deliberative democracy. The democratic part concerns exactly 'collective decision making with the participation of all'. The deliberative part stresses that this decision-making is exercised 'by means of arguments offered *by* and *to* participants who are committed to the values of rationality and impartiality' (1998b: 8).

It was the discussion about rationality and impartiality that, on the one hand, raised the theoretical debate on deliberative democracy to such a high level in the 1990s, but on the other, moved it away from more practical solutions so that it slipped into meandering and philosophical speculations. The idea that political choice in order to be legitimate must be an outcome of deliberation about ends among free, equal and rational agents, as Elster points out, was stressed by both John Rawls and Jürgen Habermas. They are seen as the intellectual fathers of deliberative democracy, and the fact that two such prominent thinkers have participated in the debate makes deliberative democracy very fashionable. Rawls's idea of *reflective equilibrium* presupposed the possibility of moral deliberation, whereas Habermas's concept of the *ideal speech situation* was intended to permit deliberation about ends as well as about means (1998b: 5). Their contribution triggered the discussion about the very nature of democracy and its foundations, rationality and so on in relation to deliberation and deliberative democracy in general.

So far, we have looked at deliberative democracy as a mechanism, but in fact, Fishkin proposes a democratic system based on deliberation, the deliberative poll. The above-described deliberative mechanism is applied to a random sample of citizens, who are to discuss a given problem, and (hopefully) come, via deliberation, to agreement. Unlike in the circles of their daily lives, participants will in this way meet virtually all other possible points of view (which they otherwise would not know about). Similar to regular opinion polls (nowadays the most important (or sometimes the only) indicator for politicians of how to adjust their policies) the samples should reflect the society as a whole, and have statistical relevance. Deliberative polling differs from opinion polls, however, in that the actual decision (agreement) that is reached is practically binding. This should make it worthwhile for individuals to participate. The outcome of such a deliberative poll does not reflect 'top-of-the-head' answers (as in the case of opinion polls and, most of the time, voting for that matter). Participants are not only confronted with each other's arguments and counter-arguments, but also get additional information from the organisers of the deliberative polls. The obvious problem is how the objectivity of this additional information can be guaranteed, but there is an attempt to solve this by inviting experts who represent several conflicting views on the matter (Fishkin 1995; 1991).

Although this system is presented as deliberative democracy, I distinguish between the deliberation (which is the mechanism) and the polling (which could strictly speaking also be applied to another mechanism). So here, I consider polling as the system, and the deliberation within the deliberative poll still as the mechanism.

The System of Associative Democracy

The discussion about associative democracy started at the end of the 1980s. Associative democracy was developed and advocated by its theorists as a democratic model in which the main role is played by voluntary, self-governing groups or associations,[3] which are internally democratic, that is, possess a democratic internal structure (for a similar definition see Streeck (1995: 188)). Although it has a distinct (qualitative) participatory character, associative democracy was, in fact, developed *not* as the outcome of a search for more participation, but rather to supplement the existing (that is, representative, parliamentary and so on) democratic system which seemed to be inadequate, especially as far as the representation of interests was concerned. It was an imaginative and innovative democratic system, with the advantage that it was, instead of inventing new institutions, taking groups that already exist and turning existing memberships and activities into political participation.

As the particular designs of associative democracy originate from different sources, their character, the type of associations involved and the functioning of these in society differ with every author.[4] Nevertheless, all designs require associations to have a democratic structure, and all reflect the idea that associations can represent interests that are not sufficiently organised through 'existing territorial politics based on majority rule' (Cohen and Rogers 1995a: 43). We can roughly divide the associative democracy designs into two streams. The first one arises from pluralist tradition, where the state plays a marginal role, and the associations are to be originated 'bottom-up' ('societal approach'). In the other stream, of a corporatist background, the state plays a more active role, in some sense controlling the associations ('top-down' or 'state approach').

We can locate the design of Paul Hirst in the first stream; in the second half of the 1980s, he formulated a design for the associational reconstruction of democracy by expanding and developing the anti-collectivist ideas of English political pluralism (and Guild Socialism) (1989; 1993; 1994). English political pluralism is a political doctrine that developed after the First World War mainly by G.D.H. Cole and H. Laski, under the strong influence of both British socialism and liberalism

(Perczynski 1995; 1998). Hirst substantially transforms English political pluralism by moving away from the functionalist limitations of this doctrine that were in contradiction with its overall freedom-oriented character. In my view, the tensions caused by this contradiction were, at the end of the 1920s, an important reason for the total disappearance of this doctrine from theoretical debate. Unlike English political pluralists, who were hostile to representative democracy and treated their doctrine as a substitute for it, Hirst treats his associationalist system as a supplement to the existing representational system. He does develop pluralist ideas on the economy, and proposes a detailed programme of economic reconstruction, which in my view seems to be not entirely realistic in the market economy of today; however, in this text, I focus on the political side of his proposals.[5] In his design, Hirst envisions associations as spontaneously arising, democratically legitimated, self-governing, and voluntary, with internal participation of the members as their main asset and with the state having minimal power over the existence and structure of such associations (1993: 12; 1994: 19; 1997: 17). He prescribes that the relations between authorities and the associations take place on the local or regional level, with (if possible) omission of the national state level (1994: 39). This can only work in cases where the issues are of a local nature.

Hirst sees associations as taking an active part in informing the government and representing the interests of their members, but also in the actual process of governance (1997: 17). They are to take over some of the important functions of central government, such as the provision of services. Because services are getting more complicated and need to be customised to the needs and preferences of individuals, a democratic and voluntary association is (because of its scale and size, and the short distance to the consumers) much better suited to provide modern services than the state. But as membership of an association is voluntary, the state is still an alternative provider for those who prefer it. Hirst considers associative democracy as a 'vital supplement', rather than a substitute, for parliamentary representative democracy (1994: 42; 1997: 24). This makes it, in fact, a 'partial' substitute: some decisions are taken away from the existing (functioning) representative democracy, and will now be taken by associations. One could also envision decisions that are not taken in a democratic context at all, and by making them the responsibility of associations, it is 'enlarging' democracy – hence, a supplement.

In fact, Hirst states that associative democracy can *strengthen* representative institutions (and thus representative democracy) because freeing them from an overload of activities allows them to concentrate better on their main functions: 'to provide society with a framework of basic laws to guide social actors; to oversee forms of public service provision to hold public officials accountable; and to protect the rights and interests of citizens' (1997: 18). His design of associative democracy should be understood as a system next to representative democracy. He does not elaborate much about the mechanisms within the associations.

Joshua Cohen and Joel Rogers designed another form of associative democracy, also meant to supplement, or partly substitute (see above), representative democracy. They build their design on (neo-)corporatist ideas, which places them in the stream of the 'state approach', as they give the state an active role in organising the associations and the relations between them. Their associations take the form of broadly understood interest groups. The list of features that groups should have (though, in fact, Cohen and Rogers put it more vaguely as 'features of qualitative variation ... that are worth keeping in mind' (1995a: 48)) includes accountability of the group leadership to members. This is an indicator of democracy, so by stating this feature, Cohen and Rogers implicitly require associations to possess an internally democratic structure. They also view the functions that groups perform in society as a contribution to an 'egalitarian-democratic order'. They mention various functions that such groups are capable of performing, and by so doing contribute to 'egalitarian-democratic order'. Similar to Hirst, in their view, associations can take an active part in 'social governance'. The role of associations as 'problem solvers' is underlined – they are not only to help to formulate public policies, but also to execute them. Closely connected to this function is the function of providing information. Although some tasks are still reserved for the state (which, as I said, plays a much larger role than in Hirst's design), associations can provide the state (much better than state agencies can) with accurate information on the preferences of their members, as well as on the impact of proposed legislation or the implementation of existing law. Cohen and Rogers write: 'Groups provide additional enforcement power, thus increasing the likelihood that *decisions made by the people* will be implemented.' (1995a: 65; emphasis added.) Note also that here they implicitly assume an underlying democratic mechanism in which members of the associations participate. This function becomes more important, since, according to Cohen and Rogers, the state is today heavily involved in regulation, and constantly extends its regulatory reach to more diverse and technically complex areas and rapidly changing processes. The function that affects the overall democratic system most directly is the function of 'equalising representation' (1995a: 43). Cohen and Rogers say that groups enrich the political debate because a wider range of proposals can be discussed seriously; in my view, this can be seen as a starting point for a form of deliberation on the intergroup level.

Another aspect of Cohen and Rogers' design is education. Cohen and Rogers stress the importance of associations as a particular type of school where their members can learn in practice how democratic norms work (1995a: 43–4). This would fit the mentioned educational ideals expressed in the deliberative democracy literature, in which the deliberation itself also has the function of acquiring knowledge and self-reflection.

Another design that we could place in the neo-corporatist stream of associative democracy is the proposal of Philippe Schmitter. Schmitter also perceives his design as an addition to representative democracy. Associations in his design are 'modern' interest groups, in an even broader sense than Cohen and Rogers – almost any organisation claiming to represent 'causes' or 'rights' could fit in. These kinds of associations already perform a variety of public functions in the dual sense that they affect the public with their actions and they carry out policies, often subsidised by the state. Schmitter envisions a design in which people could choose more directly which interests concern them the most and which associations could best represent them in these.

Such associations would have to meet several conditions of which the most important are a non-profit character and, again, an internal democratic structure. Schmitter proposes a fixed 'Charter' (or general provisions) for all groups able to play a role in his schema, which would describe their internal structure, their rights and the means by which to check on them from outside. Schmitter mentions, for example, a guarantee for democratic procedures and a guarantee that public authorities will not intervene in the internal deliberations (1995: 175). Only associations who would fulfil their duties according to these general provisions could gain and maintain a so-called 'semi-public' status and take part in 'voucher voting'. For the latter, Schmitter proposes that every individual gets a fixed amount of vouchers, which can be 'voted' with for associations that have semi-public status, by giving them one or more of the vouchers. In this setting, being a member is not a requirement for voting for the association, and likewise, membership carries no obligation to vote. Schmitter sets out quite detailed arrangements concerning the distribution of the vouchers; his idea is that they could be administered jointly with the yearly income tax. However, unlike paying taxes, people would not be *forced* to participate; in the end, funds would be distributed in proportion to the 'vote' of those who wished to participate, just like normal elections. 'Voucherism' is a distinctively participatory mechanism, parallel to the electoral mechanism of representative democracy.

Hence Schmitter's design is a democratic system, in the sense we have introduced before, and is like the previous two designs meant to function next to a representative democratic system. However, the system differs from the two previous ones *as a system*, because it involves two different types of participation within the associative democratic part: the possibility of being a member of an association on the one hand, and being a supporter (that is, a voter in the voucher system) of an association on the other. Although Schmitter, like Hirst and like Cohen and Rogers, does not give much detail about the internal democratic mechanism within associations, his proposal for 'voucherism' is extremely detailed – it can be seen as a separate *mechanism* (decision procedure, as I have defined earlier) within this system. In fact, his system includes two (new, apart from the participation needed in the representative democracy system) types of participation: voucher voting (which is not necessarily 'more' and, besides, of a quantitative nature) and internal (possibly qualitative) participation within the 'semi-public' associations, which can be compared to the internal participation in the associations of Hirst and of Cohen and Rogers.

All three designs impose democratic conditions on the groups concerned, which means they may exclude certain groups from taking part in the system at all. This exclusion is a reason for criticism of associative democracy, as some theorists state that, in reality, most groups are not of a democratic nature, so it would be more interesting to look at what one could do with the existing groups (Bader 1998a; 1998b: Mansbridge 1995; Young 1995). However, within the designs of associative democracy, the *existence* of other types of group is not denied; they are simply not considered as associations able to contribute to associative democracy (perhaps because already it would be difficult to defend the second part of that name). In fact, reducing the number of relevant associations in this way also serves pragmatic goals, such as those regarding the effectiveness of negotiations among associations[6] (deliberation on an intergroup level) and between associations and the state, as well as the overall efficiency of the 'double' democratic (associative *and* representative) system.

Associo-Deliberative Democracy?

As we have seen, associative democracy is a system without a predefined democratic mechanism. Clearly, theorists of associative democracy were much more preoccupied with the functioning of the associations in the society and less in how actual decisions would be taken within the association; unlike Guild Socialism or some corporatistic designs, there are, fortunately, no detailed (and therefore likely to be unrealistic) blueprints here. Deliberative democracy, on the other hand, is not considered a system, but a mechanism without a specified 'context'. The idea of using deliberative democracy as a mechanism inside the groups which are operating within the framework of associative democracy comes to mind and seems to be possible, as the ideas of both theories regarding qualitative participation seem to fit very well. In addition, they both must be connected to smaller scale (face-to-face) debates and decision-making. Cohen even states that 'the notion of a deliberative democracy is rooted in the intuitive ideal of a democratic association in which the justification of the terms and conditions of association proceeds through public argument and reasoning among equal citizens' (1997: 72). Hence, the fundamental feature of associations is to be the outcome of discussion. In my opinion, the daily procedures and decisions within the association can be based on the same merit.

However, apart from the (internal) decision procedure taking place within the associations, we must also look at the (external) decisions at a higher level: between the operating associations. The theorists of associative democracy see the mechanism on that level either as a spontaneous process of competition and cooperation or assume that the state acts as an intermediary in an unspecified decision process (even if its influence is mainly limited to affecting the shape of the groups). The role of deliberative democracy on this level is less obviously understood. When groups are considered participants in the deliberation, the question is what this form of debate should exactly look like. How do the groups communicate about their (group) opinion? How does one form or change the opinion of such a group? To look for answers, we could think of a scheme in which representatives of the groups take part in an intergroup deliberation. So they take part in deliberations on two levels: within their own groups and between groups. The groups discuss the actions their representatives should take in the deliberation on the higher level, and in return, the groups learn from their representatives what arguments are presented by other groups. The exchange of ideas between groups on the higher level is then, in fact, the exchange of ideas of individual group members that flow via the representatives. This will slow down such a debate, as compared to an 'isolated deliberation', such as the one present within a group, but it does preserve the small scale of deliberation on all levels.

In practice, there may not be many decisions that have to be taken on the higher level, but it may already be a problem for the associations to coexist peacefully. Iris Marion Young connected her idea of politics of difference to deliberation on the higher level, that is, between groups (1997; 1990). She understands groups in a very broad way, broader than associative democratic theorists, when she includes social movements, ethnic groups, interest groups and so on, that is, also non-democratic groups. As we have already mentioned, she was one of the critics of the theorists of associative democracy, pointing to a 'serious weakness' in not building their designs on currently existing associative forms (1995: 208). Nevertheless, her ideas about communication between groups can be applied to groups in the sense of associative democracy as well. She envisions a form of deliberation in which the notion of *social perspective* plays an essential role. As she explains, every social background gives to individuals a different perspective on reality, which they share with other members of the same social group. She writes that 'the social positioning of group differentiation gives to individuals some shared *perspectives* on social life' (1997: 385). Communication between groups is understood as mutually presenting these perspectives with the intention of enabling (members of) the other group to look from that perspective, rather than being convinced by the argument. In my view, her ideas could be used as a starting point for democratic deliberations toward decision-making between associations.

Conclusion

The common call for 'more participation' has resulted in a broad exploration of possible ways of extending representative democracy with systems that allow for more participation. I have divided participatory activities into two types: quantitative and qualitative participation. Of these types, I consider qualitative participation as the most promising (and the most realistic), because it uses and enriches the competence of the participants – unlike quantitative participation which only requires 'yes' or 'no' answers on subjects that may not be interesting or known (or both) to participants. Qualitative participation seems more realistic because it takes place in the context of one's own interests. Rather than trying to make people interested in the power they can exercise, this approach is giving them power in areas that they are interested in.

In this context, we have been analysing two innovative models of democracy, based on qualitative participation, that could function next to the existing representative (territorial, parliamentary and so on) democracy: associative democracy and deliberative democracy. The connection between them is established because they cover two different parts of democracy: the first one is a system that provides the democratic structure, without describing what decision procedures or mechanisms should be applied, and the second one is a democratic mechanism without a fixed system to apply it to. We have seen that the deliberative democracy mechanism could fit very well into a system of associative democracy, especially inside groups. The use of deliberation on the higher, inter-associational level is more problematic, but we see possible starting points with the help of some representation there. Further study of the rich literature on both deliberative democracy and associative democracy seems to be necessary if all possibilities for enriching democracy with qualitative participation are to be discovered and analysed.

NOTES

1. The terminology I introduce here comes from the fact that the first one values a high turnout, while the other tries to steer the electorate toward competent decision-making.
2. However, one might argue along the same lines that a non-democratic mechanism could also impose, for example, a voting procedure.
3. Groups and associations are treated as synonyms in the literature on associative democracy. I will do the same in this text.
4. I base this comparison of the different designs of associative democracy on my earlier analysis in Perczynski (2000).
5. Radical, anti-collectivist projects seem also to influence the associative proposals of Mathews, who, even more than Hirst, focuses on groups that are directly involved 'in shaping the economy' (Mathews 1989: 114–15). The imaginative associative design of Sabel (1995) also concentrates on the economy.
6. See Immergut (1995: 206). We find in Schmitter's design another way of avoiding inefficiency in the system: a threshold for associations, comparable to the well-known electoral threshold in some parliamentary systems. Only with a certain minimum amount of vouchers could they acquire the status of a semi-public association (Schmitter 1995: 180).

REFERENCES

Andeweg, R.B. 1985. 'De Burger in de Nederlandse Politiek' Andeweg et al, 1985.
Andeweg, R.B., A. Hoogerwerf & J.J.A. Thomassen, eds. 1985. *Politiek in Nederland*. Alphen aan de Rijn: Samson H.D. Tjeenk Willink.
Bader, V. 1998a. 'Associative democracy and the incorporation of ethnic and national minorities'. University of Amsterdam (unpublished manuscript).
1998b. 'Problems and prospects of associative democracy, revisited'. University of Amsterdam (unpublished manuscript).

Beetham, D., ed. 1994. *Defining and Measuring Democracy*. London: Sage.
Bohman, J. & W. Rehg, eds. 1997a. *Deliberative Democracy*. Cambridge, MA: MIT Press.
    1997b. 'Introduction'. Bohman & Rehg 1997a.
Cohen, J. 1997. 'Deliberation and democratic legitimacy'. Bohman & Rehg 1997a.
    Rogers, J. 1993. 'Associations and democracy'. *Social Philosophy and Policy Foundation*, 10, 282–312.
    1995a. 'Secondary associations and democratic governance'. Wright 1995a.
    1995b. 'Solidarity, democracy, association'. Wright 1995a.
Dahl, R.A. 1989. *Democracy and its Critics*. New Haven, CT: Yale University Press.
Dryzek, J.S. 1990. *Discursive Democracy*. Cambridge: CUP.
Elster, J., ed. 1998a. *Deliberative Democracy*. Cambridge: CUP.
    1998b. 'Introduction'. Elster 1998a.
Etzioni, A. 1995. *The Spirit of Community*. London: Fontana Press.
Fishkin, J.S. 1991. *Democracy and Deliberation*. New Haven, London: Yale University Press.
    1995. *The Voice of the People*. New Haven, London: Yale University Press.
Held, D., ed. 1993. *Prospects for Democracy*. Cambridge: Polity Press.
    1993b. 'Democracy: from city-states to a cosmopolitan order?' Held 1993a.
Hirst, P., ed. 1989. 'Introduction'. *The Pluralist Theory of the State*. London: Routledge.
    1993. 'Associational democracy'. *Prospects for Democracy*. Cambridge: Polity Press.
    1994. *Associative Democracy*. Cambridge: Polity Press.
    1995. 'Can secondary associations enhance democratic governance?' Wright 1995a.
    1997. *From Statism to Pluralism*. London: UCL Press.
Immergut, E.M. 1995. 'An institutional critique of associative democracy'. Wright 1995a.
Kujawinska-Courtney K. & R.M. Machnikowski, eds. 1998. *Liberalism Yesterday and Today*. Lodz: Omega-Praksis.
Mansbridge, J. 1995. 'A deliberative perspective on neocorporatism'. Wright 1995a.
Mathews, J. 1989. *Age of Democracy*. Melbourne: OUP.
Offe, C. 1995. 'Some sceptical considerations on the malleability of representative institutions'. Wright 1995a.
Parry, G. & G. Moyser. 1994. 'More participation, more democracy?' Beetham 1994.
Pateman, C. 1986. *Participation and Democratic Theory*. Cambridge: CUP.
Perczynski, P. 1995. 'Political pluralism in English guild thought'. Ryszka 1995.
    1998. 'Liberal influence on British socialist thought – the concept of combined freedom'. Kujawinska-Courtney & Machnikowski 1998.
    2000. 'Active citizenship and associative democracy'. Saward 2000.
Putnam, R.D. 1993. *Making Democracy Work*. Princeton, NJ: Princeton University Press.
Ryszka, F., ed. 1995. *Historia, Idee, Polityka*. Warsaw: Scholar.
Sabel, C.F. 1995. 'Bootstrapping reform: rebuilding firms, the welfare state, and unions'. *Politics & Society*, 23, 5–48.
Saward, M. 1998. *The Terms of Democracy*. Cambridge: Polity Press.
    2000. *Democratic Innovation: Deliberation, Association and Representation*. London: Routledge, ECPR Studies in European Political Science.
Schmitter, P.C. 1988. 'Corporative democracy: oxymoronic? Just plain moronic? Or a promising way out of the present impasse?' Stanford University (mimeo).
    1995. 'The irony of modern democracy and the viability of efforts to reform its practice'. Wright 1995a.
Streeck, W. 1995. 'Inclusion and secession: questions on the boundaries of associative democracy'. Wright 1995a.
Tully, J. 1995. *Strange Multiplicity*. Cambridge: CUP.
Wright, E.O., ed. 1995a. *Associations and Democracy*. London: Verso.
    1995b. 'Introduction'. Wright 1995a.
Young, I.M. 1990. *Justice and the Politics of Difference*. Princeton, NJ: Princeton University Press.
    1995. 'Social groups in associative democracy'. Wright 1995a.
    1997. 'Difference as a resource for democratic communication'. Bohman & Rehg 1997a.

5

Association and Deliberation in Risk Society: Two Faces of Ecological Democracy

WOUTER ACHTERBERG

This article explores in a preliminary and somewhat roundabout way some interrelationships between associative and deliberative democracy. Some theories aim at extending and broadening liberal democracy – associative democracy (in the version of Hirst on which I focus) by giving secondary associations a substantial part in economic and social governance, deliberative democracy by emphasising the necessity of more public deliberation in formal and informal political contexts. My approach to this subject will not be purely normative, though, and also not purely philosophical. I focus on a particular set of problems: the environmental or ecological problematic, and on that set of problems, moreover, in the context of late modern society, that is, the advanced capitalist countries of western Europe and Northern America among others.

There are different conceptions of this type of society on offer nowadays. One of the most challenging is Ulrich Beck's theory of late modern society as a risk society. I have chosen his sociological theory as a background and context for the subject of this article because ecological problems and the renewal of democratic politics are important in it. I have already explored in two articles the possible contribution of associative democracy to a democratic and sustainable solution of environmental problems. To enhance our understanding of what this contribution might be, it is, I believe, necessary to clarify its connection to the relevant problems risk society raises for democracy. So after summarising some results of the earlier articles, I will go on, in the second section, to delineate some basic aspects of risk society, the nature of the new risks and their implications for democracy and politics. In the last section, I continue spelling out, in a reconstructive manner, these implications and argue that deliberative and associative democracy, far from being inherently in tension, seem to be plausible candidates which can and should flesh out together Beck's so far very sketchy idea of ecological democracy. To be sure, Beck himself is quite innocent of using theories of associative or deliberative democracy.

Associative Democracy, Sustainability and Ecological Modernisation

The questions I try to answer in this section are as follows. What are some of the basic characteristics of associative democracy? How might associative democracy contribute to sustainable development? (More than the usual liberal democratic dispensation, one hopes.)

Associationalism is a political theory that, as developed by Paul Hirst, proposes institutional reforms to build new forms of 'economic and social governance'. The thrust of the proposed reforms is to broaden and enhance democracy and not to supersede liberal democracy. Neither are the new forms of economic governance intended to replace markets as the central means of decentralised coordination in liberal democratic societies. Associationalism intends to give more weight to a third principle of coordination: negotiations between secondary associations and between these and the state as the primary association. The effect of giving this type of coordination more weight is that secondary associations become much more important *vis-à-vis* the state than in the familiar liberal democratic regimes (especially in the English-speaking countries). Ideally, the secondary associations become the 'primary means of both democratic governance and organizing social life' (Hirst 1994: 26). On the face of it, this institutional proposal seems predominantly inspired by the wish to increase the efficiency of democratic governance in modern capitalism. The doctrine of subsidiarity, for example, has been adopted and becomes a mainstay of the institutional proposals. Of course, the possible efficiency gains reached in this way are not to be despised, but the impression of a proposal driven by considerations of increased efficiency is misleading. Actually, the ambition to make liberal democracy more democratic and less dependent on bureaucratic organisations, whether of the central government or of the big corporations, and more accommodating to freedom of association and to cooperation in pursuit of common purposes is at least as important, if not more so. This is evident not just from its 'central normative claim' that 'individual liberty and human welfare are both best served when as many of the affairs of society as possible are managed by voluntary and democratically self-governing associations' (Hirst 1994:

19), and from the 'associationalist ethic' (Hirst 1994: 44), but also from the three principles of political organisation which are basic to Hirst's proposal:

1 that voluntary self-governing associations gradually and progressively become the primary means of democratic governance of economic and social affairs;

2 that power should as far as possible be distributed to distinct domains of authority, whether territorial or functional, and that administration within such domains should be devolved to the lowest level consistent with the effective governance of the affairs in question – these are the conjoint principles of state pluralism and of federation;

3 that democratic governance does not consist just in the powers of citizen election or majority decision, but in the continuous flow of information between governors and the governed, whereby the former seek the consent and cooperation of the latter. (Hirst 1994: 20.)

The preferred way to get there is from below and in a manner that is decentralised, especially regionally, in marked contrast to Cohen and Rogers' modest proposals (1995), which are more top-down and centralised.

My next question is what these associative reforms might contribute to realising sustainable development. I take it that our collective use of the environment would be a suitable object of the new forms of economic and social governance envisaged by associationalism. So if the associative reforms are going to be in any way useful in achieving sustainability, then it will be by means of at least their institutional aspects.

Since the late 1980s sustainable development has become the umbrella goal of much national and international environmental policy and regulation. So it is not surprising, at least politically, that the concept has been used in such a way that it tends to mean all things to all people. At the end of the day, this weakness may be a strength of the idea, though. The least we can do is separate out a core meaning which can be embodied in different and decentralised experiments of sustainable living. The core meaning has to do with establishing patterns of production and consumption which, in principle, can be maintained indefinitely. They are sustainable in this sense when they do not overshoot the limits set by the regenerative capacities of nature, that is, the capacities which enable nature to continue to fulfil its functions, economic or otherwise, which make our patterns of production and consumption possible in the first place. Furthermore, not just our patterns of production and consumption, but also those of people in other parts of the planet and of its inhabitants in the future (at least the human ones). A lot of questions are raised by these concepts and distinctions, and I will come back to some of them later in this article. For example, the whole question of limits will turn out to be inherently controversial and so too will be the implied notions of international (intragenerational) and intergenerational justice. The notion of social justice is, of course, centrally involved in the developmental aspect of sustainable development. It is not just a pragmatic insight that without the cooperation of the poor countries on this planet sustainable development presumably will not be achieved. For now, it suffices if we use only the intuitive core of sustainability and ask ourselves what difference associative reforms might make if we try to achieve sustainability in this sense. So far, Hirst has not said much about environmental concerns in his writings on associative democracy, so we can only answer this question by extrapolation and in a tentative way. On the other hand, it is unavoidable to try to answer it because environmental problems are, or should be, a central concern for late modern societies.

I try to answer the question of what difference associative reforms may make in pursuing sustainability by describing some general social requirements which have to be met if there is going to be any chance of achieving sustainable patterns of production and consumption in modern liberal democratic societies. Using these requirements as criteria we will be able to evaluate the possible contribution of associative democracy on our way to sustainability.

To be brief (for more see Achterberg (1996a; 1996b) and Voges (1999: Ch.3)), at least three conditions should be mentioned here: a higher level of social cooperation and coordination; a more effective social embeddedness of the market; and a more equal distribution of income. The first condition derives the plausibility it has from the insight that neither government regulation or tax policy nor market incentives are in the long run sufficient to achieve a sustainable pattern of, for example, production. Necessary for this is not just the consent and cooperation of the business community, but also cooperation between firms and even coordination between firms in whole chains of production, not to forget the coordination, at the policy level, between local, regional, national and other authorities and branches of industry.

Governance by negotiation seems to have its appropriate place here (see the article by Hoekema).

The second condition is based on the assumption that a market economy and its core mechanism, the price mechanism, will not lead to a scale of resource use (in a broad sense, since the use of nature as a 'sink' is also resource use) that is acceptable from an environmental point of view unless the appropriate regulations and incentives are in place. This presupposes that the political will exists and is sufficiently effective to bring non-market points of view (for example, long-term ones) to bear on the outcomes of markets, that is to say, at the macro-economic level.

The third condition is closely connected to the second one, for an optimal (let us say a just) distribution of resources (for example, of income) has not been a historically conspicuous outcome of 'free' markets. Of course, one or another type of welfare state has taken care of all that, but in the meantime, inequality has again been on the rise since the 1970s, nationally and internationally. Furthermore, increasing inequality severely hampers the pursuit of sustainability.

What about associative democracy if we use these conditions as criteria? The evaluation is not easy because we have not seen a functioning associative order yet. On the other hand, the environmental track record of liberal democracies with a substantial admixture of neo-corporatist arrangements (for example, the Scandinavian countries, Germany and the Netherlands) seems often to be better than that of liberal democracy in the English-speaking part of the world (Dryzek 1997). So, if this is anything to go on, at least the prospects for a more associative order seem bright. From a more theoretical, but congenial point of view, Cohen and Rogers have made it clear that the difference associative environmental management may make is to be found especially in increasing the social level of cooperation and coordination (Wright 1995: 57ff; Achterberg 1996a).

As to the second criterion, participation in the tasks of social and economic governance should surely make the members of associations responsible and public-minded citizens and not just producers or consumers trying to realise their private interest by other means. This is important because trying to live sustainably is not a one-off activity but involves a society-wide learning process. The connection between the third criterion and an associative order, as envisaged by Hirst, is close because the introduction of a guaranteed minimum income (or a basic income[1]) might be most helpful in establishing a broadly based associative order. Of course, all this does not extend to the problems of achieving sustainability in a global market economy and may also not contribute much to more equality at the international level, but insofar as the rich countries will anyway have to a set an example of living sustainably, an important step will have been taken if an associative order in rich countries leads to more sustainable patterns of production and consumption.

There are some weak spots, however, in this positive picture of the possible merits of associative democracy in achieving sustainability. In the first place, there is a heavy emphasis on the production side of the process. Thus a rather strong convergence emerges between the programme of ecological modernisation (in a weak sense (Dryzek 1997: Ch.8)) and an associatively transformed industrial order which has become environmentally benign. But that cannot be all there is to sustainability. At least as important are sustainable patterns of consumption and lifestyles. So far not much attention has been paid to the problems of how to achieve these in the context of modern consumerism. Furthermore, there is not any inherent reason why decision-making in the context of associative democracy could not contribute to the societal process of learning to live sustainably.

Next, the extent of democratisation by associative reform is unclear. This reform should extend and enhance democracy, as we have seen. So, we can distinguish between a quantitative and a qualitative aspect of the associative transformation. So far mainly the quantitative aspect and its institutional embodiment in terms of rights and the stakeholder model of the corporation has become reasonably clear. What is going on *in* all those new associations is not so clear. Though more responsible decision-making and responsible citizens might belong to their output, the result might, on the face of it, just as well be something not much different from the aggregation of preferences and mediation of interests with which we are familiar from ordinary parliamentary politics (see the article by Bader). Additionally, the density of the negotiating and bargaining rounds needed to consolidate all the particular interests emerging into policies with sufficient backing in the relevant constituencies may well make parliamentary control precarious, to say the least. Although Hirst leaves the normative structure of the democratic process within and between the associations underdetermined, it is important, I believe, to elaborate this structure before we can determine whether the nature of associative democratic politics will differ enough from the traditional politics of representative democracy. Here, I believe, is where deliberative democracy comes in, at least that is what I argue for in the next sections.

Lastly, it seems to me that Hirst's concept of late capitalist society is seriously underdescribed, so that we are not quite in a position yet to establish or evaluate the function and the viability of associative reforms (as proposed by Hirst) in late modern society. To put more flesh on the concept of advanced capitalist or late modern society, I will make use of some elements in Beck's evolving concept of a risk society, elements, moreover, which tie in with the theme of deliberative democracy. In the next section, I will introduce risk society and spell out some implications of the new risks. In the last section, I will try to make connections between associative and deliberative democracy via the relevant aspects of risk society; in that context, there will be occasion to mention sustainable patterns of consumption again.

Risk Society, Sub-politics and the Nature of the New Risks

I will first discuss the thesis of risk society in rather general terms and then highlight a few important aspects relevant to the subject of this article.[2]

We are, according to Beck, in the midst of a transition from classical industrial society to risk society or, with a different emphasis, from classical (industrial) modernity to reflexive or 'modernised' modernity. Moreover, this change is potentially taking place on a global scale. Indeed, reflexive modernisation implies globalisation. What features are essential to distinguish industrial society from risk society?

Most important is that on the way to risk society risks are becoming pervasive in social life and culture as 'stowaways of normal consumption' (Beck 1992a: 40) and simultaneously transformed, leading to what Beck calls the social and political 'explosiveness' of hazards. Their ultimate source is the development of science and technology. But no longer are they just limited side-effects of a technological development which seems on the whole benign and, at least in its particular manifestations, under control; no longer can they be considered the unavoidable price of a progress which brings material benefits to most people. The development of science and technology forms part of an autonomous process of modernisation that leads inexorably in its later phases to what one may call a return of the repressed: pre-industrial hazards, the dangers of natural disasters, tend to lose their external character and become internal, manufactured and large-scale risks arising from our technological transformation of nature. They are internal because risk society has lost in its scientific and technological development any clear distinction between society (culture) and nature. At the same time, they are large scale because these internal risks, of which the ecological ones are heavily emphasised by Beck, are not limited in scale anymore, neither geographically nor in time nor socially; by the same token they cannot be covered by any insurance. They are the result of modern technologies (nuclear, chemical, bio-industrial, genetic and so on) which are actually out of (scientific and political) control, even in their development let alone in their so-called normal operation. As Beck puts it, 'this transforms society into a laboratory in which no one organization controls the conditions and the results of any ongoing experiment' (1997b: 19). An important effect of the wholesale transformation of risk is the emergence of a new legitimation crisis: the consensus over progress, the authority of (technological) science as its epistemological basis, and the social institutions embodying and supporting both are increasingly undermined. These developments and others are captured in Beck's concept of 'reflexive modernization'. This concept, as he himself states:

> does not mean (as the adjective 'reflexive' might suggest) reflection, but rather self-confrontation and self-transformation. The transition from the industrial to the risk epoch of modernity occurs *un*intended and *un*seen, inexorably in the wake of the autonomous dynamics of modernization, following the pattern of unintended consequences. One can say that the constellations of risk society are created because the certainties of industrial society (the consensus on progress and the abstraction of ecological effects and hazards) dominate the thought and action of people and institutions. Risk society is not an option that is selected or rejected as the result of a political conflict. It originates in the inexorable motion of autonomous modernization processes that are blind to their consequences and deaf to their hazards. Taken altogether, the latter produce latent self-endangerment that calls the foundations of industrial society itself into question. (Beck 1997b: 28.)

Nonetheless, one wonders where reflection might come in here. Presumably, it takes place in what one may call a second phase of reflexive modernisation. For as Beck remarks elsewhere, the 'fact that this very constellation [of reflexive modernisation] may later, in a second stage, in turn become the object of (public, political and scientific) reflection must not obscure the unreflected, quasi-autonomous mechanism of the transition: it is precisely abstraction which produces and gives reality to risk society' (1994: 6). Thus in a second stage, but only then, there seems to be an opening for the project of trying to control and manage consciously, reflexively risk society or at least those aspects of it already manifesting themselves in the present industrial society. One may infer from Beck's writings that, ideally, this control and management should take place in an enlightened, just and democratic way, but for more information on who is going to control and manage, and in what sense and in what way, we have to await the further development of the theory of reflexive modernisation.

Of course, the transition to risk society is not characterised by just the transformation of risks and hazards. Beck also discusses what he calls the 'end of tradition', with its repercussions on the way individuals conduct their life and form an identity (biography), the nature and form of the family, gender relationships and labour. I will not discuss these matters here, but it is important to be aware of Beck's view of them, if only by way of background to the parts of his analysis highlighted here.

After this very broad-brush picture we should turn to a more detailed analysis of Beck's concept of risk. Three aspects of it should be discussed in more depth: the nature and transformation of risk; the evaluation of risk, particularly from the point of view of justice; and the democratic control of risk. However, I will discuss mostly the first and third aspects. Special attention will be paid to environmental or ecological risks (see especially Beck (1995; 1992b)).

The Nature and Transformation of Risks

Within the category of risks (I am using the term here in a blanket sense) Beck distinguishes three subclasses: pre-industrial hazards, the risks of classical industrial society and the man-made, large-scale hazards of 'late industrialism' (risk society). I take it that the (external) dangers of earthquakes and hurricanes, and the risks of occupational accident and disease will persist in risk society. New are the large-scale ecological, nuclear, chemical and genetic hazards (Beck 1995: 76, 109).

What exactly is new? They differ qualitatively in an number of ways from the risks of classical industrial society (an overview is provided in Beck (1995: 73–110) and also Benton (1997: 35)). (i) They are potentially global in scope, that is, on our planet unlimited in space and time. Risk society within the bounds of the nation-state will therefore develop into a global risk society (Beck 1996a; 1997b). (ii)

They are often irreversible and irremediable ('annihilation hazards'). (iii) The calculus of risk ceases to apply in their case (predominantly on account of (i)), which does not mean, of course, that the worst case could not occur. (iv) The first three differences imply that insurance or (financial) compensation are out of the question; also, 'the idea of security through anticipatory control of the consequences fails to apply' (Beck 1995: 109). (v) Their potential reach is also socially unlimited; this includes future generations. (vi) Their identification (perception) and assessment require scientific means (Beck refers to the 'expropriation of the senses'). (vii) They are the result of the normal operation of our combined social institutions, especially the industrial system, the legal system, technology and applied science, but they cannot be attributed causally or otherwise to any of them in particular nor to the state. Beck calls this state of affairs 'organised irresponsibility'; he uses this term to explain 'how and why the institutions of modern society must acknowledge potential and actual disasters, while simultaneously denying their existence, concealing their causes and ruling out compensation or control' (1997b: 28).

Beck's account of the risks inherent in risk society (a better designation might be 'second order dangers' (Bonss 1995), since the first order ones have never disappeared, of course) raises many questions. This is not the place to pursue them. One problem merits some discussion, though, because it is linked directly to the subject of deliberative democracy. It concerns the almost completely negative picture of the new risks that Beck paints. This might have to do with his macro-sociological perspective in which risks are seen *ex post* and so to speak from above. But in the *ex ante* perspective of the acting subject, individual and collective, risks are not just chances of negative effects of action, but are also connected with chances of benefits, for example, the calculations of an entrepreneur in a market economy. This means that conscious risk-taking behaviour always implies a trade-off between, so to speak, expected (dis)utilities. On a macro-level the same goes for the development of science and technology, especially to the extent that it tends to become an object of self-regulation and even of political regulation and interference. This will make heavy demands on the deliberative capacities of the relevant political institutions. If we add to this Beck's suggestion (see next section) about the ethical point of view involved in any meaningful discussion of risks, we see that the whole subject of (the new) risks is inherently controversial, not just in a cognitive sense, but also ethically and politically. Environmental risks are, of course, no exception. Even the whole notion of limits to the regenerative capacity of nature is already controversial in the same sense as the risks incurred by ignoring or even nearing them. Of course, the same goes for the associated concepts of harms and benefits for their recipients.

We have to accept, then, that living in a 'modernised modernity' is fraught with risks, often implying chances of big harm, so that 'risk communication' (Bonss 1995), involving political debate about what the risks are and which are acceptable and therefore could or even should be taken, and which not, is unavoidable. The decisions resulting from this debate are principally revisable, so that discourse about harm and risk becomes (explicitly) or remains political. Those groups that bear the risks should be enabled and empowered to participate, directly or by means of representation, in decision-making about risks.[3] The practical importance of deliberative democracy is a direct result of the state of affairs described in the last two paragraphs. On the other hand, risk communication is also an excellent illustration of Hirst's third principle of associative political organisation, 'democracy as communication' (1994: 20, 34). So already here we see that associative and deliberative reforms should be linked.

Risk Evaluation: Risk (Society) and Social Justice

Let us now turn to the following question: what risks and hazards are acceptable to society? At least as important is the question discussed in the next section: who decides that? These are some of the central issues in the ethical assessment of risk society. Moreover, this is not a peripheral topic in the discussion of risk society. As Beck puts it: 'one must assume an *ethical point of view* in order to discuss risks meaningfully at all' (1992a: 29). The same goes for risk society. I will briefly discuss some issues of distributive justice, which is an important element in answers to the question: 'how do we wish to live?' (Beck 1992b: 119). Answers to that question have much to do with the acceptance of risks, as Beck rightly remarks (1992a: 28).

From the beginning, Beck (1992a: Ch.1; 1995: Ch.6) has emphasised that the transition to risk society implies a shift to new conflicts and patterns of distribution. Superimposed on the familiar conflicts in industrial society about the distribution of material wealth, crudely simplified, between capital and labour, appears a new type of conflict, one about the distribution of a 'poisoned cake', that is, of risks and hazards. The old conflicts do not go away, of course (Beck 1992b: 121, note 8), but connected with them there arises a new inequality in social risk positions, within and between social classes, within nations and between nations, and globally between rich and poor.

We have to take seriously, according to Beck, the possibility that for those in disadvantaged positions in (global) society the coming of risk society will make them worse off. This raises serious doubts as to whether the hazards imposed on us by the autonomous advance into late modernity are acceptable from the point of view of social justice. Furthermore, if this advance is just 'semi-autonomous', instead of autonomous, then social justice might ask us at least to slow down the advance into global risk society. Of course, there are very different theories of social justice and even more ethical theories, and anyway invoking them might not have much more effect, globally, than using a 'bicycle brake on an intercontinental jet' (Beck, 1992b: 106). On the other hand, we cannot just forget all about ethics when the going gets rough. Perhaps the promise of sub-politics, as Beck envisages it, may be seen here: in the interstitial tissue of the formal institutions of (global) society, there may grow pockets and networks of an ethically inspired resistance against what often looks like a free fall into global risk society. Here we might also see new prospects for associative democracy. In the meantime, we can perhaps put into order our ethical thoughts or at least our ideas about social justice.

Recently, Beck has stated that 'turned political, the ecological crisis amounts to a *systematic infringement of fundamental rights*' (1997b: 26; 1996a: 137). If this is right then the techno-industrial order which has produced this crisis, so to speak as a side-effect of its normal operation, stands condemned from the point of view of justice, and the liberal democratic political order which allowed this to happen is in danger of losing its legitimacy. But there may be hope for liberal democracy if democracy can be extended and enhanced, or so I argue in the next section.

Risk and Ecological Democracy: Deliberative and Associative

Beck discusses two answers to the organised irresponsibility that allows the transformation of risks into unmanageable global hazards: an empirical and a normative one. If successful both are steps on the way to an enhanced democratic risk management. Central in the empirical answer is an analysis of what he calls 'subpolitics'. The focus of the normative answer is radical or even ecological democracy. As will become clear, the two answers are only contingently connected, which does not exclude a fruitful combination. I will first discuss them briefly before I explore some aspects of ecological democracy in more depth than Beck has been inclined to do until now.

Sub-politics is described by Beck as, in essence, politics outside the formal political institutions and channels of parliamentary democracy. It is not itself necessarily democratic. Sub-political action has been taking place all the time in the areas of industry, science and technology, areas innocent of democratic procedures. It has led, on the one hand, to the autonomous 'techno-economic' development we used to call progress in classical industrial society and, on the other hand, to our 'truncated' version of representative democracy which has become increasingly less able to protect its present and future citizens, let alone the others within and outside its boundaries, against the hazardous (side-)effects of that development (Beck 1992a: Ch.8). In the meantime, an oppositional version of sub-politics has arisen between the market and the state, a true politics of difference, embodying seemingly an object lesson in reflexive modernisation. Its mode of operation is direct politics; it is thematic and issue-oriented, a fountain of mediagenic actions. Its seat is to be found in the new social movements and its self-selected task is to challenge the risk definitions and evaluations of the official and industrial 'safety bureaucracies'. Increasingly, they have become important parties in 'adversary risk assessments' (Shrader-Frechette 1991) and the home of experts, critical ones, of course. Beck is fond of using as an example the Greenpeace action (summer 1995) against Shell's decision to sink the Brent Spar oil rig in the Atlantic. This oppositional sub-politics has acquired an international dimension in the plethora of NGOs globally campaigning on issues of environmental policy, human rights and aid. Beck sees here the beginning of a globalisation from beneath (1996a: 136).

One may discern some tension, though, between Beck's enthusiasm for NGOs and his democratic commitment. The problem is that the democratic quality of these organisations (for example, Greenpeace) is often dubious. This may concern their internal functioning or the democratic legitimacy, especially globally, of their policies. Democratic legitimacy may be undermined by tendencies to ethnocentrism and deficient representation, which are not compensated for by increasing dependence on science (Yearley 1996: 86–92, 134–40). All this may be remediable or at any rate transitional in the light of an enhanced understanding of what democracy requires in (global) risk society. Let us turn therefore to Beck's views of radical democracy, that is, ecological democracy.

'In political theory,' he announces, 'a programme to deal with large-scale hazards might require revolutionary changes.' (Beck 1995: 180.) The changes he proposes seem rather modest, though. How could it be otherwise if one admits, as Beck does, that adequately functioning institutions of liberal democracy are presupposed for the success of oppositional sub-politics: apart from parliamentary democracy itself, he mentions a free and independent mass media and a strong and independent judicial system (1997b: 30; 1992b: 116). What, then, might be the direction of the 'revolutionary changes'? Basically, the transition to risk society offers us the opportunity to broaden and enhance democracy beyond its 'truncated' version in classical industrial society, in which 'questions of the technological change of society remain beyond the reach of political-parliamentary decision-making' (Beck 1992b: 119). Now, we are on the eve of a 'second' modernity, that is, a 'responsible modernity' in which we, having become 'ecologically enlightened', will bring more rationality and reason to the task of regulating technological change to the benefit of all affected. This is, for Beck, the utopian meaning of an 'ecological democracy' (1997b: 32–3; 1992b: 118–20). In a more practical vein, he suggests some reforms to bring about an 'ecological extension' of democracy (Beck 1992b: 109, 119): 'the production of accountability, redistribution of the burdens of proof, division of powers between the producers and the evaluators of hazards, public disputes on technological alternatives' (Beck 1992b: 119). Science is emphatically involved in the reform; in cooperation with the public sphere there should be a kind of 'public science' (Beck 1992b: 119). This is as it should be if reflexive modernisation also touches science itself, leading to a 'reflexive scientization' (Beck 1992a: 155).

What are we to make of all this? Reflexive modernisation does not leave democracy untouched. Even democracy has become reflexive! In the vertical sense of this, it implies 'deliberate and reflexive questioning of fundamental principles of democracy' (Beck 1997a: 43). Unfortunately, Beck is rather hazy about this. Taken in a horizontal sense, it implies efforts to extend democracy beyond the conventional political sphere of the nation-state, either into other realms of social action, for example, the economy, the family and the sphere of social security, or above the level of the nation-state to, ultimately, global democracy (Beck 1997a: 40–46). I will first comment on the second direction before coming back to the first.

In the horizontal direction, there is, of course (but here I am *adding* to Beck, and to Hirst), ample room for associative reforms of the type proposed by Hirst. This seems possible in two ways so that some of these may even take on a *new* function: to contribute to the governance of scientific and techno-industrial change, whether or not in oppositional (sub-political) terms; some others (in the sphere of social movements and NGOs) may begin to give shape to experiments in living sustainably (consumption and lifestyle) and to live outside the shadow of the experts, sometimes at least. To the first kind of contribution belong proposals aiming at a more democratic process of risk assessment, evaluation and management.[4]

It remains to be seen whether we can give more substance to the rather tenuous idea of ecological democracy. What type of democracy could accommodate adequately his responsible, ecologically enlightened modernity? Beck does not give any clear answer to this question but, I submit, there is at least one fitting model, that of deliberative democracy (actually a family of models). The alternative would be what has been called 'democratic pragmatism' (Dryzek 1997: Ch.5) to which Beck's own meagre practical suggestions would seem to belong. I will briefly describe both and then argue why I belief that some version of deliberative democracy would be more appropriate to Beck's concerns.

As Dryzek describes it, democratic pragmatism is marked by 'interactive problem solving within the basic institutional structure of liberal capitalist democracy' (1997: 85). The term pragmatism can be used here in the everyday sense of a practical or realistic attitude to problems. The core of the position is that 'problem solving should be a flexible process involving many voices, and cooperation across a plurality of perspectives. As long as this plurality is achieved, there is no need for more widespread public participation in problem solving.' (Dryzek 1997: 85.)

This approach is not confined to debates within parliaments. To its instruments also belong: public consultation (for example, in the preparation of environmental impact assessments or in the form of 'broad societal debates'); alternative dispute resolution (with the aid of neutral third parties); policy dialogue; public inquiries; and so-called right-to-know legislation. They reflect so many ways to mitigate or even replace a purely top-down regulatory approach to environmental policy. Democratic pragmatism is not without its achievements and even promises in environmental policy, but its limits are apparent too. Before I mention these, it has to be said that some type of associative reform fits in rather nicely here. I am thinking of the proposals of Cohen and Rogers (1995), for example, their ideas about how to improve the level of coordination and cooperation with a view to environmental management. But, I believe, the potential of associative democracy is not exhausted by such ideas and extends beyond the confines of democratic pragmatism.

The first limit of this pragmatism is the existence of power which may distort debate and decision-making. Powerful interests, resisting any attempt to change the existing structure of the capitalistic market economy, restrict the elbow room of a government oriented toward democratic pragmatism. Its first imperative will be to maintain the 'confidence of actual and potential investors' (Dryzek 1997: 99; 1996: Chs.2, 3). The second limitation is that in the actual practice of democratic pragmatic discourse, public interests and the particular interests (of producers or consumers) are treated as equally legitimate. This may have something to do with the origin of the discourse in the context of distributive issues. According to Dryzek (1997: 101), once 'environmental issues reach the agenda, they too are treated in distributive terms, with the main question being how to strike a balance between winners and losers, such as economic and environmental interests. General interests in (say) the integrity of ecosystems or the quality of common resources are less easily represented.' It is deliberative democracy, on the other hand, which gives a central place to general interests or even the common good.

Theories of deliberative democracy and the debates between adherents of its different varieties are sophisticated and complex. So I cannot even begin to do justice to the complexities involved.[5] It should suffice here to characterise the common core of deliberative democracy and to indicate why it would provide an appropriate context for deliberation about the normative issues in Beck's (reconstructed) agenda for ecological democracy.

Using Elster's distinction between the market and the forum as two different ways in which social decisions may come about, one can say that deliberative democracy belongs unambiguously to the forum. The 'market', especially when it fails, of course, stands for politics as an aggregation of given, pre-political preferences, reached by way of conflicts between interests and compromise. Voting, in the economic theory of democracy, is essentially a private act similar to buying and selling, and guided by considerations of instrumental rationality. The 'forum' stands for the possibility of 'transformation of preferences' through rational and public discussion (Elster 1997: 4, 11, 25). The procedures and institutions of the forum should be divorced from those of the market. The 'forum' implies public deliberation between free and equal citizens which, ideally, is oriented toward public interests or the common good. Public deliberation is a 'dialogical process of exchanging reasons for the purpose of resolving problematic situations that cannot be settled without interpersonal coordination and cooperation. ... Deliberation is not so much a form of discourse or argumentation as a joint cooperative activity.' (Bohman 1996: 27.)

I leave aside here the question whether public deliberation is intrinsically valuable or has only instrumental significance in that it leads to better decision-making than otherwise might occur. That it should lead to improved and more legitimate decision-making is not contested. I also leave aside the question, hotly debated between adherents of different varieties of deliberative democracy, of whether agreements reached by rational and public deliberation are right in some sense or correct just because they have been reached in that way or via an idealised procedure (fair or pure proceduralism) or because they meet some (independent?) epistemic standard of justification.[6]

It is not contested that the procedures of deliberative democracy should be informed by liberal and egalitarian values. For some theorists of deliberative democracy, this means that citizens should have not only an equal opportunity of participation in political decision-making, but also, for example, an 'equal opportunity of access to political influence' or 'equally effective social freedom' (Bohman and Rehg 1997: xxiii). Not surprisingly, deliberative democracy turns out to be a demanding ideal. 'The ultimate test', as Bohman and Rehg rightly say (1997: xxvii), 'of the fully developed conception of deliberative democracy will be practical: whether its proposed reforms can enrich and improve democratic practice and overcome the many obstacles to the public use of reason in contemporary political life,' such as increasing inequality, increasing complexity and pervasive pluralism. It should be pointed out that the practice of deliberative democracy is not confined to the formal political institutions of liberal democracy, but can flourish in the deliberative fora created by a more extensive democratisation of society, for example, as envisaged by theories of associative democracy.[7] It is also important to remember that deliberation does not need to take the form of an exchange of formal arguments, meeting standards of impartiality and ideally resulting in consensus between the participants. Public deliberation is not about the justification of morality. In a political context, it better had not take that form: it suffices if the 'outcome is such that citizens may continue to cooperate in deliberation rather than merely comply' (Bohman 1996: 187) with the decisions resulting from it.

It remains to make clear that a substantial affinity exists between Beck's ideal of ecological democracy,[8] as reconstructed by me, and the conception of deliberative democracy.[9] To show this, it is sufficient to point out Beck's call for the liberation of one-sided dependence on experts, critical or not, and to connect that with his emphasis on the need to change thinking in order to break through the prevailing relations of definition. Moreover, we have a list of still open normative questions, which are public-interest oriented and answers to which can only acquire democratic legitimacy if they are reached by way of public and rational deliberation between concerned parties or their representatives. To sum up, we have questions regarding how and according to what standards to regulate technological development and the (globalising) market economy; how to determine, in situations of conflict, the relation between social and environmental justice; how to determine the limits (and for whom) to environmental consumption, that is, how to determine specific requirements of environmental justice in the context of pursuing sustainable patterns of production and consumption; and, lastly, how to evaluate environmental risks, locally and globally, and global hazards in general.

Conclusion

Central tendencies in late modern society, conceived as a risk society, make it prudentially and morally unavoidable to extend and enhance democracy beyond the level reached in present-day liberal democracies. Associative and deliberative reforms show the desired direction of fit. But associative democracy without deliberative content is blind, and deliberative democracy without embodiment in associative and other institutions soars like a powerless spirit above the turbulent waters of present-day risk society. United they may stand, divided they stand to drown in the end, at least insofar as extending democracy is concerned.

NOTES

1. In Achterberg (1999), I have argued for a basic income and for its importance in achieving sustainable patterns of production and consumption.
2. The picture I draw in this section is rather eclectic, with an emphasis on Beck's publications in the 1990s. A very useful overview and critique of Beck's sociology of risk is to be found in Goldblatt (1996: 154–87).
3. See Bonss (1995: 233–51) for all this and more.
4. See also Shrader-Frechette's much more elaborated 'populist' reforms (1991).
5. See especially Bohman and Rehg (1997), an impressive recent collection of essays by the most important protagonists (not only the late Rawls and Habermas) in the debate on deliberative democracy. See also Bohman (1996). An other recent, very interesting and accessible elaboration is to be found in Gutmann and Thompson (1996).
6. See Bohman and Rehg, 'Introduction' (1997), for these and other important tensions within the theory of deliberative democracy.

7. For some rather formal remarks on how to combine deliberative and associative ideas in 'realizing democracy', see Joshua Cohen's 'Procedure and Substance in Deliberative Democracy' in Bohman and Rehg (1997: 424–30).
8. Dryzek defends his own brand of ecological democracy (1997: 197–201). Aside from its deliberative aspects, his view is remarkable for its emphasis on ecological communication as an important part of communication in ecological democracy.
9. There are some indications that Beck would be rather critical of the (or a) Habermasian version of deliberative democracy or so I gather from Beck (1996b).

REFERENCES

Achterberg, W. 1996a. 'Sustainability, community and democracy'. Doherty & de Geus 1996: 170–87.
    1996b. 'Sustainability and associative democracy'. Lafferty & Meadowcroft 1996: 157–74.
    1998a. 'Democracy, justice and risk society'. Paper ECPR, Joint Sessions Warwick, 23–28 March 1998.
    1998b. 'Ethiek en Risicomaatschappij' ('Ethics and risk society'). Rekenschap, June 1999, 96–103.
    1999. 'From sustainability to basic income'. Meadowcroft & Kenny 1999.
Beck, U. 1992a (1986). Risk Society. London: Sage.
    1992b. 'From industrial society to the risk society: questions of survival, social structure and ecological enlightenment'. Theory, Culture and Society, 9, 97–123.
    1994. 'The reinvention of politics: towards a theory of reflexive modernization'. Beck et al. 1994: 1–55.
    1995. Ecological Politics in an Age of Risks [translation of 'Gegengifte' 1988]. Cambridge: Polity Press.
    1996a. 'Weltrisikogesellschaft, Weltöffentlichkeit und Globale Subpolitik'. Diekmann & Jaeger 1996: 119–47.
    1996b. 'Risk society and the provident state'. Lash et al. 1996: 27–43.
    1997a. The Reinvention of Politics. Cambridge: Polity Press.
    1997b. 'Global risk politics'. Jacobs 1997: 18–33.
Beck, U., A. Giddens & S. Lash. 1994. Reflexive Modernization. Cambridge: Polity Press.
Benton, T. 1997. Beyond Left and Right? Jacobs 1997: 34–46.
Bohman, J. 1996. Public Deliberation. Cambridge, MA: MIT Press.
    Bohman, J. & W. Rehg, eds. 1997. Deliberative Democracy. Essays on Reason and Politics. Cambridge, MA: MIT Press.
Bonss, W. 1995. Vom Risiko. Hamburg: Hamburger Edition.
Cohen J. & J. Rogers. 1995. 'Secondary associations and democratic governance'. Wright 1995: 7–98. (Originally published in Politics and Society, 1992: 393–472.)
Diekmann, A. & C.C. Jaeger, eds. 1996. Umweltsoziologie. Opladen: Westdeutscher Verlag.
Doherty, B. & M. de Geus, eds. 1996. Democracy and Green Political Thought. London: Routledge.
Dryzek, J. 1996. Democracy in Capitalist Times. New York: OUP.
    1997. The Politics of the Earth. Oxford: OUP.
Elster, J. 1997 (1986). 'The market and the forum'. Bohman and Rehg 1997: 3–33.
Goldblatt, D. 1996. Social Theory and The Environment. Cambridge: Polity Press.
Gutmann, A. & D. Thompson, 1996. Democracy and Disagreement. Cambridge, MA: Harvard University Press.
Hirst, P. 1994. Associative Democracy. Cambridge: Polity Press.
    1997. From Statism to Pluralism. London: UCL Press.

Jacobs, M., ed. 1997. *Greening the Millennium? The New Politics of the Environment.* Oxford: Blackwell.

Lafferty, W.M. & J. Meadowcroft, eds. 1996. *Democracy and the Environment.* Cheltenham: Edward Elgar.

Lash, S., B. Szerszynski & B. Wynne, eds. 1996. *Risk, Environment and Modernity.* London: Sage.

Meadowcroft, J. & M. Kenny, eds. 1999. *Planning Sustainability.* London: Routledge.

Shrader-Frechette, K.S. 1991. *Risk and Rationality.* Berkeley, CA: University of California Press.

Voges, I. 1999. 'Sustainable development and the socially embedded firm. An inquiry into the nature, causes and transformation of structural unsustainability in contemporary liberal capitalism'. Dissertation, University of Stellenbosch, South Africa.

Wright, E.O., ed. 1995. *Associations and Democracy.* London: Verso.

Yearley, S. 1996. *Sociology, Environmentalism, Globalization.* London: Sage.

6

Associationalism for 150 Years and Still Alive and Kicking: Some Reflections on Danish Civil Society

LARS BO KASPERSEN and LAILA OTTESEN

Associationalism is an old doctrine with roots in various strings of nineteenth and early twentieth century European social and political theory. It has its origins in the works of, among others, Tocqueville, Proudhon, Durkheim and Duguit in France, the English pluralists (Cole, Figgis, Laski, Barker and Maitland), and von Gierke in Germany. In other words, it is a genuine European social theory. Associationalism has been revitalised in recent years, mainly in a British context and most notably by Paul Hirst (1994; 1997a; 1997b), but also by some important contributions in the USA (Cohen & Rogers 1995). This history of the theoretical development of associationalism is probably quite familiar to most scholars interested in this area of social and political theory. It is far less well known that associationalism as a model of governance has been developed and implemented as a political practice in Denmark for more than 100 years. This is the central concern in this article.

The purpose of the article is twofold. First, we shall demonstrate that associationalism is not an old-fashioned idea or pure utopia. As already indicated, associationalism is a model of governance which has a long tradition in Danish society. It contributes to a strengthening of the democratic aspect in education, social and cultural life and other welfare areas. The second purpose concerns the state-civil society relationship. By examining some associational features of Danish society we seek to point out that civil society did not emerge from nothing. Civil society is not an autonomous sphere clearly separated from the state, on the contrary, it is a sphere of social life dependent on the state. The state is the precondition of the development of civil society. Thus we reject the conception of civil society which can be found in much of the work on civil society, for example, Cohen and Arato (1992) and Habermas (1996).

The structure of the article is as follows. First, we outline the history of the rise of associational principles in Denmark going back to the end of the eighteenth century during the time of absolutism. We proceed with an overview of the development of associationalism and see how Denmark became a representative democracy supplemented with some associational features. It is beyond the scope of this article to outline the quite complex model of governance we find in Denmark. Rather, we shall limit ourselves to illustrating the associative dimension by examining more closely two areas in particular: first, we look briefly into primary and secondary education which, surprising to many, has an element of associationalism; second, and more extended, we examine social and cultural activities, such as sport, youth political organisations, religious organisations, various cultural organisations, disability organisations and others – social activities which from the point of view of the state can be called cultural political activities. Lastly, we shall discuss the problems and prospects of associationalism in the future in Danish society. Will associationalism be a path to help out the Danes with their problems with immigrants and asylum seekers?

The Emergence of Civil Society and Voluntary Associations in a Danish Context

Civil society is not a given, nor did it exist as an entity prior to the state. Civil society is a modern phenomenon created by the modern state (Hegel 1991). Before the modern state existed, Europe contained a number of different state forms coexisting and competing with each other. None of these state forms, such as the feudal state, the *ständestaat*, the church, the city-states or the city-leagues, contained a civil society in the modern sense of the word. Civil society is a sphere separated from, but conditioned by the state. This sphere developed with the transition to the modern territorial state in late-Renaissance Europe. One important element in this development was the restructuring of the defences of the states. New types of military technologies, fortifications, tactics and siege techniques were adapted to existing technologies, but this process required capital. This stimulated the emergence of a money economy and a capitalist market. Kings stimulated this development by extending the use of a currency to a territory so that they could extract resources from (civil) society in order to strengthen the state. In order to tax people, surveillance and control are necessary. This required developing an administration, civil servants and a codified law. Consequently, the development of the modern state created conditions of a sphere in which the individual becomes a person with some rights and obligations based upon a law, which is given and guaranteed by the state. In civil society, each individual can seek to fulfil his needs and satisfaction, but this cannot be accomplished to a full extent without reference to others. Indeed, as Hegel adds, 'these others are therefore means to the end of the particular ... and through its reference to others, the particular end takes on the form of universality, and gains satisfaction by simultaneously satisfying the welfare of others' (1991: 220–21). Hegel's civil society is placed between the family and the state, and for Hegel civil society is mainly the market economy. Civil society is the realm in which individuals exist as persons. They own private property, and they can decide their own life-activities according to needs and interests.

There is, however, more to civil society than the market in a Hegelian sense. In Hegel's work, civil society also expresses genuine social relationships between people and gives rise to a 'principle of universality' within civil society. Later in European thinking, we see a development toward the distinction between state, market and civil society, where civil society is separated from the market. Civil society is now social relations determined neither by the state, nor by the utilitarian exchange relations of the market. This is seen in various corners of sociological theory by, for instance, Durkheim, Tönnies and Gramsci, and also by more modern thinkers such as Habermas, Cohen and Arato. This article operates with the distinction being made between state and civil society and, consequently, the market is here contained in the notion of civil society. In this context, civil society is not what is left after we have defined the state and the market. On the contrary, civil society includes individuals, corporate bodies, associations, and large and complex organisations.[1]

Many of the changes that gradually led to the rise of the modern state and civil society in Denmark go back to the sixteenth century, but the advent of absolutism in 1660 is a crucial event. Absolutism in Denmark occurred as an unintended consequence of the war against Sweden. The king had outmanoeuvred the nobility and forced through absolutism as a response to the defeat and as a way of reconstructing the defence and cohesion of Denmark. With the introduction of absolutism external and internal sovereignty fused into one subject – the king's person. The various estates were deprived of their privileges; even the old nobility was deprived of most privileges. The king was now the sovereign active subject and society, or the people, had become a passive object. In practice, the mediating link between king and subject was the government official and the civil servants. This was codified in the Royal Law.[2] This strict separation of king (state) and people (society) mediated by the civil servants and the bureaucracy created a more transparent society and transformed the existing structure of closed feudal spheres into one public social sphere. Here we find the germ of civil society, which only became full-grown when the modern nation-state developed during the nineteenth century.

During the years of absolutist rule, we see a further development and extension of civil society. An indicator is the emergence of voluntary associations, which took place from the late eighteenth century. No associations could develop without some acceptance from the state. Censorship still existed, but the state remained silent as long as it found the associations useful for its own purposes, or as long as they did not undermine absolutist rule.

The state had an interest in this development not least because many of the late eighteenth century associations united people from different professions and estates and different parts of the country in common patriotism. This patriotism as a common ideological denominator generated stronger cohesion, which was crucial for keeping together the Danish unitary state which consisted of the present Denmark, Norway, Iceland, the Faeroes, Greenland, Schleswig, and Holstein. It strengthened the country against external enemies. An example is the 'Farm Household Society' (*Landhusholdningsselskabet*) founded in 1769 with the purpose of propagating knowledge and know-how among the peasants. Its members were mainly civil servants in the upper part of the state bureaucracy and businessmen in Copenhagen. Also, the members' background indicates a clear relationship between the state and the association.

A number of associations were created with direct support from the government. Thus, the Farm Household Society was supported with direct subsidies and free postage. Moreover, the state provided buildings for its meetings and offices. Apart from the patriotic element, the state had a great interest in motivating the conservative peasants to use more modern technologies. The entire economic foundation of the Danish state was the agricultural sector. Consequently, it was vital to the state to encourage and educate the peasants by supporting all local initiatives aimed at strengthening the agriculture of the country. During the first half of the nineteenth century the state and the king supported many other associations with the aim of reducing and preventing poverty or to generate better conditions for businesses.

The smaller associations or 'clubs' did not have the same direct relationship to the state. They were social, scientific or aesthetic in purpose, and did not as such oppose or support the state. They were, however, in a longer perspective important in developing public opinion (Clemmensen 1987: 31).

Gradually, by involvement in societal matters, these associations became more politicised and more anti-aristocratic, and this created more self-consciousness among the new classes – the bourgeoisie and the petit bourgeoisie, including the new farmers. The increasing politicisation was stopped by a setback in the otherwise liberal situation in the country in the late eighteenth century.

In the period between 1800 and 1840, a large number of political and religious associations saw the light of the day. King Frederik VI decided in 1831 to introduce the Consultative Provincial Assemblies in Holstein, Schleswig, Jutland and the islands. Only three groups were allowed to vote: landowners, landlords in the towns and property-owners in the countryside, that is, those who owned the larger farms. Together with the government, these assemblies introduced a system of local self-government in Copenhagen (1837), in market towns (1840) and the rural municipalities (1841). These reforms provided the institutional preconditions of a public sphere with a political content. New associations such as the 'Society for Appropriate Use of the Freedom of the Press' (*Selskabet for trykkefrihedens rette brug*) and the 'Reading Society 1835' (*Læseselskabet 1835*) are examples of more politicised associations. They were still mainly dominated by conservative and liberal civil servants and people from the liberal bourgeoisie and academic circles.

In contrast to these political associations, the religious movements and associations which opposed the 'national' church succeeded in engaging a broader public. Various puritan and pietistic movements challenged the foundation of the official absolutist church ideology,[3] and the state made no attempt to prevent this development. The 1849 Constitution introduced freedom of religion, and the radical character of the movement was gradually reduced.

A strong politicisation of the associations took place in the 1840s. The conflicts inherent in the state and society led to a political mobilisation of the peasantry in alliance with the liberal bourgeoisie. In other words, the politicisation must be seen as a result of the state and its hesitation to remove the last obstacles to a complete freeholder society of peasants. In particular, the peasants struggled to become recognised as equal members of the Danish state. Consequently, they protested against being the only class subject to conscription and demanded conscription for all men, citizenship rights and a smoother transition to becoming freeholders. The 'Rural District Associations' (*landkommunalforeningerne*) and the 'Society of the Friends of the Peasants' (*Bondevennernes selskab*) were crucial in strengthening the self-consciousness of the peasantry. These associations were the political forums created for the political and social demands of the peasantry. The key points of their agenda were general conscription and a removal of the feudal manorial system by the 'compulsory transformation of the remaining leasehold farms to freehold ownership' (Bjørn 1990: 285; Clemmensen 1987: 127). The peasant and farmer organisations were far more effective than the liberal bourgeois associations as a channel for a social movement because the former had a stronger hierarchical organisation with local committees.

It was not only the peasants and the national liberal bourgeoisie who organised associations as instruments for political pressure. The old ruling class, the landowners, formed associations and so did the craftsmen and workers in towns. With the abolishment of the guild structure they had to counterbalance increasing liberalism and the expansion of the free market, which was a threat to their conditions of existence.

Throughout the nineteenth century, many associations developed as an aid to self-help. Small local banks and credit unions were established as voluntary associations. From 1810 onward, a number of local savings banks (*sparekasser*) emerged in most towns all over the country. Their only activity was savings, and these banks offered private solutions to social problems caused by the transition away from an agrarian society based upon a closed system in which the copyholders were tied to the landowners. Society moved toward a new agrarian structure with freeholders, an emerging new farming class. The very process of transformation brought about severe problems because many servants, orphans or single parents no longer had a security net. The old, almost feudal structure of strong communities had protected the poor to some extent. This was now no longer the case, and poor relief was very limited. The banks attempted to 'teach' the peasants and the poor good morals, a protestant ethic, and individualism. By hard work and saving they could buy land and become free. The members of these savings banks (*sparekasser*) and their executive committees were recruited among civil servants of the absolutist state and the big landed proprietors. The members reflected the interest of the state, which strongly supported these banks and accepted their establishment as voluntary associations because from the point of view of the state, they relieved the pressure on poor relief, and they contributed to making peasants, servants and so on independent and self-reliant. After the abandonment of absolutism the development continued. Between 1865 and 1874, more than 250 local savings banks were created, and farmers and local primary school teachers now took over as the key persons in this process. Also, cooperative stores and sick-benefit associations started as aids to self-help organisations. The sick-benefit organisations emerged in the 1830s, formed by craftsmen who needed a replacement for the guild, which for centuries had guaranteed the craftsman some social security and sick benefit. The principle of voluntary sick-benefit associations spread to other groups in society, and during the nineteenth century it became crucial to most of the population. The liberal state found an advantage to this principle and supported it warmly. In order to improve the situation, the state issued the Sick-Benefit Associational Law in 1892. The associations were now officially recognised by the state, and the state contributed to the associations partly by paying a fixed amount per person supplemented with one-fifth of the total member contributions. The associations paid when a member needed a doctor, a hospital or sick payment.

The Constitution of 1849 and the 'Age of Associations'

The Constitution of 1849 is crucial to the development of the associative structure of Danish society. Here are two clauses of vital importance:

§92: Citizens shall, without previous permission, be free to form associations for any lawful purpose.

§93: Citizens shall, without previous permission, be at liberty to assemble unarmed. The police shall be entitled to be present at public meetings. Open-air meetings may be prohibited when it is feared that they may constitute a danger to the public peace.[4]

As demonstrated above, a number of voluntary associations developed before the 1849 Constitution. They contributed to the creation of a public sphere and some of them were important as channels for a critique of the absolutist regime. In general, however, most of these associations formed in the pre-constitutional period existed with the silent approval of the state because they took care of specific problems or functions which needed to be solved, for example, education of the peasantry, poverty relief and so on. Moreover, in the latter part of the eighteenth century, most of them furnished the general feeling of patriotism in the country. In the nineteenth century, this patriotism turned into nationalism, and here also many of the associations helped to strengthen the country in this respect (Damsholt 1995).

Between 1866 and 1915, the role of the voluntary associations became even more important because political life changed character. The big landowners gained greater power through amendments to the 1849 Constitution. The government and power of the country was now in the hands of conservative forces – the big landowners and the civil servants. The revision of the constitution in 1866 led to some democratic restrictions, which gave the voluntary associations considerable democratic importance (Gundelach & Torpe 1999: 74). They functioned partly as pressure groups against the government, aiming at redemocratising the constitution, and partly they were important because the very associations contained democratic structures and practices.

Thus the voluntary associations had an important role in sustaining democratic structures, practices and ideals in the latter part of the nineteenth century. After their emergence in the late eighteenth century, associations gradually developed more and more democratic structures. Each association was based upon certain democratic principles. The members were a 'demos' and a set of clauses and principles (a miniature constitution) was decided and passed by the members in a constituting meeting. Each association had an annual general meeting at which the old executive committee reported on the association's activities and accounts and a new executive committee was elected. This structure has survived, and even today it is an important pillar of the Danish democratic structure.

The history of the development of associations in nineteenth-century Denmark cannot be completed without a look at religious movements and their related associations. Many people living in the eastern part of Denmark took part in a religious revival in the 1820s, which through lay preaching urged personal acceptance of Christian principles. However, in the 1850s and 1860s, facilitated by the 1849 Constitution, this revival became more widespread, and it divided into two variants. The Home Mission, originally established as a layman's association in 1853, became a strong revival movement within the Danish National Church in the 1860s. Its popularity continued throughout the century and peaked in the 1890s. The Home Mission had its roots in evangelicalism and was characterised by the demand for personal conversion. The other movement, Grundtvigism, also developed during the last part of the nineteenth century. It was based upon the priest N.F.S. Grundtvig's belief that baptism, Holy Communion and Profession of Faith were the most important elements of the concept of Christianity, and it became one of the most comprehensive popular movements in Danish history (only matched by the labour movement). As it spread, free schools and folk high schools were established. Also, a number of elective congregations as well as independent congregations began to appear. In contrast to the religious movements emerging in the eighteenth century, these two groups did not oppose the Danish National Church as such. They were both contained within it and had lasting effects on Danish society. They were more than religious movements: they established schools and youth clubs and were involved in the economic sphere as well. They took part in the foundation of savings banks, dairy production and other economic activities (Clemmensen 1987: 56–60). They were an important part of the 'great transformation' of Danish society in the last three decades of the nineteenth century.

The last third of the nineteenth century has often been characterised as the 'age of associations'. The peasant movement with its involvement in political, cultural, religious and economic matters contributed to a transformation of the peasantry into a more self-conscious class of farmers. Combined with the emerging labour movement's growing size and strength in the breakthrough of industrialism in Denmark (Hyldtoft et al. 1981; Hyldtoft 1984), this indicates a transformation of the country in terms of modes of production, financial structures, and class, organisational and democratic structures. From the 1870s, the working class began to organise, and within a few decades became a force to be reckoned with by the other classes.

The fundamental structure of the Danish society changed considerably during the nineteenth century, from a feudal economy at the end of the eighteenth century to a smallholder economy with farmers in particular, but also with craftsmen in a key role. After the abolishment of the Law of Adscription in 1788, which had tied the peasant to the estate, the smallholder economy, with freeholders purchasing land, developed. The flourishing grain trade made them quite wealthy, and more money meant more land for the freeholders. The many savings banks benefited from this economic boom, and many new freeholds were established (Hull Kristensen & Sabel 1997: 357–8). When Danish farmers were hit by a decrease in grain prices due to cheap grain from America, Australia and Russia, a deep reorganisation of the Danish agrarian sector took place. A class and a sector of society embedded in a strong associational structure responded better to these changing external conditions than many others in Europe. The associational tradition was one crucial reason for the fast and efficient transition and reorganisation of the Danish agricultural sector. The change from cultivation of plants to livestock farming saved the economy. Agricultural products accounted for 85–90 per cent of the country's exports and this transition to new farming practices saved the export trade. The cooperative movement (dairies, slaughterhouses, bacon factories, savings banks, free schools, free congregations and folk high schools) was one of the most obvious signs of the successful restructuring, with a point of departure in a special Danish variant of associationalism which took place in the second half of the nineteenth century. The principles of associationalism were found not only in the cooperatives, but also in the church, the education system and in social and cultural areas. The old peasant culture was replaced by a more self-conscious and self-sufficient class of farmers with family farms at its centre.

What role did the state play in this whole transition period? The state as such did not intervene much, but provided the general conditions of existence for the farmers and their project. The Act of Freedom in 1857, property rights and the right to form associations were guaranteed by the state. In general, again, the state upheld the principle of self-help. The state generated some specific conditions for the development of civil society (including the market), to a large extent in interaction with the various actors and interests in civil society. Of course, as always, the state's rationale was higher than the individual interests in society: to be a strong and coherent state and society in order to maintain independence and sovereignty as a state. The state did not oppose the development of the farmers as a new and independent class. On the contrary, the state had for almost a century an interest in this development, partly for military reasons (the free peasant could be conscripted) and partly for economic reasons (they could be taxed directly). The farmers were far more productive and efficient than the big landowners, and the wealth creation of the country depended on the farmers. Consequently, even during the years governed by the conservative landowner Estrup, the state did not set up severe obstacles to the farmers and their associations because, in the last instance, most politicians knew it was crucial to the development of the country. On the contrary, Estrup sowed the seeds of the welfare state by introducing social aid on the state budget to help the farmers who otherwise had to pay for the old and the poor who were left in rural areas after the migration to towns and cities.

After this overview of the emergence and development of associationalism, we shall now focus on two areas with strong associational features: the education system and the cultural and social arena.

Associationalism in the Education System

In 1814, Denmark enacted its first school law, which gave all children, including those living in rural areas, the right to receive teaching. With the democratic constitution in 1849, some of the educational reformers, most notably N.F.S. Grundtvig and C. Kold, influenced the clause of the constitution related to education. According to the clause 'all children of school age shall be entitled to free instruction' (section 76 of the constitution). Thus the clause stipulates general compulsory education, but not compulsory school attendance. This is a crucial clause, since it gave the two education reformers the opportunity to develop other types of schools as alternatives to the state school. The first *friskole* (free school or, somewhat misleadingly, 'private' independent school) was founded in 1852,[5] and it was meant to serve children from rural areas. Today, the 'free schools' still exist, and they are more popular than ever. About 12 per cent of all children at basic school level attend 'free schools'. They are privately established and run by teachers and parents, but the state subsidises them. In 1995, 68,000 children attended the 415 'free schools', while 515,000 pupils between seven and 16 attended the 1,700 municipal schools.[6]

There are roughly seven categories of 'free schools':

- Small 'Grundtvigian' independent schools in rural districts
- Academically oriented lower secondary schools
- Religious or congregational schools, such as Catholic or Danish Mission schools
- Progressive free schools
- Schools with a particular pedagogical aim, such as Steiner schools
- German minority schools, and
- Immigrant schools.

Regardless of the ideological, political, religious or ethnic motivation behind their establishment, these free schools are recognised by the state and receive public funding. As long as they do not violate the constitution, they are free to provide the sort of teaching and education the persons involved find pertinent. Since the free-school system was established in the mid-nineteenth century, a consensus has prevailed in the parliament to ensure the legislation for and public funding of these schools. Even today the free schools are seen as important, partly because the opportunity to create and attend these schools is seen as important, and partly because the municipal schools benefit from the competition offered by the free schools.

The relationship between the free schools and the state is quite simple. The government has made detailed rules about public funding. The Ministry of Education does not exercise strict control when it comes to the content of the education itself. Here there are only very general rules: the free school has to provide an education which measures up to that of the municipal schools. However, in principle, it is not up to the government, but to the parents of each free school to check that its performance measures up to the demands of the municipal schools. The parents have to choose their own supervisor to check the pupils' level of achievement in basic subjects. Parents who are dissatisfied with the free school may move their child to the local municipal school. In principle, the local municipal school must always admit the child.

In 1991, parliament passed new legislation regarding free schools, which changed the public grant system. Now, public funding follows the pupil, but the parents still have to pay a modest tuition fee (approximately £650 a year) while the government pays on average £2,300 per pupil a year. It depends on the size of the school. Small schools receive more. Special grants are given to pupils with learning disabilities or other special difficulties. Other grants are allocated to each free school, for instance for rent, maintenance, construction and so on.

The free-school system as it developed from the 1850s and as it exists today expresses an attempt to solve the minority problem in Danish democracy. Within certain areas, the Danish constitution and the legislation based upon the spirit of the constitution attempt to provide minority protection. In the Act on Free Schools, minority protection becomes a minority right, which is visible in other areas as well. The minority does not have to beg the majority for permission to exist. On the contrary, the law provides civil, political and economic rights to oppose the opinion of the majority. Protection of a minority by permitting the minority to establish its own schools is found in several other countries, but we rarely find legislation or a practice in which the state actually subsidises the minorities exercising their rights.

The state provides conditions of existence which enable minorities to fight back against the majority (Balle & Balle-Petersen 1996: 11).

Over the years, the Danish state has had a clear interest in this system. Among other things, this school structure reflects the socially liberal character of Danish society. The constitution and its amendments indicate this social liberalism. The small social liberal party (det Radikale Venstre), which has shared power with the Social Democrats several times throughout the twentieth century, has left clear fingerprints on the development of the Danish state and society in a period otherwise dominated by the Social Democrats. The Social Democratic Party itself has seen it as an advantage to keep a more pluralistic education system because it also provided opportunities for the working class to develop their own voluntary associations, including schools. Also, the free-school system was a continuation of the liberal state which emerged in the nineteenth century, stressing help for the self-help principle. The state benefited from this system because any pluralistic tendency could be contained within the state by allocating these sets of rights and opportunities for self-governance. As long as no one attempted to undermine the state, it was a fruitful way to develop schools and education for everybody. Lastly, it is important to stress that this institutional structure did not emerge as a 'result of spontaneous and natural will to associate' (Hirst 1994: 45). The state clearly provided the conditions for the existence of these schools, of course, in interplay with various social movements, not least Grundtvig and his followers. The state, however, did not just give in to the pressure of people and the movement. The state only accepted the demands of Grundtvig and his supporters because it was no major threat to the existence of the state. On the contrary, the Grundtvigian movement generated a strong Danish nationalism which strengthened the state and the cohesion of society.

Some fundamental associational principles can be found in the Danish free-school system. The associative principles outlined by Hirst (1997a: 149–50) are easy to detect in the Danish school model, as follows.

1. Education is provided by free schools which are voluntary self-governing associations 'that are partnerships between the recipients and the providers of the service: such associations will be at least formally democratic and recipients will have the annual right to exit' (Hirst 1997a: 149). Free schools in Denmark contain the double democratic principle expressed in the right to stand for and

to vote for the executive committee in the association and the right to leave the school and move to another. Thus, the schools are internally accountable to their members.

2. These associations or organisations are funded from public sources. The parents contribute with a small amount as well, and the schools are free, within certain limits, to earn their own money.

3. The free schools are subject to public inspection and standard setting. No school can violate the constitution. Public funding will automatically be reclaimed and then terminated. The Danish free schools are obliged to provide an education which measures up to the standard of the municipal schools, and most free schools use the final examination of the municipal schools in order to demonstrate their level and standard.

In the next section, we shall see how some of these principles are also found in another area.

Voluntary Associations, Associationalism and Social and Cultural Activities in a Danish Context: Development, Continuity and Change

In the previous description of the historical development of civil society, a public sphere and the voluntary associations, we saw how the establishment of associations in one area is often closely linked to the development in other areas. We saw how farmers and freeholders created a network of cooperative dairies, slaughterhouses, savings banks, folk high schools and other associations. A similar development can be found in the labour movement. In this section, we will examine the associations developed in relation to social and cultural activities, such as evening and adult education, youth and leisure clubs and, not least, sports. As indicated, the development of these associations cannot be seen as an isolated phenomenon, but must be situated in a wider context of associationalism.

These associations have been and still are extremely important in Denmark, partly as places for learning basic democratic skills, and partly because the majority of the population is involved in these organisations. Most people spend many hours of their life in these associations and, consequently, these associations are an important part of public life and the public sphere.

There is a consensus in Denmark that a wide scope of cultural activities organised by voluntary associations is the best way to learn basic democratic principles and thus prevent crime and delinquency among young people. Also, these associations are regarded as an important means to educate and reskill the adult population and at the same time provide the basis for meaningful leisure time. Consequently, it is an area which politicians also have found important to support and develop.

The Origin of Shooting and Sports Associations

In retrospect, the formation of shooting associations was important to the development in this area. The shooting associations were mainly established as a response to the defence problems after the defeat by Germany in 1864. A strong nationalism prevailed and most people, despite class differences, realised the necessity for stronger defence. A conflict emerged between the left (mainly farmers) and the right (big landowners and civil servants) about the character of defence forces. The right argued for a preservation and extension of the standing army, while the farmers (representing the people or general public) preferred a militia, a people's army. The disagreement led to a division in the shooting movement. The conservatives saw the voluntary shooting clubs as a pre-school to the army, while the farmers wanted them to be the core of a national militia. The conflict between the left and the right was not only about defence; it was a more comprehensive cultural struggle which had its material side as well – the struggle between the small freeholder economy and the big landowners, the emerging capitalist and large-scale industrial production. The cultural struggle also manifested itself in the debates on education (free schools, adult education and folk high schools), religious matters, and education of the body (gymnastics). It also contained a constitutional conflict, which worsened after the revision of the constitution in 1866. This revision implied a restriction of democracy and strengthened the position of the big landowners.

The cultural battle reflected in the shooting movements was extended into other areas. The clubs put gymnastics on the agenda from the 1860s. For several decades, gymnastics became a battleground for farmers versus conservative forces. From the 1870s, people formed independent associations with gymnastics and other get-together activities. Also, rowing, various ball games, sailing, tennis and horse racing became activities which spawned clubs and associations. Whereas the shooting associations and later the rifle associations were directly supervised and subsidised by the state, the other associations did not at this point rely on financial aid from the state. It was, of course, the 1849 Constitution which had provided the legislative foundation for the voluntary associations, but direct financial support did not occur until the twentieth century (Korsgaard 1997).

The state had a clear interest in the formation of sports clubs. From the point of view of the state, a better system of physical education would benefit the country. A healthier and stronger population would contribute to stronger defence and would also be a more productive and efficient workforce. Officers, philanthropic landowners and schoolteachers all tried to encourage peasants to do gymnastics or sport to improve their fitness and the national defence. Later, the strong interest in the physical education of peasants led to strong governmental support of sport and leisure activities.

Adult Education and Evening Schools

Many attempts were made to encourage peasants to learn to write, read and reckon. This brought about a considerable number of evening schools. Various types of adult education for the peasants and the general public go back to 1856, when the state permitted local parishes (small municipalities) to support evening classes financially in order to improve the reading and writing skills of the peasants. Mainly voluntary associations organised evening classes. From 1895, adult education was supported directly by the state without approval from the local parishes. The support increased considerably in financial terms from 1895 to 1920. Adult education and folk high schools developed in the nineteenth century, primarily in the countryside, driven by the farmers' movements. Subsequently, in the late nineteenth century and in the twentieth century, we find a similar development in towns, but here the labour movement was the driving force. Despite their differences and disagreements, the two important political parties, that is, Venstre (the farmers' party) and the Social Democrats (the workers' party), maintained a policy guaranteeing financial support for associations offering adult education. They competed (and still do) under almost equal conditions. In 1930, an act was passed which gave adult education (evening schools) the same conditions in towns and countryside. The act had the consequence that a number of subjects previously not regarded as education acceptable for governmental financial support now became legitimate subjects, for example, cooking, sewing, knitting, and later on, gymnastics, dance and singing. During the following decades, a continuous redefinition of adult education and pertinent subjects took place. Almost every activity defined as meaningful for a group of interested persons has been able to obtain government support, either as membership support or as free rooms for organising meetings.

Today, evening and adult education is also organised by voluntary associations, which compete with each other for members. In principle, all types of associations can offer adult education regardless of their religious, ethnic, political and pedagogical foundation, as long as they stick to the legislation based upon the constitution. Today, the associations offer education without constant control from the government, and they obtain a contribution from the government corresponding to their number of members. The state and municipal government govern this area in a similar way to the free-school area. Furthermore, the evening-school associations have democratically elected executive committees, and consequently the voice-exit aspect is also a key dimension to this area.

Sport and Leisure Associations

As the last example of associationalism, we turn to the organisation of sport and leisure activities. This area is another example of how the state influenced and, in some respects, created a strong civil society. As indicated above, sport has been organised by voluntary associations since the 1860s. Again, the constitution with the associative and assembly clauses facilitated the establishment of sports associations. Gradually during the next 150 years, the state and governments based upon different ideologies have all had an increasing interest in encouraging the population to take part in sport activities. The various governments have also preferred that the organisation of sport takes place through voluntary organisations with a democratic structure. Again, the principle of aid for self-help has been maintained. Partly it reduces the burden on the state, and partly the state, by decentralising power to other levels, contributes to local democracy and a variant of associational democracy. The latter has the effect that members are brought up with democratic processes which they can influence themselves. Moreover, the activity only exists as long as members find it interesting and useful.

After the Second World War, the new generation (youth) became the focus of the state in its attempt to reconstruct and develop the country. The government established a Youth Commission, which had to come up with proposals for examining and improving living conditions for the future generation in terms of work, accommodation, education and leisure opportunities. The commission suggested direct public support of youth and sports associations, scout clubs and political youth associations in two ways: financial support should be given partly to the education of leaders and coaches and partly to physical facilities (fields, courts, meeting rooms, assembly halls and sports halls). In the same period, the government passed the Football Pool Act (1948) which permitted football pools. However, it was under government control, and the surplus was allocated to the central sports federations and other voluntary associations targeting youth. The sports federations mainly allocated the money to educate leaders and coaches in the local clubs. The government passed an act in 1954 which decided that local municipalities were under an obligation to provide rooms, halls, fields, sports courts and to contribute financially to the rent or mortgage any local club or association may have.

The report from the Youth Commission and the Football Pool Act clearly demonstrate a Danish solution to the problems of governance in these areas: the state is responsible for allocating resources to youth activities, but the criteria of allocation and the actual allocation are undertaken by the nationwide sports or youth federations. This is an example of self-governance developed partly as a result of a social-liberal state tradition and partly because the government found that the organisations themselves would always know best how to allocate the financial means and the criteria to be used. As long as the federations and local associations stick to the rules, the state has no intention to intervene or control. Also, the Youth Commission stresses the importance of providing reasonable and healthy leisure opportunities as a compensation for the uniform and repetitive work most people do in industrial society. Moreover, the Youth Commission found the principle of help for self-help of major importance because it contained an element of democratic education: the state provides the physical facilities, but youth must learn how to create the content themselves in a democratic way. They have to contribute by doing voluntary work in the association and by paying a membership fee.

The Leisure-Time Act of 1968

At the end of the 1960s, we find the peak of the welfare state in terms of extending legislation on leisure. The Leisure-Time Act (*Fritidsloven*) passed in 1968 was called the 'best legislation on leisure in the world'. The act intended horizontal (geographical) and vertical (social) support to leisure and cultural activities, mainly adult education.

The act was developed in order to improve facilities and conditions for adult education, but included provisions making it possible to subsidise child and youth organisations. Apart from subsidising evening classes for the adult population, the local municipalities now had to provide facilities for adult sports, something which proved especially significant for sport and sports associations.

Most municipalities found it too difficult to administer the act, and many associations involved argued that it was too bureaucratic. Consequently, most towns and municipalities in the countryside developed their own set of rules within the framework of the act. These rules were inspired by existing practice in other towns. The essence of this practice corresponds closely to some associative democratic principles. Financial support from the public authorities is only given to voluntary associations based upon democratic principles according to the constitution. The associations, whether they offer sports, scout activities or adult education, must be open for all to join. Their financial means come from membership fees and contributions from the state or municipalities. The state and municipalities offer a certain amount per member, and if a member leaves to join another club or evening school, the financial means follow the member to the other club or association. She or he can shift association and so on as often as she or he wants, but the contribution from the state will stay with the association where the membership fee was paid for a year. In order to reduce administration, each club reports annually to the municipality how many members have paid their membership fee. This number determines a certain contribution to the associations from the municipality, which also contributes in other ways to associations offering leisure activities (including sports, scout and political youth organisations and evening education). They can by estimation offer financial support according to the actual expenses of each association, and they cover expenses for the education of leaders and coaches. The actual size of the contribution from the municipalities to the associations could vary. Due to the decentralised structure of Danish society, the municipalities have considerable power to raise taxes and decide the level of services they offer. The Leisure-Time Act obliged municipalities to contribute financially, but again they alone can decide how much.

The Leisure-Time Act supports not only sports and evening education, but all associations with a more general purpose defined as being of general interest for the public and democracy, including scientific associations, theatre associations, consumer and production associations, housing associations, architectural associations, associations for improvement of the physical environment, political youth organisations, temperance movements and sports associations (but not professional sports).

The Leisure-Time Act was an important piece of legislation for the development of civil society. A number of principles embedded in this legislation were a continuation of principles going back to the mid-nineteenth century. Thus, again the principle of aid for self-help was sustained, but the government and parliament found it important to strengthen civil society further and thus enable the voluntary associations within the leisure area to provide better services for their members, but still with the intention that members must give something back to the club or association in the form of voluntary work, participation in their democratic procedures and, if nothing else, a membership fee. From the preparation of the act, it is evident how important most political parties found this as a general initiative with a higher purpose: to enable the whole population to create meaningful leisure time in a society in which less work and more leisure was seen as imminent. The act demonstrates that the state and the municipalities regarded people's leisure time as important for both the state and the people.

The Act of *Folkeoplysning*

Participation in sports has always been the most popular leisure activity in Denmark; it has been a tradition for most people to join clubs and associations to do sports. This pattern has changed during the 1980s and 1990s. More people began to do sports, but in addition to voluntary clubs, they also joined activities offered by commercial institutes or clubs.

These changes in the participation pattern combined with an increasing focus on sports as a health-creating factor (this was strengthened after Denmark signed the WHO's declaration on 'Health for all in the year 2000') led to a critique of the traditional strong support for sports organised in voluntary associations. Since a part of the population participates in sports activities outside the traditional sports clubs, critics suggested that some of the resources should be allocated to them also. This critique fused with a critique of the Leisure-Time Act that argued that the act was too bureaucratic and too centralised in the state, with too little competence resting with the municipalities. This led to the introduction of a new act in 1990, The Act of *Folkeoplysning* (literally, 'The Act of the Enlightenment of the People'). The purpose of the act is an 'empowerment of people', to educate them as citizens and enable each individual to become independent and capable of deciding and choosing.

The act guarantees public financial support and room for free general education (enlightenment of people) respecting the particularity of the participants and originators of the activity. The Act of *Folkeoplysning* is a framework law which gives a lot of freedom to the municipalities. They receive money from the state, but they decide how and where to spend these funds. This makes it easier to adapt the act to local structures and needs. Two types of activities need to be subsidised: (i) adult education and (ii) other activities, including sports, political and religious organisations, scout movements, and other associations with the purpose of offering activities aimed at 'empowering' the people and educating the general population. In principle, it is up to the municipality to define *folkeoplysning*. However, only voluntary associations can be recognised as recipients of public support.

A red line can be found in acts and legislation running from the early postwar period to the Leisure-Time Act in 1968 and later acts such as the Act of *Folkeoplysning* in 1990. The constitutional rights to assemble and to form associations are still closely linked to Danish policy within sports, political and religious associations.

Another red line can be found in the division of labour between state and municipalities. Also, the Act of *Folkeoplysning* (1990) is a very decentralising law, with room for each municipal government to govern according to local traditions and needs. Another continuous aspect concerns the principle of voluntarism, activation of users and membership contributions.

The picture of the development of voluntary associations within adult education, leisure and sport illustrates how the Danish state over the years has kept a strong interest in developing this aspect of civil society. The flourishing life of voluntary associations within sports, cultural activities and adult education did not just grow up from below. Throughout the period the state stimulated this growth and responded to ideas and suggestions from civil society. Consequently, the state generated a set of conditions of existence for the voluntary association which offers social and cultural activities. Moreover, as the development clearly demonstrates, the principle of governance within some areas has been a variant of associationalism.

Problems and Prospects: The Future of Associationalism in the Danish Context

The history of the emergence of civil society is a story about how the state has preconditioned and shaped civil society. At crucial moments (during 'states of exceptions') due to external pressure and in order to survive as a sovereign state, the state has been forced to reorganise its own society and change the conditions of existence of the people. Consequently, the very structure of Danish civil society has been conditioned by the Danish state.

The history of the development of Danish civil society reveals strong elements of associationalism at least from the mid-nineteenth century. The two areas examined in this article demonstrate that the state by new legislation over the years has accepted and even encouraged strong associational features in Danish society. The organisation of sport and other cultural activities is a clear example of an area in which we find a strengthening of associative democratic principles over the past 150 years. Also, the primary and secondary school system, which allows room for the 'free schools', illustrates how associative principles have been deeply embedded in the Danish social structure despite the general conception that the Danish welfare state is a top-down system where all schools are uniform state schools. Consequently, the Danish case reveals the presence of associationalism as a model of governance supplementing liberal representative democracy. Historically, the two models of governance developed hand in hand and have, to some extent, been interdependent.

This article is not an attempt to idealise the Danish 'model' or to claim that it can be replicated by other societies. Specific historical conditions have paved the way for this development, and just because it works in Denmark (and, of course, not without problems) it might not work in another socio-economic, political and cultural context.

However, we can conclude that it has contributed to the governance of, first, a specialised agricultural society based upon small freeholders and later a highly specialised, differentiated, industrialised society with an economy based upon small and middle-sized companies utilising advanced technologies. Moreover, this complex democratic structure has worked as a means to develop a welfare state with a high degree of decentralisation, but still based upon some universal principles. Compared to the other Scandinavian welfare states, Denmark is more social liberal and more decentralised and less social democratic and centralised. The structure of the Danish welfare state and the structure of governance have been important at a time when welfare states in Europe have been under pressure from recession, geopolitical and economic changes. So far, the model has proved to be fairly adaptable to these new external conditions, and so far, the Danish welfare state has not run into a severe legitimation crisis (Goul

Andersen 1997a; 1997b). We claim that this very decentralised structure of governance based upon representative and associative democratic principles is the key to understanding this readiness to meet changes. The present situation is not unique in that Denmark has faced serious challenges several times during the past 100 years: the deep recession in the 1870s, the situation after the two world wars (especially after the Second World War, which led to the abandonment of neutrality and a close alliance with the USA) and again in the 1970s and 1980s. The ability to change and adapt is related to the structure of governance, but whether this structure will prove successful in the future is, of course, difficult to predict.

Today, Denmark is facing other challenges which might test the 'Danish model' in other respects. During the past 30 years Denmark has become a more pluralistic society in terms of lifestyles, subcultures and so on. After the first wave of guest workers in the 1960s and later refugees and asylum seekers from the Middle East, and the Balkans in particular, but also from the east and Africa, a multicultural society has emerged. Denmark no longer has, as usually claimed, the most homogeneous population in the world with the same ethnic, religious and linguistic background. The increasing pluralism and multiculturalism challenge a society which during the past 150 years has developed a strong nationalism, a strong belief in the 'people', in the 'folk'. The Danish self-consciousness of being Danish, belonging to the Danish Folk, developed as a response to the threat from an expanding Germany in the nineteenth century. During the past two centuries, Danish politicians have supported any strategy which strengthened the feeling of belonging to the Danish 'folk', to the Danish nation. It has been seen as a necessity because in case of war Denmark would lose its independence and sovereignty. Denmark, it was argued during the last part of the nineteenth century and the first half of the twentieth century, would never be able to resist German military power, but could survive as a nation and a people if it developed strong national welfare institutions, such as a national health or a national education system.

This strong belief in the concept of 'folk' and the Danish national identity has now become an obstacle, because multiculturalism requires a rethinking of identity, including political identity. Here, the associational aspect can prove to be either a strength or a weakness. It is still an open question whether the existing civil society with its large number of associations will be able to absorb new cultures, or if the system will be flexible enough to allow the variety in cultures and lifestyles to form their own associations. Some critics argue that the voluntary associations in Denmark have functioned as a means to transcend class segregation in society. Associations, whether 'free schools' or sports clubs, recruited members from all social strata – the wealthy lawyer played football with the unskilled worker (Gundelach & Torpe 1999: 76ff). Implicitly, these critics reject associationalism as a help in integrating the 'foreign' part of the populations. A more extended associationalism is seen as a way of fragmentising and disintegrating a society which, until recently, possessed strong social cohesion. To transfer more power to associations and support Islamic organisations which offer day nurseries, schools and hospitals or to accept that specific groups, more or less, can build up their own small communities based upon certain ideals and ideologies which do not correspond to a more general set of norms is regarded as segregation rather than integration by many Danes.

We claim that it is a myth that voluntary associations assembled people across social and cultural barriers. Moreover, we claim that the key aspect of the Danish version of associative democracy is the democratic structure and function of the associations. The educational aspect of participating in an association where each member to some degree had to relate to democratic procedures is far more important than the cross-cultural or cross-class aspect. Consequently, we do not see it as a problem for democracy that many different and contrasting cultures and lifestyles organise themselves and receive public support as long as basic principles, for example, the constitution, admittance, and the voice-exit principle are not violated. The only consensus necessary in this society is some set of minimum rules, which, in the case of Denmark, are mainly codified in the constitution. As long as the very associational structure of society is democratic, it is not too serious a problem that social and cultural differences are sustained. Such differences are impossible to remove anyway. If people, regardless of cultural or social background, are brought up with democracy, are learning democracy in practice, it will be easier for them to respect the Danish model of governance and contribute to a consolidation of representative democracy as well. The key problem is not democracy, but the way democracy has developed in a Danish context. Since the development of democracy closely corresponded to the emergence of the nation-state, the Danish version of democracy became closely embedded in a nationalistic veil in which democracy equalled the Danish 'folk' (people).

Also, associationalism in Denmark is closely linked to the national project, and this is the real challenge for Danish society. Can the concept of a Danish folk be reinterpreted to include everybody living in the country? Can our structure of governance based upon representative and associational democracy change into a new structure relieved from nation building and a nationalistic framework? The presence of the associational structure today has already led to Jewish, German and Islamic schools. Ethnic minorities dominate several sports clubs. A strengthened associational democracy might prove to be one accessible road to reach a new platform for defining identity. It is important, however, to rethink the Danish associational model. In the modern world, with a highly international economy screaming for more regulation and with membership of a regional organisation such as the EU, Denmark must think of associationalism on a larger scale. Associational democracy can no longer be a Danish national project only. This is a key challenge for the Danish model.

NOTES

1. Hegel's own configuration of the state implies that the state is constructed from 'within' and from 'below'. First, we have the individual and the family, civil society and then the state, but the state is still seen as the precondition of the development of the others. We conceptualise the state as an entity conditioned by external recognition from other states as well as internal recognition by the key estates or classes.
2. See the Royal Law of 1665, for example, sections 4 and 5. See Danske Forfatningslove (1958: 17).
3. It has to be mentioned that the first voluntary associations in Denmark developed shortly after the Reformation. It was religious groups, which as a consequence of the Reformation and Luther's message took the bible into their own hands and sought to escape the local priests' interpretation.
4. In the revised constitution, these clauses are now section 78 and section 79.
5. 'Free schools' are often translated into English as 'private schools', but this is misleading. The free school is the perfect example of the removal of the private-public distinction, which only naive liberal thinkers are struggling to maintain.
6. The figures are from the Minister of Education (1995), and can be found at www.uvm.dk.

REFERENCES

Andersen, H. 1994. 'Det civile samfund i teoretisk lys'. *Social Kritik*, 29.
Balle, T. & M. Balle-Petersen. 1996. *Den danske friskole – en del af den grundtvig-koldske skoletradition*. Faaborg: Dansk Friskoleforening.
Betænkning om idrætten og friluftslivet. Afgivet af det af ministeren for kulturelle anliggender nedsatte udvalg. Betænkning nr.709. København 1974.
Betænkning om eliteidrætten i Danmark. Ministeriet for kulturelle anliggender. Betænkning nr.992.
Betænkning om breddeidrætten i Danmark. Betænkning fra kulturministeriets Breddeidrætsudvalg. Ministeriet for kulturelle anliggende. Betænkning nr.1094, bd.I–III.

Bjørn, C. 1990. *Fra reaktion til grundlov.* Gyldendals og Politikens Danmarks historie. Copenhagen: Gyldendal/Politiken.

Charter for Sports for All. 1966 (revideret 1992). The Council for Cultural Co-operation (CCC), a subcommittee of the Council of Europe.

Clemmensen, N. 1987. *Associationer og foreningsdannelse i Danmark 1780–1880.* Øvre Ervik: Avheim & Eide.

Cohen, J. & A. Arato. 1992. *Civil Society and Political Theory.* Cambridge, MA: MIT Press.

Cohen, J. & J. Rogers. 1995. *Associations and Democracy.* London: Verso.

Damsholt, T. 1995. 'On the concept of the "Folk"'. *Ethnologia Scandinavia,* 25.

Danske Forfatningslove 1665–1953. J.H. Schultz Forlag.

Finansministeriet. 1952. *Ungdommen og fritiden.* Betænkning udgivet af undomskommissionen. København.

Folkeoplysningsloven. Lov nr.410 af 13 juni 1990 om støtte til folkeoplysning (The Act of *Folkeoplysning).*

Fritidsloven. Lov nr.233 af 6 juni 1968 om fritidsundervisning m.v. (The Leisure-Time Act of 1968).

Goul Andersen, J. 1997a. 'Beyond retrenchment: welfare politics in Denmark in the 1990s'. Department of Economics, Politics and Public Administration, Aalborg University.

    1997b. 'The Scandinavian welfare model in crisis? Achievements and problems of the Danish welfare state in an age of unemployment and low growth'. *Scandinavian Political Studies,* 20/1, 1–31.

Goul Anderson, J., P. Munk Christiansen, T. Beck Jørgensen, L. Togeby & S. Vallgårda. 1999. *Den demokratiske udfordring.* Copenhagen: Hans Reitzels Forlag.

Gundelach, P. & L. Torpe. 1999. 'Befolkningens fornemmelse for demokrati: foreninger, politisk engagement og demokratisk kultur'. Goul Andersen et al. 1999.

Habermas, J. 1996. *Between Facts and Norms.* Cambridge: Polity Press.

Hegel, G.F.W. 1991 (1821). *Elements of the Philosophy of Right.* Cambridge: CUP.

Hirst, P. 1994. *Associative Democracy.* Cambridge: Polity Press.

    1997a. *From Statism to Pluralism.* London: UCL Press.

    1997b. *Globalisering, demokrati og det civile samfund.* Copenhagen: Hans Reitzels Forlag.

Hull Kristensen, P. & C. Sabel. 1997. 'The small-holder economy in Denmark: the exception as variation'. Sabel & Zeitlin 1997.

Hyldtoft, O. 1984. *Københavns industrialisering, 1840–1914.* Herning: Systime.

Askgaard, H. & N. Finn Christiansen. 1981. *Det industrielle Danmark.* Herning: Systime.

Indenrigsministeriet/Sundhedsstyrelsen. 1985. *Sundhed for alle i år 2000 – WHO's sundhedspolitiske mål for Europa – En dansk introduktion.* Komiteen for Sundhedsoplysning.

Korsgaard, O. 1982. *Kampen om kroppen.* Copenhagen: Gyldendal.

    1997. *Kampen om lyset – Dansk voksenoplysning gennem 500 år.* Copenhagen: Gyldendal.

Sabel C. & J. Zeitlin, eds. 1997. *World of Possibilities.* Cambridge: CUP.

The Minister of Education. 1995. Homepage: www.uvm.dk.

Tipsloven. Lov nr.278 af 9 juni 1948 om tipning.

7

Globalisation and Multilevel Governance in Europe: Realist Criteria for Institutional Design, or How Pessimistic Should One Be?

EWALD ENGELEN

Although a myth, globalisation has proven to be an effective one. By means of this ideological construct economic and political elites have wrestled far-ranging concessions from labour movements, social democratic parties and other left-wing organisations. The idea that economic competition puts clear restrictions on the governing capacities of nation-states, especially with regard to macro-economic regulation, has become one of the dogmas of today. It has not remained uncontested, however. Critics of the myth of globalisation come in two shapes. The first type of critic emphasises the mythical character of globalisation by confronting it with a plethora of macro-economic data. The upshot of this exercise is that globalisation is all rhetoric, no reality. The second type of critic is more careful. She too relativises the globalisation thesis in its 'strong' form, but at the same time she does admit that 'things' have changed beyond recognition since the mid-1970s, and, moreover, that these changes matter for domestic power balances. Yet that does not imply that each and every mode of economic governance has become obsolete, as some globalisation theorists state. The conclusion is rather that some of the old modes of governance have become obsolete. This is good news for progressives, of course. If the necessities of globalisation are proven to be false, a case can be made for a viable and convincing left socio-economic alternative to neo-liberal market-making. It is evident, however, that such a case depends heavily on the ability of theorists, policymakers and politicians alike to find forms of governance that cut the link of yesteryear between governance and 'top down' state intervention. The possibility of a left politics under post-Fordist, post-industrial or post-

Keynesian conditions,[1] in other words, is equivalent with the possibility of institutional design of a 'market correcting' mode.

The issue I will address is the conceptualisation of institutional design in the European context by Paul Hirst and Grahame Thompson (1996; 1999), Wolfgang Streeck (1996; 1998a; 1998b; 1999; Streeck & Vitols 1995) and Fritz Scharpf (1999) respectively. As the title of my article suggests, one can distinguish between pessimistic and more optimistic approaches to issues of institutional design. At first sight, Hirst and Thompson's emphasis on 'contingency' and 'diversity' seems to be the more optimistic one, whereas Streeck's and Scharpf's more 'structural' approach appears to be more pessimistic. Instead, I will argue that the mere demonstration of contingency does not suffice. Lacking a description of the institutional logic to be able to identify institutional constraints as well as institutional possibilities with enough detail and precision, the analysis by Hirst and Thompson ultimately resorts to a rather naive voluntarism. Streeck's and Scharpf's analyses, on the other hand, seem to introduce a certain degree of institutional determinism. Yet this need not be so. The case of the European Work Councils as reconstructed by Wolfgang Streeck does fit into the deterministic mould. Scharpf's examples of multilevel problem solving within a European setting, alternatively, reveal that the logic inherent in the institutions of European decision-making is much more indeterminate than Streeck presupposes. In the conclusion, I will present a set of realist criteria for institutional design, to overcome the gap between philosophical optimism on the one hand and sociological pessimism on the other, as well as the rift between theory and practice.

Voluntarism and Political Will

Hirst and Thompson's (revised and expanded) *Globalization in Question* (1999) evidently belongs to the second strand of criticism. They describe globalisation from the outset as an ideological construct that serves primarily as a weapon ('a necessary myth', they call it) in international and intranational negotiations and exchanges. The bulk of their book is thus devoted to debunking globalisation with the explicit aim of creating space for political manoeuvring.[2] At the same time, they do acknowledge that structural transformations have been caused by changes in the international economic environment from the mid-1970s onward. Their list contains the following (well-known) items: the collapse of the Bretton Woods system; the oil crises of 1973 and 1979; the debt crisis of the early 1980s; the liberalisation of financial markets; deindustrialisation in the developed economies; the rise of the South-East Asian economies; and the flexibilisation of production processes and the fragmentation of consumer and producer markets. Together, these changes add up to an economic order that is characterised by increasing internationalisation, growing uncertainty and decreasing predictability, but that is anything but 'globalised' (Hirst & Thompson 1999: 5ff).[3]

Their conclusion is based on an ideal typical distinction between an international and a global economy. A global economy is an economic system in which 'distinct national economies are subsumed and rearticulated into the system by international processes and transactions' (Hirst & Thompson 1999: 10), that is, lose their distinctiveness. To operationalise it Hirst and Thompson sketch four characteristics which ought to be 'visible' to be able to speak of a global economy. The first is an increasing degree of ungovernability. Through a process of negative (regulatory) competition and conflict the global economy would increasingly lack public agencies for reinsurance against external shocks and risks. Instead, spontaneous attempts to spread risks and costs by private agencies should abound. The second consequence is the transformation of multinationals into truly transnational corporations. This process of 'transnationalisation' must result in the relocation not only of plants and other production units, but also of vital functions such as research and development or the location of the head office, the place of 'incorporation' and the make up of the board of directors. The third consequence is the marginalisation of organised labour. The globalisation of some labour markets would disrupt solidaristic strategies and would enhance current trends toward increasing inequalities. The fourth consequence is the 'multipolarisation' of the international political system. The international domain would cease to be a one-dimensional bargaining arena for national governments, but would become a chaotic, multidimensional sphere of temporary agreements between private players, national governments, non-profit organisations and multinational organisations. National governments would not only become merely one type of actor among others, but would also lose their control over the national territory and its inhabitants.

In an internationalised economic order, on the other hand, 'the principal entities are national economies' in which 'trade and investment produce growing interconnection between these still [sic] national economies' (Hirst & Thompson 1999: 8). This implies that economic activities are primarily nationally based, that national economies are dominated by multinational corporations which have clear historically grown national roots, that the national regulatory regime is in large part based on the bargaining power of national labour movements *vis-à-vis* domestic employers, and that the international political sphere is very much the product of agreements and negotiations between national actors. It should be stressed that this does not preclude a growing importance of 'foreign markets' for multinational corporations, a tendency toward internationalisation of the labour movement or a growing importance of non-governmental organisations, multinational organisations and international bodies within the international domain.

In a second step, Hirst and Thompson combine these ideal types with more or less uncontroversial indicators for the level of internationalisation or globalisation of the world economy, such as foreign direct investment (FDI), international trade and the organisation of international business activities. Some of their findings are well known, others are more surprising. They state that the emerging international economy is more adequately described as 'triadising' than as globalising because 80 per cent of trade takes place within the area of the members of the Organisation of Economic Cooperation and Development (OECD) and because 70 per cent of FDI occurs within the Group of Five (the USA, UK, Germany, Japan and France). Moreover, transnational capital flows, according to Hirst and Thompson, were more substantial (relatively speaking) before the First World War than they are now. In addition, the increase that has taken place has not been a 'natural process', but is the effect of 'political decision making'. With regard to trade flows, they observe that, even though there has been a noticeable increase, trade still adds up to only a small percentage of the gross domestic product of most countries, small trading countries such as Sweden, Singapore and the Netherlands excluded. Their last qualification addresses the numerous regional trading blocks that have recently been set up in answer to the process of European integration, especially the creation of the common market. According to Hirst and Thompson, this has set in motion the development of trilateral relations between the EU, the USA and Japan and satellites, representing the construction of new non-national modes of economic governance, mainly dealing, however tentatively, with FDI, trade policy and exchange rates. In their opinion, these developments reflect protectionist sentiments, although no longer on a national scale, but at a regional one (Hirst & Thompson 1999: 2–3).

These important and informative qualifications serve the goal of debunking neo-liberal 'necessities' that welcome regulatory competition and the ensuing 'race to the bottom' as an elegant means to do away with 'social justice'. Exemplary is the chapter on the welfare state. There they state that it is evident 'that welfare states in the advanced countries are now under a variety of strain that push up both costs and the demands for services' (Hirst & Thompson 1999: 163). Hirst and Thompson rightly point out, however, that these 'strains' (at least within the European Union) have more to do with a politics of self-restraint (that is, the Maastricht 'convergence criteria') than with global economic forces. Due to the liberalisation of capital markets and the ensuing internationalisation of capital flows, national governments have been robbed of some important macro-economic policymaking instruments, especially those of monetary policy and fiscal reflation. Liberalised capital markets have forced national governments into a politics of restraint. So much for necessity. The diversity of state reactions does highlight the importance of institutional trajectories and indicates that there is (still) substantial room for political manoeuvring.

Hirst and Thompson substantiate this thesis with four examples, one of state failure (Sweden) and three of state success (Denmark, the Netherlands and Italy). The case of Sweden is used as an example of the postulated inevitability of the so-called 'race to the bottom'. At first sight, the Swedish welfare crisis does seem to corroborate the neo-liberal proposition that a high level of equality and high public expenditure is incompatible with economic growth under conditions of a borderless economy. The cases of Denmark and the Netherlands, however, show that this is not an iron law. All three are known to be relatively generous welfare states with a high level of public spending and a concomitantly high level of taxation, especially when compared to the level of spending and taxation in the residual welfare states of the UK and the USA. According to the neo-liberal logic, all three of them should have been in severe macro-economic trouble by now, but only Sweden is (or has been). How come? The answer is that apparently some institutional arrangements are easier to combine with current economic and political demands than others, without sacrificing the social arrangements that guarantee a decent living for all. According to Hirst and Thompson, this has to do with the specific mix of different modes of governance within the three countries. Following Streeck and Schmitter (1985) and Boyer and Hollingsworth (1997), they distinguish between 'governance by hierarchy', 'governance by negotiation' and 'governance by markets'. Neo-liberalism is then characterised as the attempt to dispense with negotiation, and to rely solely on the combination of a strong state hierarchy and extensive coordination via the market. The alternative, thus the lesson from the Netherlands and Denmark, is 'enough corporatism to win the commitment of the social partners in certain policy spheres and enough hierarchy to remove blockages and to unravel serious policy failure' (Hirst & Thompson 1999: 179). Yet, it needs to be stressed that this is not identical with old-fashioned corporatism, that is, a combination of centralised bargaining, huge corporations and Keynesian demand management. Rather, the Dutch and Danish success is based on a form of meso-corporatism, that is, a dense network of corporatist institutions, a consociational political structure and a high degree of decentralised decision-making. Within such an institutional setting, thus Hirst and Thompson, the willingness to learn is the effect of a shared history of successful conflict reduction and problem solving (1999: 178, 224). Although they merely state that a neo-corporatist regime 'can deliver the goods better than strong states enforcing free markets' (Hirst & Thompson 1999: 180), implicit within their argument is the assumption that the moral and (even) prudential costs of neo-liberalism are too high.[4] This is because market outcomes tend to be highly unequal (hence the moral deficit) and because market actors are unable to overcome the paradoxes of collective action by themselves, whereas central state agencies lack the local knowledge necessary to do so (hence the prudential deficit). Governance by negotiation is thus an indispensable part of any effective system of societal coordination.

Italy, the third case of state success, is introduced to counter the riposte that no general conclusions can be drawn from the cases of Denmark and the Netherlands since these are small-trading countries with a relatively high degree of internal cohesion. Relative homogeneity implies a level of solidarity, so the riposte goes, that makes it possible to pursue policies that are out of reach of larger countries. What is more, Italy is characterised by a 'weak state' that does not conform to the preconditions of corporatism, that is, highly monopolised interest representation and a state strong enough to reward cooperation and punish defection (Schmitter 1981; Lehmbruch 1984). Nevertheless, from the early 1990s onward, through an interesting combination of will-formation at the workplace and basic, framework-setting agreements at the national level, Italy has been able to cut unsustainable welfare entitlements and to redesign pensions in a more equitable direction. Thus, Hirst and Thompson (1999: 185) conclude, 'If Italy, with its history of militant industrial conflict and dogged defence of acquired privileges, can reform then it is possible that other medium-sized nation states could do so too.' The main lesson Hirst and Thompson derive from these examples is 'that history is not fate and that given the right political conditions, societies can change and adapt' (1999: 224). But they do not tell us how to do that, nor what the right political conditions are, let alone which agent, or coalition of agents, is to carry out these changes and adaptations. Lacking specifics such as these, Hirst and Thompson's analysis raises the spectre of voluntarism to pre-empt the accusation of a 'utopianism' of the wrong kind. Their conclusion that 'policy does have an effect and that there are options at the political level' (1999: 167), while correct, implies that further steps are up for grabs, if only the political will is there.

Voluntarism is also what boils up in their treatment of the possibilities of economic governance at the European level. Neither downward harmonisation, nor upward harmonisation is likely, thus they state that: 'Even if there can be no levelling up, equally there can be no levelling down of European social standards to create a common norm that serves as a level playing field for competition' (1999: 186). This is mainly because of enormous institutional differences (1999: 251–4). What can be perceived within a European context, though, is the widespread adoption of so-called 'social pacts' between governments, employers and labour unions. These social pacts are seen by Hirst and Thompson as an 'alternative mechanism' to contain inflation at the national level and enhance the competitiveness of the national export sector – alternative, that is, to downward or upward harmonisation. At the same time, these pacts tend to reduce domestic growth by limiting domestic spending power. The way out in the form of an expansive monetary policy is precluded in the form of an independent European Central Bank (ECB), which is carefully kept out of reach of politicians and is officially wedded to the ideology of monetary orthodoxy. To realise the goals of containing inflation, enhancing economic growth and diminishing unemployment simultaneously, a reformulation of the mandate of the ECB in a more growth-enhancing direction is needed, as well as a coordinated, concerted effort at the European level between the member states to contain inflation. The solution to this riddle is thus, according to Hirst and Thompson, a division of labour with regard to governance tasks between the different layers of the European polity, that is, the supranational, national and regional level. As it stands, however, such a division of labour is lacking, not only at the institutional level,[5] but also at the theoretical level. Hirst and Thompson observe that the subject of multilevel governance (or in their terminology, 'polycentric governance') is still a theoretically underdeveloped one. They state that 'we need a new ... theory' (more or less mimicking the theory of the 'mixed economy') 'which recognises that certain key aspects of economic activity can no longer be under direct control and that a changed international environment needs new governance strategies and institutions' (Hirst & Thompson 1999: 193). Lacking such institutions and such a theory, we must rely on 'political will', 'political leadership' and conducive 'political conditions' to build them. 'The main limits of possible policy in Europe are political and concern the capacity of Brussels to mobilise citizen support for continental-scale policies involving major fiscal commitments and political risks,' suggest Hirst and Thompson (1999: 255).

A voluntaristic conclusion such as this is based on the idea that the subsumption of the genealogy of specific institutions under the category of the political suffices to create room for institutional change. Political agreements, however, can be just as restraining as 'natural laws', and institutions, whether or not the product of political will formation, differ with regard to the costs (intellectual, financial, economic and mental) their transformation entails. Hence, the political should not be equated with what is 'socially constructed', meaning not naturally given, but should be used in a more restricted sense, that is, what is politically viable in terms of institutional design, given the fact that not everything can be changed simultaneously, that some changes are more costly than others, and that institutional complexes have their own functional logics.

Institutional 'Logic': the Case of the European Works Council

In a number of articles, Wolfgang Streeck has formulated his scepsis concerning the attempt to see European integration as a solution to the regulatory 'race to the bottom' that has been set in motion by the phenomenon of globalising markets. Streeck's scepsis has to do with the increasing inability of the European Council to counter 'market making' policies with 'market correcting' social policies. The attempt to create a European equivalent to national codetermination legislation is a case in point. As early as 1972 (after the labour unrests of

1968–72) a proposal for European codetermination was launched. The proposal aimed for harmonisation of national systems of corporate governance at the German level, that is, a two-tier board with mandatory employee representation in the supervisory board. Because of a slow and burdensome legislative trajectory, a changing ideological climate, diminishing labour union power, increasing nationalism and ever-louder protests from employers and their representatives, the 'fifth Directive' (as the proposal was called) was unable to make it. A revised version that was presented by the European Commission (EC) in 1983 doubled the floor for mandatory codetermination from 500 employees to 1,000, and gave employers the choice between the German model of the earlier proposal and an upscaled British one, meaning a one-tiered board of directors with employee representation (as 'non-executive directors') and a works council of a functional equivalent. Under each model the codetermination rights were to be the same.

Apart from harmonisation of corporate governance systems the European Commission strove for a body of European corporate law that was meant to enable the 'incorporation' of economic activities under European law. As this initiative too was formulated during the high tide of social democracy (1975), German corporate law once again served as the model to be emulated. The ensuing 'European corporate-statute' (as it was named) prescribed a two-tiered board and a full-blown works council. This initiative shared the fate of the 'fifth Directive'. The watered-down version that was presented in 1989 consisted of the same set of choices as the revised Directive of 1983. Moreover, all references to 'co-management' and 'co-determination rights' were deleted and replaced by 'softer' 'information' and 'consultation rights'.

The third attempt dates from 1980. In contrast to the earlier attempts, this one did not aim at institutional innovation within 'hard' corporate law but at changes within 'soft' labour law. Building upon existing proposals for extending information and consultation rights for employees during corporate restructuring, the Dutch commissioner Vredeling pleaded for a further extension of these rights to all corporations, disregarding their economic situation. While agnostic *vis-à-vis* the institutional format, the 'Vredeling-Directive' did specify in great detail the scope of these rights. The extension was also meant to be mandatory for all companies within the territory of the European Community, wherever their head office might be located. The Directive immediately encountered fierce resistance from employers, aimed as much at the proposal itself as at the social democratic agenda of the European Commission of which it was part (Streeck & Vitols 1995: 251). Even in a trimmed-down version (higher entrance level, restricted scope and less rights), the proposal proved to be politically untenable.

In 1990, when the 'neo-liberal turn' had put the social democratic agenda on ice, the issue of a European Works Council reappeared, no longer as part of a broad social and participatory legislative offensive, but as the social counterpart of the economically motivated creation of a common market. Although harmonisation as a goal was explicitly skipped from the Directive, which merely demanded non-discriminatory treatment of diverging codetermination practices within the national territory, the Directive did demand that subsidiaries of British (and Japanese and American) multinationals, located in member states of the European Union other than the UK, had to conform to national codetermination laws. The British government and British business organisations reacted furiously. The main counter-argument was that it implied foreign intervention in British property. The fury of the British protest was in part due to the fact that 332 of the 880 European businesses and almost half of the 280 non-European corporations that would have to accede to the demand, according to 1992 figures, were British or were known to have a substantial British share (Streeck & Vitols 1995: 252).

Until 1986 decision procedures within the European Commission were based on the unanimity rule. In 1986, a two-third majority rule was introduced to reduce deadlock, but only for issues dealing directly with the creation of a common market. Codetermination rights were explicitly kept out of the project of 'market making'. Thus a British veto was imminent. Attempts to subsume the Directive under the heading of working conditions, as a means of dodging the unanimity requirement, failed. This changed in 1992 with the 'treaty of Maastricht'. Then it became apparent that the proposal to lift the unanimity requirement for social issues could find agreement by all except the British. The prospect of years of political deadlock could only be avoided by accepting British 'exceptionalism' with regard to the 'European Social Treaty' (Streeck & Vitols 1995: 248–58).

As from 22 September 1994 the 'Directive regarding the implementation of a European Works Council' has been installed, which gave the relevant corporations two years to conform.[6] In broad strokes, the Directive states the following. Before 22 September 1986 corporations with more than 1,000 employees and plants in more than two member states, each with more than 150 employees, had three options. The first (Article 13) is any form of voluntary consultation which encompasses all employees and grants them at least information and consultation rights. The second (Article 6) concerns the formation of a 'special negotiating unit' which is supposed to negotiate with the board of directors over a form of employee consultation which is acceptable to all. The third is consultation according to a format as stipulated in the addendum to the Directive. The format is a European works council with information and consultation rights regarding all issues that are relevant for the corporation as a whole. Entailed within the Directive was the deadline of 22 September 1996 to put pressure on the negotiating process. Every corporation which had not reached agreement on a mode of consultation under Articles 13 or 6 before that date had to implement a European works council as described in the addendum.[7]

Even though it is still too soon to cite research into the empirical effects of the Directive, the meandering genealogy of this piece of legislation does allow us to draw some preliminary conclusions regarding the question of whether the Directive will reduce the downward pressure on the codetermination laws and practices of Germany and the Netherlands. The first thing that catches the eye is the gradual restriction of the scope of the respective proposals. While the first initiatives proposed modes of codetermination which concerned *all* businesses above a certain scale, the ultimate Directive concerns only multinationals, that is, corporations with subsidiaries in at least three countries. The second conclusion is that the prescriptive mode of the first proposals has been replaced by a set of options from which corporations can choose. It is clear that this is done anticipatorily, to pre-empt possible protests. The effect is too, that the Directive in its current formulation does meet business interests as they have been formulated by the Union of Industrial and Employers' Confederations (UNICE) especially (Streeck & Vitols 1995: 255; Hugo Sinzheimer Instituut 1995: 6), but also growing fears from national labour unions that a European Work Council modelled on the German format would interfere with their representative monopoly (Streeck & Vitols 1995: 254). The third conclusion is that direct legal regulation has been transformed into the obligation to find local solutions by means of negotiations. The result has been that codetermination has become less a topic for the legislator and more a topic for self-government by the social partners, that is, employers and workers. In the actual Directive, two of three options depend on negotiation. The legislator merely puts a floor underneath them. By shifting the main focus from the legislative power to negotiations between capital and labour, the EC is actually distancing itself from its earlier preference for a dual system of worker representation based on the German model, and thereby from the attempt to force upon national systems of industrial relations a more substantive level of economic citizenship. The fourth and last conclusion concerns a gradual farewell to legal and institutional harmonisation. Even though the Directive of 1994 does suggest the installing of a uniform European works council, because of its high degree of voluntarism it *de facto* leaves existing national differences as good as intact (Streeck & Vitols 1995: 251–5).

According to Streeck, this illustrates a broader trend within European law-making. Although the pace of European legislative initiatives has been unrelenting, substantial qualitative changes have taken place in the nature of European social law. Four characteristics in particular stand out. First, social law has increasingly become 'soft law'. The legislator has a strong and growing preference for measures that leave as much space for individual choices as possible; options and exclusionary clauses are becoming ever more frequent. The percentage of law that is binding has decreased from 74 per cent in 1958–72 to 36 per cent in 1992–98. Corrected for amendments on existing laws, the percentages are respectively 62 and 22 per cent (Streeck 1998b). The overall effect has been a further fragmentation of social arrangements within the European territory. This in turn has increased the degree of institutional competition and has enlarged the threat of convergence at the lowest common denominator. According to Streeck, this trend reflects a neo-liberal interpretation of the principle of subsidiarity, even though it is a 'neoliberalism with a nationalistic face' (1996: 68–9). For national political and economic elites subsidiarity has the triple function of proving their good European citizenship, enabling them to pursue national interests, and continuing the project of supranational 'market making' at the same time. Second, there has been increasing use of instruments such as recommendation, information and consultation. Third, there has developed an increasing preference for flexibility, options and voluntarism, instead of direct legislation and univocal directives. Fourth, increasing use has been made of what could best be called 'governance through unintended diffusion'. Via comparative research assignments so-called 'best practices' are being identified, which are diffused by means of closed meetings and public media at the same time. It is then up to the member states to decide whether and to what degree these examples should influence state policymaking (Streeck 1996: 77–83). The competitive powers of the supranational 'policy market' have replaced the earlier project of European institution building and institutional harmonisation. Streeck speaks of 'neovoluntarism' in this regard, meaning a decentralised and multilayered system of governance which has an inherent institutional preference for 'market making' over 'market correcting' policies.[8]

Joint-Decision Traps

'Neovoluntarism', according to Streeck, is the unintended effect of institutional characteristics (a decision-making procedure based on unanimity and 'opt out' options) and diverging interests. The logic inherent in configurations of this type has been the main topic of interest of Fritz Scharpf for two decades now. From the early 1970s onward Scharpf and his collaborators have identified, described and analysed so-called 'joint-decision traps' within the German federal system (Scharpf et al. 1976; 1977; Scharpf 1978; 1988). The German federal system consists of two houses, the *Bundestag* and the *Bundesrat*, of which only one is based on direct elections (*Bundestag*). The other provides for the representation of the constituting states or *Länder*. Moreover, the executive powers of the federal state are limited. For the execution of services, the federal state thus has to rely on the administrative apparatus of the *Länder*. Because the distribution of sovereignty between the federal state and the *Länder* is constitutionally delimited, attempts to introduce state-wide policies aimed at distribution and coordination between the *Länder* require qualified majority voting in both houses, *de facto* introducing just as many veto points as there are *Länder*. Even with regard to issues where no qualified majority was required though, the Länder voted *en bloc*. This was mainly the effect of an earlier attempt by federal officials to 'divide and rule'. The combination of *de facto* unanimity rule and veto points was not deadlock, but a cartellised decision-making procedure generating suboptimal outcomes. According to Scharpf, the policy outcomes were suboptimal in four respects. They were: (i) inefficient, that is, they tended toward overspending; (ii) inflexible, that is, they were too rigid to be adaptable to changing circumstances; (iii) unnecessary, that is, they were being maintained even after the reason for their introduction had disappeared; and (iv) undemocratic, that is, they present parliaments (whether at the state or federal level) with *fait accompli*, by using matching schemes they lower opportunity costs at each level of government thereby perverting political preferences, and they increase the salience of federal political issues at the state level (Scharpf 1988: 247–50). This is the so-called joint-decision trap (JDT): 'an institutional arrangement whose policy outcomes have an inherent (non-accidental) tendency to be sup-optimal [but which] nevertheless [represent] a "local optimum" in the cost-benefit calculations of all participants that might have the power to change it. [Hence] there is no gradualist way in which joint-decision systems might transform themselves into an institutional arrangement of greater policy potential' (Scharpf 1988: 271).

From the mid-1980s onward the emphasis has shifted to the rather more complex decision-making procedure of the European Union. According to Scharpf, the parallels with the German system of joint decision-making are obvious. In both cases, we are dealing with intergovernmental decision-making. In the European case, that is evident: the locus of sovereignty and legitimacy is and will remain the member state. In the German case, the intergovernmental aspect lies in the fact that the federal state is dependent on the operative apparatus of the *Länder* (giving *Länder* a *de facto* veto right) and because the current division of labour is institutionally backed. In both cases too, the decision-making procedure requires unanimity or near unanimity. As was highlighted in the example of the European Works Council, all European legislation requires unanimity, except laws and directives that can be subsumed under the heading of 'market making'. In the German case, unanimity appeared to be as much constitutionally enforced as inherent to the decision-making process itself; cartellised voting enabled the *Länder* to pool powers *vis-à-vis* federal officials *and* gain outcomes which for each of the participants represented a 'local optimum'. The third similarity has to do with the style of decision-making. Scharpf, following Richardson (1982), distinguishes between 'problem solving', 'bargaining' and 'confrontation'. Leaving the confrontational style aside, the main distinction between problem solving and bargaining is the notion of a common orientation underlying problem solving. This orientation can be based on ethnic or cultural homogeneity, on a shared history of successful conflict resolution or, even more minimal, on a perceived common vulnerability.[9] Bargaining does not presuppose any notion of commonality and does thus appear the most robust type of decision-making; 'It is premised upon the assumption that participants will pursue their individual self-interest, and that agreement can only be obtained if its anticipated utility is at least as high for each participant as the anticipated utility of no co-operation.' (Scharpf 1988: 260.)

Whereas the German joint-decision system was initially characterised by a problem-solving mode, the 'social contract' of the first postwar decades has gradually eroded and been replaced by more antagonistic confrontations between political parties – fissures which were replicated in the joint-decision system, ultimately forcing participants to fall back upon bargaining. The European system of joint decision-making, however, lacked such commonality from the outset (or at least since the failure of a common defence policy). A bargaining mode of decision-making has thus been prevalent from the start. These characteristics, Scharpf suggests, have resulted in 'pathologies of public policy' (the failure of the Common Agricultural Policy, the Sectoral Fund and the Social Fund) and the disappointment of integrationist dreams, both of which have severely undermined the legitimacy of the project of *political* integration, if not that of *economic* integration. The effect has been a prevalence of 'negative integration' or 'market making' over 'positive integration' or 'market correcting'. This is not only because 'market making' does not fall under the unanimity rule, but also because 'negative integration' has much less political salience and is thus much less politically divisive. Hence, Scharpf concludes rather pessimistically, 'If the iron grip of national governments cannot be broken the decision logic of European institutions will continue to reproduce ... substantive pathologies.' Political will, even political will that is not at variance with the logic of JDT, is (*pace* Hirst and Thompson) rather powerless against this 'logic': 'the dynamic movement toward greater European integration may have been retarded and, perhaps, reversed, not by the ideological strength of nationalism or by the instructions of a Charles DeGaulle or a Margaret Thatcher but by the pathological decision logic inherent in its basic institutions' (Scharpf 1988: 269).

Countervailing 'Logics'

The institutional 'trap' of joint decision-making turns out to be much less determinate and much less constraining than Scharpf stated;[10] the logic of joint decision-making does not predetermine the outcome of the decision-making process, nor is the logic of the JDT the only one at work within joint-decision systems. This has been the outcome of a series of more recent investigations into the role of sub-national regions within the European multilevel governance structure and into the way in which these regions adapt themselves and their supporting institutional structures to the ongoing process of Europeanisation.[11]

To start with the point of 'countervailing logics', Benz points out that the new prominence of governance at the sub-national, regional level has not resulted in increasing deadlock and growing intransparency, as was to be expected following Scharpf's analysis, but rather that the logic of JDT was countered by a dynamics of self-structuration consisting of 'joining' (actors, levels and domains) as much as 'dis-joining' them. The answer to problems of deadlock is not only 'problem solving' by means of 'common orientations', as Scharpf maintained. They can also be avoided through institutional and functional differentiations and variabilities. This is what Benz (borrowing from systems theory) calls 'loose couplings' ('*lose Kopplung*'). Benz's main thesis thus falls apart in three parts. The first part is that not all joint-decision systems are prone to fall into the JDT. The second one is that 'common orientations' are not the only solution to JDTs and the third one is that the European joint-decision system falls into the category of those joint-decision systems that are not prone to fall victim to the JDT and for other reasons than for the existence of 'common orientations' among the participants.[12]

JDTs, suggests Benz, only arise (i) if participants are delegates who are subject to control by delegators and thus to the antagonistic logic of particularistic interest definitions;[13] (ii) if none of the participants can act as 'hegemon'; and (iii) if participants are unable to opt out, either because of institutional constraints or because of the pay-off structure. All three conditions are met in the European system of joint decision-making only in a very qualified sense. First, not all actors are delegates, some are autonomous. Examples range from the European Commission to national experts, corporations, and labour and business federations, which are only indirectly subject to the 'logic of membership'. Second, even though a real 'hegemon' is absent within the European system, actors do differ significantly within specific policy domains with regard to their structuring and agenda-setting powers. The Commission in particular possesses important initiating capacities. Equivalent actors can be identified in the other levels of governance. Third, the institutional structure of the European system is such that the institutional constraints enforcing unanimity are more often than not supplemented by flexible forms of cooperation and interaction between territorial and functional governing bodies, whether public, semi-public or private. The most important difference, however, is that JDTs only occur under conditions of multilateral bargaining between actors at two levels of governance. The European system of joint decision-making does not only consist of more levels, at which a wider token of actor-types is active, it is also a system that shows huge differences with regard to both levels and actors between policy domains.[14] The effect is, according to Benz, that the European system 'is not as easy to stabilize' and, I would like to add, rigidify, as is the case with joint-decision systems within a national context (1998: 561–2).

Adding new levels inevitably increases the number of participants as well as their heterogeneity. The neo-corporatist literature teaches that this entails an inevitable loss in effectiveness and governing power.[15] Within the European setting this problem is dealt with, not by excluding parties from the 'third level' completely (which would be not only undemocratic, but also inefficient[16]), but by unravelling the decision-making process itself. Following Bader (1981) one can, schematically, distinguish between the following phases of decision-making: (i) problem definition, (ii) decision-making preparation, (iii) deciding, (iv) implementation, and (v) evaluation and feedback. Within the European joint-decision system a distribution of actors can be perceived, more or less along these lines, thus squaring democratic inclusiveness with effective government. Benz speaks in this regard of 'islands of bargaining' (1998: 564), the borders of which can be strategically manipulated to isolate delegates from their delegators to increase the manoeuvring space of the former. This, in turn, raises the problem of coordination between these 'islands'. Benz sketches two possible solutions. The first one conforms to Simon's 'architecture of complexity' (1978) and is based on hierarchical ordering. The second one consists of simultaneously operating bargaining arenas which are loosely linked. In contrast to the first solution, which entails a top-down logic in which all aspects are determined at the highest decision-making level (lower levels merely adding detail), the solution of loose couplings is based on the idea of a division of labour according to the criteria of knowledge, expertise, interest or contribution (see Figure 1).

FIGURE 1

SYSTEMS OF COORDINATION

'Loose coupling'	'Hierarchical coupling'
Bargaining with exit options	Enforced bargaining
Free mandates	Binding mandates
Informal 'joining'	Institutional 'joining'
Consultation	Codetermination
'Embedded games'	'Connected games'

Source: Benz 1998: 565.

Benz lists the following advantages of 'loose couplings' compared to 'hierarchical coupling': (i) enforced bargaining and its suboptimal outcomes can be avoided by informal consultation between participants with free mandates; (ii) they are less exclusionary and thus have a greater capacity to break up vested interests; (iii) there is more scope for deliberation and negotiating over power broking; (iv) access to leading positions within the decision-making process are more based on expertise or strategic positioning, or both, than on structural power; and (v) there is more innovative competition between arenas.

The riposte (left unaddressed by Benz) that complexity and opaqueness also entail costs in terms of diminished democratic accountability, though correct, can be countered in two ways. The first has to do with the terms of comparison. If a system of 'hierarchical coupling' is taken as the norm, it should be kept in mind that formal lines of responsibility hardly ever coincide with the informal division of labour, distribution of discretionary powers and concomitant responsibilities. Formal appearances should not be taken for the informal realities they are hiding. Hierarchical coupling, in other words, is no guarantee of transparency and accountability either. Second, democratic accountability is a moral ideal that presupposes not only clearly delineated powers and responsibilities, and thus a certain degree of organisational transparency, but also a certain level of inclusiveness; the decision-making process must be open enough to accommodate as many relevant interests and perspectives as possible (and preferably all). The tension between inclusiveness, effective governance and organisational transparency could well be unresolvable. The trade-off thus seems to be between inclusiveness on the one hand, and accountability on the other – systems of 'loose coupling' scoring higher on the criterion of inclusiveness and systems of 'hierarchical coupling' in turn scoring higher on the criterion of accountability. Yet both systems entail moral costs.

'Trading Up'

Not only does the so-called 'logic' of the JDT thus appear to be much less 'logical' in practice, its outcomes, moreover, are much less determinate than Scharpf still presupposed in 1988. In his most recent work, *Governing in Europe* (Scharpf 1999), the nefarious effects of 'negative integration' are weakened substantially. Scharpf does admit that there are constraining circumstances for rational decision-making within the European context. These circumstances have primarily to do with enlarged exit options for mobile factors of production (that is, capital and scarce competences), setting in motion a process of regulatory competition that reduces severely the regulatory capacities of national governments, especially with regard to employment maintenance (let alone creation). Yet, the assumption that regulatory competition between states automatically entails competitive deregulation is false. He demonstrates this with two examples of regulatory 'trading up' instead of 'scaling down', taken from work done by Vogel (1995; 1997) and others. Starting from the observation that in some domains re-regulation has taken place in spite of competitive pressures, an attempt is made to explain such anomalies.

In his summary of this body of research, Scharpf identifies two mechanisms that might explain these instances of 'trading up'. The first one is the so-called 'California effect'. What this effect describes is the type of environmental upscaling that was set in motion by the American Clean Air Act of 1970 that allowed California to set stricter standards for automobile emissions. In 1990, the federal government adopted the Californian standards and once again allowed California to adopt higher standards. Other states could choose between either adopting federal standards or Californian ones. In 1994, 12 states decided to adopt the stricter Californian standards. These standards once again will be upgraded nationally in the next round of federal legislation: 'Thus, instead of states with laxer standards undermining those with stricter ones, in the case of automobile emissions precisely the opposite has occurred: California has helped to make American mobile emissions standards steadily stronger.' (Vogel 1997: 561.)

According to Vogel, this has to do with market access. State-enforced product standards make market entrance conditional on adopting those standards. If the gains are large enough (as they are in the Californian case), external producers will adapt their products, and will even force the governments of their home country to adopt stricter standards to gain competitive advantages in the home market *vis-à-vis* foreign competitors: 'Political jurisdictions which have developed stricter product standards often force foreign producers in nations with weaker domestic standards ... to design products that meet those standards, since otherwise they will be denied access to its markets. This, in turn, encourages those producers to make the investments required to produce these new products as efficiently as possible. Moreover, having made these initial investments, they now have a stake in encouraging their home markets to strengthen their standards as well, in part because their exports are already meeting these standards.' (Vogel 1997: 562–3.) The crucial variable, thus, is the extent or depth of the market of the 'first mover'. Small economies will see foreign companies turn away from higher entry markets. To this Scharpf adds the condition of anticipatory upgrading because of imminent tightening of regulation. In the absence of this 'threat', the dynamics of 'trading up' will come to a standstill (Scharpf 1999: 94ff). A third limitation of the dynamics of environmental upgrading has to do with the fact that process regulation can be abused to shield domestic interests from foreign competition. Environmental upgrading by means of market pressures hence appears to be restricted 'to a relatively small number of highly visible and largely "symbolic" products, usually associated with natural resources' (Vogel 1997: 564).

The second mechanism is called the 'certification-effect' (Scharpf 1999: 93). This mechanism is based on the distinction between price competition and quality competition. Regulatory competition too can take two forms. Competitive deregulation is more or less comparable to price competition. The reasoning is as follows: regulation increases production costs and thus product prices, which, in turn, decreases national competitiveness. Deregulation, on the other hand, decreases production costs and thus increases competitiveness. In this line of thought, regulation is only legitimated in case of market failures. Yet market failures abound in really existing markets. One of the most ubiquitous is market failure by asymmetrical information. Certification by a third party, whether private or public,[17] does do the job here, signalling good quality to aspirant buyers and driving out bad-quality goods. According to Scharpf, this mechanism can also be perceived on a national scale. If national regulation aims at quality competition, the regulatory framework could become known to be synonymous with good quality if consumers are sufficiently informed about the differences and their underlying causes and care enough about those differences. Given these conditions, 'stringent national regulations may become a competitive advantage for national firms competing in the international market for quality products – in which case there is indeed no reason to think that regulatory competition should induce competitive deregulation' (Scharpf 1999: 93).

Conclusion

It is obviously true, as Hirst and Thompson emphasise, that sovereignty does not come in fixed amounts and hence that what one polity gains another polity loses (1999: 235). Sovereignty as well as governing capacities are (and can be) distributed among different levels, different agents and among different levels and different agents in different combinations. From this observation it follows that we should stop thinking about European integration in terms of a fully sovereign nation-state that never was. Indeed, the theory of multilevel or polycentric governance ought urgently to be developed further, as Hirst and Thompson press us to, especially if we want to come up with a progressive alternative to neo-liberalism that enables us both to account for the huge political, social, economic and cultural changes of the past two decades (globalisation) and to save the tradition of human emancipation that is the core of the Enlightenment project.

Hirst and Thompson aim to do just that. To do so they follow two strategies. The first one is stressing the political origin of the globalisation process. The internationalisation of markets, corporations and economic associations is shown to be the result of political interventions aimed at deregulation, flexibilisation, liberalisation and privatisation. The second strategy is of a comparative nature. The diversity of the reactions of different national welfare states to comparable socio-economic pressures demonstrates the continuing relevance of the national level as well as the actual manoeuvring space for political actors at the national, supranational and regional levels. This is what Hirst and Thompson do, and they do it convincingly. Yet it is not enough – not enough, that is, if your aim is a progressive alternative to neo-liberalism. That it is not sufficient is reflected in the voluntarism on which Hirst and Thompson fall back. The transformative strategy underlying their analysis goes something like this: if only the political will were there, the future would be ours. But the political will is not there, and there are good reasons why the political will is not there. In order to identify those reasons much more stress needs to be put on structural constraints. With this aim in mind I sketched Streeck's reconstruction of the European Works Council directive as a clear case of institutional determinism. According to Streeck, the European institutional logic is thus that only 'market making' initiatives will get off the ground. 'Market correcting' measures, on the other hand, are doomed from the outset. Reformulated in terms of a joint-decision trap it appeared that Streeck's institutional 'logic' can be avoided. Whether or not joint-decision systems fall into 'traps' depends on the orientation of the participants, the mode of decision-making, as well as the division of democratic labour between the different levels. In other words, precisely because the European system of multilevel governance is much more complex and opaque than comparable systems within a national setting, tasks, powers and responsibilities can be distributed much more easily, not only between different levels, but also between different actors, whether private or public, thus creating opportunities to avoid deadlock and rigidity. At the same time, it was shown that regulatory competition is not equivalent with regulatory downscaling but can, given certain conditions, result in regulatory 'trading up'.

What does this teach the political theorist involved in progressive institutional design? In the first place that it is not enough to stress contingency and indeterminacy. The battle against 'false necessities' must of course be fought. But this battle is also relatively easy to win. The second step is much harder to make. It consists of a sober analysis of the institutional constraints and institutional openings confronting real actors. Although sociological generalisation has a restricted validity, we can make educated guesses concerning the intended and unintended effects of institutional change. The same criteria with which we evaluate institutions can be used prospectively as principles for institutional construction. That would be the first constructive task for political theorists. The second one has to do with strategy and tactics. Proposals for institutional design, in order to have real impact, must not only be attractive from a moral (more individual autonomy and less exploitation) and prudential (economic welfare) point of view, they must be realistic as well.[18] Therefore, they must be based, first, on 'thick' comparative descriptions and analysis of institutional structures and their structuring effects on human actions and practices. These descriptions must at the same time be general enough to generate rules of thumb that cross functional boundaries and are contextual enough to estimate the costs of transformation. Second, proposals should be based on an incremental path of transformation, keeping to the middle way between piecemeal engineering on the one hand, and revolutionary radicalism on the other.[19] Third, proposals need to be able to identify winners and losers, and they must find ways to relieve the costs of change for the latter. Only then will the political theorist be able to bridge the gap between theory and practice, and be able to infuse sociological pessimism with a healthy dose of moral cheerfulness.

NOTES

1. I use these terms not in any substantial way, but merely to highlight the rupture of the 1970s within the capitalist mode of social reproduction, without any further theoretical pretension.
2. This is what Hirst and Zeitlin have called the 'normative empirical mode'. This mode of research is characterised by normatively informed social-scientific and historical investigations into alternatives and possibilities, which are explicitly aimed against the deterministic premises of teleological social theories (Hirst & Zeitlin 1997: 228ff).
3. See Marglin & Schor (1990) and Kitschelt et al. (1999) for analysis of the social, economic, cultural and political causes behind this rupture.
4. This is explicit in Hirst, where the economic liberalism of the Thatcher years is being castigated for serving 'rentier' interests 'at the expense of the public sector, the low-paid, the unemployed, welfare recipients generally and capacity in the manufacturing sector' (1994: 92).
5. See the following quotes: 'The EU has still failed to develop an effective division of labour in economic governance with the member states in order to manage a continental-scale economy successfully,' (Hirst & Thompson 1999: 190) and 'Europe is still at the point where a great deal of institutional work needs to be done to ensure that its effective integration is irreversible.' (Hirst & Thompson 1999: 254.)
6. The evaluation of the Directive started in September 1999.
7. See Lamers (1995: 127ff) for the text of the Directive.
8. '"Neo-voluntarism": an emerging commitment to a decentralized regulatory regime with a preference for "soft" over "hard" law, and "private" over "public" order, operating under a "variable geometry" of participants that are protected from central intervention by ample opportunities for "opting out", as well as by a general presumption of precedence of both local traditions and market forces over universal normative regulation.' (Streeck & Vitols 1995: 255.)
9. It has been said that the origins of the European project lie in the wartime experiences of the participants, and thus in their common vulnerability. A Hobbesian starting point, however, does not preclude the accumulation of thicker notions of commonality. It thus does not need to come as a surprise that the European project has survived the failure of a common European defence policy. However, whether the thickness of the common identity suffices to back up substantial redistribution between the regions, for example, is a matter of debate, as is the question of whether a common identity is indeed what is needed for a more substantial European social policy.
10. 'There is no "gradualist" way in which joint-decision systems might transform themselves into an institutional arrangement of greater policy potential. In order to be effective, institutional change would have to be large scale, implying the acceptance of short-term losses for many, or all, participants. That is unlikely, but not impossible. And, of course, the system might be jolted out of its present equilibrium by external intervention or by a dramatic deterioration of its performance which would undermine even its "local optimality" for crucial participants. Thus, *I have not described a deterministic world, even though the logic of the "joint decision" trap may provide as close an approximation to structural determinism as one is likely to encounter in the social sciences.*' (Scharpf 1988: 271.) (Emphasis added.)
11. This research project was supervised by Gerhard Lehmbruch, Burkard Eberlein and Arthur Benz, conducted by the University of Konstanz and financed by Baden-Württemberg. See Benz (1998: 558–60) for a short description of the project.
12. Compare Benz's conclusion: 'The extension of joint-decision systems with three or four levels of governance does not automatically imply a concomitant decrease of governability. There are "traps" for sure, but there are also sufficient ways out. To

perceive them, one must distinguish analytically between different types of joint-decision systems, their internal differentiations, different mixes of modes of governance (market, hierarchy, community, association [EE]) and, finally, the dynamics of self-structuration of these systems.' (Benz 1998: 586.) (Translation by Ewald Engelen.)

13. This is, of course, the well-known conflict between the 'logic of membership' and the 'logic of influence'. See Streeck (1994) and Schmitter and Streeck (1999).

14. Benz refers to the establishment of representational offices by German *Länder* and cities in Brussels to promote their causes at the European level on the one hand, and the search for closer cooperation with regional actors by European agencies directly, effectively circumventing the national level, on the other (1998: 563).

15. It is implicit within Scharpf's earlier analyses: problem solving does not result in suboptimal outcomes, but is dependent on the existence of a 'common orientation' which presupposes a restricted number of participants.

16. Insufficient democratic input lowers the quality of the output. This is, of course, derived from Scharpf's distinction between 'input-oriented legitimacy' and 'output-oriented legitimacy' as the two sides of democratic legitimacy (1970; 1999: 6–15).

17. According to Werle (cited by Scharpf) not every type of certification or standardisation can be left to voluntary agreement. Werle distinguishes between coordinative standardisation and regulatory standardisation. The first type merely aims at technical compatibility. It is this type of standardisation that is best left to self-regulation. The second type deals with the prevention of externalities. Due to paradoxes of collective action any system of self-regulation will tend to be unstable, that is, actors will be tempted to defect. With regard to this type of standardisation state intervention is inevitable, if only in the form of a mere 'shadow of hierarchy' (Werle 1993; 1997; Scharpf 1999: 91).

18. See Engelen (2000) for elaboration.

19. Sabel's 'bootstrapping reform' is an excellent example of an incremental strategy. Compare Sabel (1995), also Unger (1987: 395–441) and Hirst (1994: 40–43, 96–101).

REFERENCES

Bader, V. 1981. 'Entscheidungstheoretisches Modell zur theoretischen Strukturierung der Fragenkomplexe zum Problemgebiet: Demokratische Kontrolle und Fachqualifikation im System der ökonomischen Planung und Leitung'. (Unpublished manuscript.)

Benz, A. 1998. 'Politikverflechtung ohne Politikverflechtungsfalle – Koordination und Strukturdynamik im europäischen Mehrebenensystem'. *Politische Vierteljahresschrift*, 39/3, 558–9.

Berger, S., ed. 1981. *Organizing Interests in Western Europe*. Cambridge: CUP.

Engelen, E. 2000. *Economisch burgerschap in de onderneming. Een oefening in concreet utopisme*. Amsterdam: ThelaThesis.

Goldthorpe, J., ed. 1984. *Order and Conflict in Contemporary Capitalism*. Oxford: Clarendon.

Hesse, J., ed. 1978. *Politikverflechtung im föderativen Staat*. Baden-Baden: Nomos.

Hirst, P. 1994. *Associative Democracy. New Forms of Social and Economic Governance*. Oxford: Polity Press.

Thompson, G. 1996. *Globalization in Question*. Oxford: Polity Press.

1999. *Globalization in Question*, 2nd edn. Oxford: Polity Press.

Zeitlin, J. 1997. 'Flexible specialization. Theory and evidence in the analysis of industrial change'. Hollingsworth et al. 1997: 220–39.

Hollingsworth, J.R. & R. Boyer, eds. 1997. *Contemporary Capitalism. The Embeddedness of Institutions* Cambridge: CUP.

Hugo Sinzheimer Instituut. 1995. *De Europese ondernemingsraden en de medezeggenschap per overeenkomst*. Handelingen van de HSI-conferentie, 27 September 1995. Amsterdam: Hugo Sinzheimer Instituut.

Kitschelt, H., P. Lange, G. Marks & J. Stephens. 1999. *Continuity and Change in Contemporary Capitalism*. Cambridge: CUP.

Kubicek, H. & P. Seege, eds. 1993. *Perspektive Techniksteuerung. Interdisziplinäre Sichtweisen eines Schlüsselproblems entwickelter Industriegesellschaften*. Berlin: Sigma.

Lamers, J. 1995. *Medezeggenschap in concerns. Effectiviteit van de nationale wetgeving en de Europese richtlijn*. Alphen a/d Rijn: Samson.

Lehmbruch, G. 1984. 'Concertation and the structure of corporatist networks'. Goldthorpe 1984: 60–80.

Marglin, S. & J. Schor, eds. 1990. *The Golden Age of Capitalism. Reinterpreting the Postwar Experience*. Oxford: OUP.

Marks, G., F. Scharpf, P. Schmitter & W. Streeck, eds. 1996. *Governance in the European Union*. London: Sage.

Richardson, J., ed. 1982. *Policy Styles in Western Europe*. London: George Allen and Unwin.

Rogers, J. & W. Streeck, 1995. *Works Councils. Consultation, Representation and Cooperation in Industrial Relations*. Chicago: University of Chicago Press.

Sabel, C. 1995. 'Bootstrapping reform. Rebuilding firms, the welfare state, and unions'. *Politics & Society*, 23/1, 5–48.

Scharpf, F. 1970. *Demokratietheorie zwischen Utopie und Anpassung*. Konstanz: Universitätsverlag.

1977. *Politikverflechtung II. Kritik und Berichte aus der Praxis*. Kronberg: Athenäum.

1978. 'Die Theorie der Politikverflechtung. Ein kurzgefaßter Leitfaden'. Hesse 1978.

1988. 'The joint-decision trap. Lessons from German federalism and European integration'. *Public Administration*, 66, 239–78.

1999. *Governing in Europe. Effective and Democratic?* Oxford: OUP.

Reissert, B. & F. Schnabel. 1976. *Politikverflechtung. Theorie und Empirie des kooperativen Föderalismus in der Bundesrepublik*. Kronberg: Scriptor.

Schenk, K.E., D. Schmidtchen & M. Strait, eds. 1997. *Jahrbuch für neue politische Ökonomie, 16. Neue politische Ökonomie der Integration und Öffnung von Infrastrukturnetzen*. Tübingen: Mohr.

Schmitter, P. 1981. 'Interest intermediation and regime governability in contemporary western Europe and North America'. Berger 1981: 282–327.

Simon, H. 1978. 'Die Architektur der Komplexität'. Türk 1978: 94–120.

Streeck, W. 1994. 'Staat und Verbände. Neue Fragen, neue Antworten?' *Staat und Verbände*, 25, 7–34.

1996. 'Neo-voluntarism. A new European social policy regime?' Marks 1996: 64–94.

1998a. 'The internationalization of industrial relations in Europe. Prospects and problems'. *Politics & Society*, 26/4, 429–59.

1998b. 'Europese integratie en de toekomst van de verzorgingsstaat'. (Lecture in De Balie in Amsterdam, 9 November 1998, at the invitation of the Dutch social democratic delegation in the European parliament.)

1999. 'Social citizenship under regime competition. The case of the European works council'. *Korporatismus in Deutschland. Zwischen Nationalstaat und Europäischer Union*, 124–58. Frankfurt: Campus.

Streeck, W. 1999 (1981). *The Organization of Business Interests. Studying the Associative Action of Business in Advanced Industrial Societies*. MPIfG Discussion Paper, 99/1, http://www.mpi-fg-koeln.mpg.de.

Streeck, W. & S. Vitols 1995. 'The European community. Between mandatory consultation and voluntary information'. Rogers 1995: 243–81.

Türk, K., ed. 1978. *Handlungssysteme*. Opladen: Leske + Budrich.
Unger, R. 1987. *False Necessity. Anti-necessitarian Social Theory in the Service of Empowered Democracy*. Cambridge: CUP.
Vogel, D. 1995. *Trading Up. Consumer and Environmental Regulation in a Global Economy*, Cambridge, MA: Harvard University Press.
    1997. 'Trading up and governing across. Transnational governance and environmental protection'. *Journal of European Public Policy*, 4, 556–71.
Werle, R. 1993. 'Politische Techniksteuerung durch europäische Standardisierung?' Kubicek & Seege 1993: 129–42.
    1997. 'Technische Standardisierung im deregulierenden Europea'. Schenk 1997: 54–80.

8

Reflexive Governance and Indigenous Self-Rule: Lessons in Associative Democracy?

ANDRÉ J. HOEKEMA

Associative democracy is a concept which builds on a multitude of empirical tendencies of pluralisation of the state and restyles it into a normative political ideal. Let me cite some of these tendencies. Between state and market operate those public-private inter-organisational networks that are less hierarchical, more flexible and less exclusively interest oriented than (still existing) neo-corporatist institutions of governance. I shall call them reflexive institutions of governance.[1] Streeck and Schmitter (1985), from whom I took the 'beyond state and market' expression, qualify governance by these networks as an 'associative model of social order'.[2] 'Associative ownership' is a concept with which the Ethiopian scholar Desalegn Rahmato (1994: 13) indicates a form of community-based, non-state-institution tenure of land, often called communal land tenure. He perceives this as a way to empower the poor local farmers and to counter and make transparent state control of the land. It purports a reshuffling of relations between the state and social actors too. The rediscovery of communal tenure as an effective and democratic institution in development theory helps to propel a movement toward politically and legally upgrading existing community-based tenure regimes and inventing new ones.

The last example concerns the newly emerging multicultural institutions of state and law now springing up in many states harbouring national minorities, immigrant groups and particularly indigenous peoples. All these tendencies, and more, could be summarised under the heading of Hirst's (1994) concept of associative democracy although each of them in some important features falls short of the pure associative case. In the important tendency to come to terms with indigenous demands for more autonomy and respect, one sometimes hears the slogan of 'new partnership relations' between these distinct peoples and the dominant society and its state – clearly an associative tendency.

Pluralisation of the state has been very much in my mind for the past couple of years when I studied 'interactive' public-private networks at home, indigenous self-rule abroad and communal land tenure everywhere. They all have to do with ways of regionalising state power and the empowerment of regional (and functional) collectivities: groups, communities, organisations and peoples. On the basis of these experiences I hope to be able to present two of the tendencies in more detail and thereby to show that important impulses of renewal of democracy, citizenship and institutions of governance are going about their work already. At the same time, I should like to point to the specific conditions that give rise to these tendencies to pluralise the state. These conditions provide opportunities, but also obstacles, for cooperative or associative forms of governance. To focus my analysis, my main theme will be the conditions for the growth of an attitude of trust and cooperation as a necessary element in a process toward a genuine co-production of policies by state and private actors.

Let me make clear at the outset that 'governance' in this article carries one of the meanings Mayntz (1998: 7) discussed recently: 'a new mode of governing that is distinct from the hierarchical control model, a more cooperative mode where state and non-state actors participate in mixed public-private networks'. While this definition does not include all forms of cooperative policymaking, it is broad enough to cover the tendencies I want to treat here.

In the next, the second section, reflexive governance will be analysed more fully, and in part three the case of indigenous self-rule. Community-based or communal forms of resource tenure will not be discussed in this article. In part four some conclusions are drawn.

Reflexive Governance

Regarding this relatively new and penetrating phenomenon of reflexive governance, the Dutch organisation for pure scientific research (NWO) financed a series of six empirical and conceptual studies which I had the pleasure to help to coordinate. From this experience stem some of the following observations.

Already I have suggested a difference between two forms of institutional arrangements through which public and private actors co-produce public policies. Instead of, or next to, top-down, interest-oriented, rather durable and firmly institutionalised neo-corporatist networks, another type of network shows up, particularly under the conditions of 'intractable policy controversies', defined by Schön and Rein (1994) as those controversies that cannot be solved by recourse to the facts, which means recourse to evidence to which all of the contending parties will agree. Controversies around issues such as poverty, crime, abortion, drugs, resource depletion and so on are immune to resolution by appeal to the facts. People argue from different frames, 'structures of belief, perception and appreciation', not unlike what I could call: frames of interpretation. It is the post-modern condition of western culture not to possess a unity in conceptions of the common good any more. This gives rise to the problem of 'issue definition'. Take the problem of an excess of manure because of a unprecedented growth in pig-farming in the Netherlands. Is it a problem of exporting the manure from the south to the north, a distribution problem, or is it an environmental problem? A common definition of the problem in itself is not emerging. It has to be worked out in a cooperative effort, which Schön and Rein call frame reflection.

From this condition some typical elements of the new networks spring up: deliberations do not start with interests and exchange, but with reflection about issues and problem definition, while partners in the network are less often national federations and tend to be more often regional organisations, both public and private. The networks are far less institutionalised: they surface for a while, say five years, and then disappear.

The main partners in these new networks are not individuals; neither are they voluntary self-governing associations of the sort Hirst has in mind, although some might be involved. They are, as Michels identified, organisations that are already subject to the iron law of oligarchy: they are selected as partners according to the criterion of whether they are reliable as a partner or not. This means: have they proven to be willing and able to discipline their followers? This in itself, however, does not disqualify them as voluntary associations, because some form of group constraint on the individual is also indispensable in a society that functions like an association of associations.[3] Although the driving force behind the new networks is not the recognition of a pluralism of responsible individuals nor the desire to empower them, in the new networks, responsible citizen groups are to be found as partners in governance. Clearly, there is a break away from bureaucratic styles of governance.[4]

The new networks are structures that develop through communication, not hierarchy, market exchange or community. Under favourable conditions the process itself can produce the sort of trust that keeps communication going and makes it more ground-breaking. The trust I have in mind has a broader reach and a longer duration that the trust needed to keep market exchange going, or for that matter that keeps neo-corporatist networks going. Following in the footsteps of the Dutch legal sociologist Dorien Pessers (1999), the principle of interchange prevalent in the new networks will be called reciprocity, whereas the moral of markets will be called mutuality.[5] Trust is everywhere. It underpins any relationships of people living and cooperating together. But a gap yawns between the mutuality on markets, with its stress on formal and precise rights and obligations which are restricted in time, and reciprocal trust that is underpinned long-term, 'vaguely' (non-specified) and not time specifically. Very often the ethos of reciprocity, studied by anthropology through the ethics of the gift, is misunderstood as a tit for tat type of mutuality. It is different from that. It is this relationship's cooperative relations that are needed to inspire associative democracy.

Communication feeds on, but also builds, trust. It takes a while before the actors involved start to refrain from calling each other names: 'those softies that want to save the last duck nestling near the Airport' versus 'those blind-eyed business people that want to put asphalt even over the last green parts of our country'. They have to learn to appreciate the opposite interests and to come to see the mutuality of interests in the solution of the problem. Here, we come across the problem already alluded to: a common definition of the problem is wanting. Frame reflection is needed. So, it is not clear from the outset which interests are at stake at all. A great deal of deliberation is consumed by trying to reach such a common definition. Only afterward can interests be pinpointed. A salient feature of these reflexive governance institutions is the tendency to discontinue traditional interest positions, that is, the tendency to perceive organisational interests differently from before.

Here, we should briefly mention another form of public-private governance that takes a middle-way position between neo-corporatism and reflexive governance: win-win negotiations. These negotiations proceed in a less open way than reflexive arrangements. Corporate actors do not change their views and preferences as to the interests of their organisation or group. They are not only willing to appreciate the fact that although interests clash, the overriding interest is to stick together, as in all networks of co-production of public policies, but the partners even tend to move toward an expansion of the range of interests. In this way, they hope to find an encompassing exchange that is favourable to all.[6] Although the range of relevant interests is expanded much to the benefit of the outcome, in win-win negotiations the interests in themselves are continuous in each (corporate) actor.

Not so in reflexive networks. During sessions over many years, in search of a common definition of the problem, slowly each protagonist comes to see the position of the other and then, together, they persuade each other that it is wise or necessary, or both, to see their own interests differently. This changing of minds will be put to the test in concrete proposals asking sacrifices from all the parties, which they now no longer perceive as sacrifices. Entrenched interest positions are given up. Hence, in due time fierce debates start with the followers, the rank and file members, because these members have not reaped the fruits of frame reflection.

In taming their followers, we see these negotiating partners exercising constraints on their followers lest they be written off as reliable partners in the cooperative effort. There is even a formal procedure of disqualification in a proposed brand-new 'constitution' for interactive governance, I happened to read. One of the biggest Dutch state agencies (the one undertaking big infrastructural works on waterways, railways and motorways) has elaborated a model of an agreement which will serve as a framework for future 'multiple cooperative relations' with stakeholders and other relevant interests involved in the planning and execution of these works. It includes just such a formal procedure of disqualification.

Let me return to frame reflection. It presupposes a common morality of cooperation that might check selfish or short-sighted behaviour both in policy development and in the implementation phase. Interactive policymaking is rightly hailed as a structure of coordination that facilitates a moral foundation which in its turn may help to overcome the obstinate sticking to short-term interests and to open up toward the needs of next generations and (other) unrepresented or weak interests. I submit that this morality of cooperation is the cornerstone of any scheme of associative democracy. These reflexive networks under favourable conditions provide, as some commentators have said, the social capital needed to address the real problems of society. This morality of reciprocity means a curb on free-riding and a mobilisation of 'altruistic' commitments for national or regional policies that are sometimes cutting into one's own corporate flesh.

The proof of the pudding is in the eating. Indeed, out of these interactive processes do come good and effective solutions to intricate problems. We have some cases in our research that can be hailed as quite successful in terms of reshuffling social forces, redefining a problem, eventually designing a new and hitherto unheard of solution, and even implementing it smoothly because of the strong commitments that were built up. A case at hand is the new plan for a complete rearrangement of functions in a complicated zone in the west of our country, where extensive bulb fields (causing massive pollution), nature conservation, urban relocation and so on competed (and compete) for scarce land. The plan first developed and then stalled within provincial bureaucracy was discarded and a new and long process of communication started – a success story. The case of the so-called Dutch Aids platform designing an array of public health and other measures to diminish the physical and social risks of this epidemic is another such success story.

Success does not happen automatically. A variety of crucial conditions ask for further consideration. Briefly, I want to point to the most crucial one indeed: sufficient autonomy of all the participants involved. With regard to the private partners this means, *inter alia*, the ability to resist the temptation to let their behaviour and thinking be determined either by the higher federation or mother organisation or by their most clamorous followers or members. Responsive government means taking into account a wide range of relevant interests not just the ones that are represented formally. This means working against the closure that is so often scorned with regard to neo-corporatism. It can be assumed that one crucial condition to have is an independent posture by the networking partners. In one of the empirical studies financed by our Dutch sponsor, precisely this empirical condition was put to a comparative test. It was found that in a negotiating process where actors such as regional unions or employers groups, or both, safeguarded their independence from their higher federations, the agreed upon policies showed more consideration for the interests of non-represented weak parties (Sol 2000). The same holds for the independence of public authorities. Should the participating authority tell the partners that on this particular item no deliberation is possible because 'my council has already decided upon this point', the interactive process is over. The evidence is clear cut: with independent actors more responsive policies result.

Frame reflection is a precious possibility as is the ethos of cooperation. It does happen, but it is predicated on very special conditions that are not often met. Why not praise this practice unconditionally? Precisely because of the point that Metcalfe (1994) makes so well. This way of governance is not accountable along the lines set out by the system of binding government to substantial legal rules, adhering to a strict principle of legality. Reflexive governance tends to loosen itself from the formal rule of law required of 'good governance'. It is the informal process that reigns supreme. To qualify this, one has to bear in mind that the interactive process needs the shadow of the formal procedures and rules to keep the process going, to remind private actors of the powers the government has to deal with the problem one-sidedly (not very credible, but nevertheless, one never knows) and not least to ratify results and make these binding on all, participants and third parties alike. But, notwithstanding this 'shadow of hierarchy' as Mayntz (1998: 13) calls this, the structure of formal public competencies is not able to keep the informal process in check. Should the formal structure of public competencies forbid unconditional public commitment to elements of the co-produced policy, too bad for the law. Sometimes breaches of formal law have to be condoned officially in the cause of a successful problem-solving outcome.[7]

But I stick to the old principle that trust must be organised, or to put it better, must be made accountable. This, however, in my view needs not to lead to an all out war against interactive governance, which certainly is here to stay. Some ideologists brand any deviance from a strict liberal rule of law as the first step toward serfdom. But, in day-to-day practice, other ways have been found to call reflexive government to account. Let me cite from the experience of the case I have already referred to. In that bulb-growing area, a platform of public and private negotiators was meddling with competencies in the hands of municipal and provincial councils. It is true to say that no council could steer this negotiating process; no law or by-law could do that job either. Representative democracy lost? True, but there are alternatives, which we saw at work. The council could and did officially start the interactive process. Individual members of the council henceforth played a role in it, or at least kept themselves informed about its progress. Moreover, the participants saw to it most carefully that at regular intervals formal and less formal meetings were held with politicians. Obviously, members of the council or the council itself are not in a position to strike down the outcome of this process that lasted for years, but they can and do influence the process while it is under way. This is not a standard, let alone formal and general, solution for democratic accountability; it is certainly no solution for third parties who have had no invitation. But solving important social problems is worth a price in formality, provided the parties develop a framework of conditions, structures and procedures that keep the discussion table visible, and as far as possible open to the public.

Analysis of the Incorporation of Distinct Communities through Forms of Self-Rule

In the case of indigenous peoples and (other) distinct communities, such as national minorities or immigrant groups, we witness important tendencies to step down from assimilationist policies and change to 'federal' policies. How then might a multi-ethnic state (and society) be instituted formally? A ready example at hand is the Ethiopian case with which I happen to be somewhat familiar.

The Ethiopian Constitution, which was adopted in 1991 after the overthrow of the Derg by the liberation movements, in many of its provisions declares itself in favour of a federal state structure of a *special kind*. It is this kind of structure that interests us here. Rather broad powers of legislation, adjudication, administration and taxation are attributed to nine regions, known as states, which together comprise the whole of the territory. This in itself does not differ from an ordinary federal state structure. But this constitution goes beyond this: it is specifically intended to address the desire of various 'nations, nationalities and peoples' of Ethiopia (as it is expressed in this constitution) to be supported not only socially and culturally, but also legally in their quest to preserve or strengthen their own identity within (and, on rare occasions, outside) the state's politico-legal borders. After the devastating period of the Menghistu regime a most generous federal state structure was set up, with the emphasis on the sub-federal state level of powers.[8] Of course, this constitution can be explained as a political answer to the enormous problems of a multifarious Ethiopian society, which in the past was held together more or less brutally by an emperor and his clan and then by a socialist populist dictatorship. There used to be and to a lesser degree still are fervent feelings of discrimination, aversion and wrath of various peoples against other groups (such as peoples from the south versus those of the north and other cleavages). Constitutionally, care is also taken to keep the federal state viable and not to fragment it too much. Also, a special Federal Council was created in which every nation, nationality and people has one or more seats, which shows the endeavour to foster the unity of civil society on the basis of full recognition of the specific, distinct features of its collective parts. In practice, however, this council seems to be utterly weak.

Thus, seen from the formal plane of the legal and political order, Ethiopian society is explicitly recognised as a pluri-national and pluri-cultural society. This calls not only for special legal protection for the use and development of specific languages, religions, social customs and cultures, but also for the recognition of distinct political and legal institutions at the regional level. The various regions are called 'states'. Through this set-up the various distinct communities are conceptualised as collective partners in a cooperative whole.

Admittedly, in the formal aspect of the federal structure, the ethnic and cultural heterogeneity does not show itself directly. To recognise and empower self-ruling states does not necessarily require self-ruling powers *in the hands of a specific people*. If it were otherwise, if the federal set-up were to call directly upon specific ethnic, cultural or other communities, then we would be dealing with a system that is often called 'ethnic' self-rule. Technically, this means direct consociationalism. This situation is defined by Asch and Smith (1992: 99) as follows: 'State ideology expressly acknowledges the existence of various ethnonational collectivities ... and thus protection is afforded explicitly to specified (and named) ethnonational communities.' Not so in Ethiopia. It conforms to the first part of the above definition, but not to the second.

However, the underlying and expressly stated rationale behind the new Ethiopian Constitution opens up possibilities to enter into *indirect consociationalism*. This means that the boundaries and composition of autonomous entities are determined in such a way that as a matter of social fact some of the different nations of Ethiopia will have a majority in the governmental, executive and judicial institutions of that entity and therefore might embark on a social, cultural, political and legal course of their own. The same system was instituted on 1 January 1999 in Canada, where the new province ('state' in Ethiopian terminology) of Nunavut took shape in the Northern Territories of the Canadian Federation. Inuit people make up an overwhelming majority of the population and will undoubtedly maintain that majority, as few non-Inuit will be tempted to move to that harsh, northern zone.

In some other countries, however, direct consociational models are in the making, which means an even more outspoken federalism of a special kind. Distinct communities conquer the (collective) right to govern themselves within a certain territory, according to their own institutions. For political elites this issue of the direct consociational way of renewing democracy, citizenship and institutional forms of governance is a very tricky one. It is not possible any more to suggest to the public that nothing changes (a note often struck while defending indirect consociationalism) and one has to confront head-on the accusation of handing out privileges to one group of the population, and cries of 'Why not to us, too?'

Along either of the two lines, the right to be different as a distinct people will make itself felt in the set-up of the national or federal state, or both, as well as in law. It need not go that way. Returning to Ethiopia again, I feel most uncertain about the future course of events there. After all, the leadership of a self-ruling state within the federation could as well opt for the maximum feasible uniformity in its own laws and institutions of governance, thus ruling out any local plurality which often exists within such an autonomous state (for instance, in the Southern Nations Nationalities and Peoples State, the official name of a large territory in the south of Ethiopia). And what is more, local rulers might also try to copy the dominant federal institutions of law and governance, for example, because they feel that loyalty to the ruling elites will pay. Besides, in the constitution itself several fields of law are officially under the competence of the federation only. Be this as it may, I cannot escape the feeling that after a while the persistent and strong socio-cultural diversity of Ethiopia and the insistence on it being respected as such will show itself in the political and legal institutions of the nine member states.

Ethno-National Collectivity

It is particularly the concept of an ethno-national collectivity as used by Asch and Smith that provokes poignant questions. In the literature on multiculturalism, many concepts are used to indicate those social entities that provide their members with a sense of belonging, a sense of identity, while entertaining many specific social institutions and cherishing a specific set of values and world-views. Some call these communities 'constitutive' communities, or 'encompassing' communities, yet others refer to them as 'involuntary', 'self-collecting', or as a community of fate like Hirst does. I prefer the simple notion of 'distinct' communities. The social and moral boundaries of these communities are neither static nor very solid. People usually orient themselves toward more than one community even if their 'original' one has cast a great spell over them. The sheer necessities of life as well as a growing market orientation force people out of their distinct world into the other world and make them adapt themselves to other visions, principles and ways of doing things. They normally adopt some or many of these other principles both for strategic reasons and as new elements of their own identity. As we shall see, within such communities we should not expect eternal peace and harmony. There are minorities within such communities, the members of which may adopt 'the majority culture' and its institutions for the sake of, say, protecting their individual autonomy against local intolerance. There is no justification for holding the romantic vision of the unspoiled, eternal and non-changing character of an indigenous or other distinct community.

These days, such distinct communities are manifesting themselves far more strongly than in the old days of so-called normal assimilation in a melting-pot society. New traditions are being invented, and old customs dug up. Leaving aside the political rhetoric, it is fair to say that for many people the prime object of identification is not something called 'the nation', but primarily something called 'my people' or 'my nation'. This at least seems to be the case in Ethiopia, though not everywhere, and not regarding all the nationalities, but certainly in some places and in some nationalities. This is where the most acute and difficult task surfaces: that of organising the peaceful coexistence of these communities, while at the same time nurturing a common plane of shared values and, particularly, shared political and legal institutions on the level of (Ethiopian) society as a whole. The call is for associative institutions of common governance, allowing for regional pluralism.

In relating this new pluralism to the concept of associative governance, I need to tackle the non-voluntary character of these distinct communities. People tend to stick to their distinct communities of origin even at great cost. On first sight, then, this case can bear no fruit for this concept, as the partners in governance are communities of fate, not of choice. I want to show below how official law could deal with this problem in terms of how far and on what grounds members of communities of fate will be forced under the authority of their leaders. To prepare the ground for this exposure of some case law, I want to introduce, rather in passing, the concepts of formal or official legal pluralism and that of conflict rules.

Official legal pluralism refers to a concept in law referring to the formal inclusion within the national legal order of a principle of recognising 'other law'. Legal pluralism in another (that is, the anthropological or empirical) sense, however, covers any situation in which within the jurisdiction of a more encompassing entity (for example, a state) a variety of differently organised systems of norms and patterns of enforcement effectively and legitimately control the behaviour of specific parts of the population. This concept of *empirical* legal pluralism concerns factual social practice. The two are not intrinsically connected.[9] Of course, official legal pluralism in cases of strong cultural diversity is the more complicated case both in terms of legal theory and in terms of how to organise this. Any system of official legal pluralism knows informal or formal conflict rules, a term and concept borrowed from private international law. These rules can be defined as *those legal rules and procedures that allow for the peaceful coexistence of the legal systems of various distinct communities (nations, nationalities and peoples) within one socio-political whole.*

These rules define the nature and content of distinct autonomous legal orders, provide for special law to govern cases of 'multinational' transactions or dealings, determine the material and personal competencies of the various legal orders, and lastly indicate procedures with which to solve problems of competence between these orders as well as with the federal order.

As I reserve the concept of conflict rules for a situation of official legal pluralism of *distinct* communities, it is of necessity a concept loaded with far-reaching and sometimes intractable problems. Different outlooks regarding man and his world, different concepts of what constitutes an individual and under what conditions an individual merits protection against the collective order are to be accommodated officially in a united politico-legal order. To convey a feeling of such tasks and also to come back to the topic of communities of fate versus those of choice, I now set out to summarise some cases very briefly.

Equality of Communities Versus Individual Equality

One of the moot points here is the one concerning the question of under what circumstances and how far a restriction on the human rights of an individual member of a self-ruling distinct community can or must be tolerated in national law. What institutions and practices in the exercising of public authority can be accepted? There is also the reverse question, which I shall only summarily touch upon before entering the human rights issue. This reverse question is: how far may national or federal state agencies encroach on the competencies legally conferred upon local communities? This latter question is one of the *external* relations between a self-ruling community and the national state referring to the legal demarcation of mutual competencies in law-making, administration, planning and execution of national plans and development schemes, criminal justice and such like. Here, to have a collective right of self-rule means to have a line of defence against encroachment by the majority society (provided there is a judiciary who dares to tackle these problems, or an important power base on the part of the self-ruling group). I would rather stick to the *internal* question of to what degree individuals within the self-ruling community have a line of defence against their own local authorities. It is here that we meet the problem of how to reconcile collective with individual autonomy. This case also preoccupies Hirst in his analysis of associational relations between distinct communities.

The notion of conflict rules helps us to see that in any system of official pluralism principles, rules and procedure have to be developed and will be developed with the mission of making the various domains of legal power compatible. In my case, it is a matter of reconciliation between vastly different and often contradictory principles. The art of doing this job is to do it *without generally sacrificing one set of principles and world-views for another*. This is frame reflection *in optima forma*.

As an example I take a case of freedom of religion. At times local leaders feel forced to repress or completely forbid the admission of, for example, Protestant sects, as is the case with the New Tribes in Latin America. These religious congregations engage in a forceful campaign of proselytising in that specific community. Should they have some success, which they usually do, the converted members of the community sometimes refuse to engage in ceremonies or to pay tributes connected with the creed they no longer profess. As religious categories permeate many aspects of social life, particularly in the communities we are now dealing with, according to their leadership, the communities' survival is at stake. Therefore they no longer admit missionaries and sometimes even expel their converts and confiscate their property and assets (without due compensation). How then do individual rights, such as the right to freedom of religion and freedom of movement, stand against the collective right of a community to preserve its culture and basic institutions? The question gets nastier the moment we realise that sometimes these community leaders are usurping a position of authority and even nurture strong ties with the national dominant and repressive regime. These 'caciques' use this way of bringing into line converted members to bolster up their authority position against internal opposition not restricted to those converted members.[10]

In the light of the intractable problems of how to deal with the many-faceted problem of local autonomy versus individual autonomy, the views of shrewd and learned observers part company. Some claim that as a matter of course all internationally recognised, and often legally binding, human rights must be upheld without reservation. This is the well-known liberal view. In the view of others, however, this would cripple local self-rule. These others, such as the judges in the Colombian Constitutional Court of whom we will talk now, claim that constitutionally backed respect for cultural differences implies a more reticent point of view. According to the reasoning of this Colombian Constitutional Court, in cases such as the one mentioned above, one has to determine which constitutional rights are of the same rank as the rights to ethnic and cultural diversity, and to then look for an ethical minimum of essential human rights to be used as a yardstick to judge when legitimately to intervene in a local authority's decisions (Cor Constitucional, T 523 1997, 15 October 1997). As such the Colombian court identified the right to life, the right not to be tortured, and the right not to be enslaved. It also came up with a fourth essential limit to local jurisdiction and authority: the right to *legalidad* (legality) of procedure and judgement, which means roughly the right not to be exposed to procedures or punishments that go beyond what a reasonable member of that community could expect. On this basis, this court upheld the sentence by an indigenous court in which a member of that community was to be punished by flogging according to the local cultural traditions and afterward was to be banished from the territory, a punishment Colombian national law and the international human rights treaties declare to be infringement of human rights.

This Colombian court, in its (hotly debated) sentence, started a process of intercultural dialogue aimed at reaching a shared view about a common body of very high-ranking principles to be accepted by (and acceptable to) all the distinct communities (Indian and African) of that society.

It stands to reason that the path indicated by the Colombian court is a thorny one. We are dealing with very sensitive problems here. From the point of view of the emancipation of individuals, we come across local practices that are considered repugnant in the eyes of outsiders, such as female circumcision, corporal punishment, arranged marriages, expelling people, not tolerating religious freedom, unequal gender relations and so on. Here, the first question that a court has to deal with is that concerning the identity relatedness of these practices.[11] If practices only superficially touch local life, it is far easier to declare them null and void than in the other case.[12] But solving this most complicated problem (with the anthropologist as an expert witness?) does not solve the problem of the weighing of collective versus individual rights. Even in the case of identity-related practices one might come to the conclusion that intervention in local practice is fully warranted in the name of a high-ranking individual right. But let us be clear: following its own criteria, the Colombian court would not strike down local decisions supporting unequal gender practices such as local institutions favouring men over woman in matters of public leadership or matters of inheritance. Here one can easily imagine hearing a roar of indignation, I suppose.

This problem cannot be solved by a rather simplistic reference to cherished formulas in several constitutions over the world: 'any law or customary practice ... that contravenes the Constitution is invalid' in Article 9 of the Ethiopian Constitution (and the Colombian Constitution has a similar clause). Taking this clause literally, judges (and administrative bureaucracies) could strike down a great many practices as unconstitutional (not mentioning the case of a constitution invalidating any practice which runs against 'the laws of the Republic'). Such automatic prevalence of the constitution (and the human rights and other fundamental rights enshrined in it) bears little resemblance to granting full respect to other cultures. Respect for difference of cultures and related social practices, in this view, requires acceptance of the theorem that individual human rights do not *automatically* prevail over the collective right invoked in such a conflict. Adherence to this theorem opens up a wide field for legal and social philosophy and practical judicial wisdom to look for a common point of view that steers clear both of a penetrant cultural relativism and a no less penetrant cultural hegemony.

In view of the problems sketched here, such scholars as Tully (1995) and De Sousa Santos (1997) rightly stress the need for an intercultural dialogue through which, on the basis of mutual recognition and consent, the various socio-culturally differently embedded citizens of the society discuss the acceptability of each other's practices. This means not only that the majority society cannot claim adherence to all the liberal individual rights of the constitution as an unquestionable principle, but also that local communities cannot claim automatic immunity for practices that violate those rights.[13] Matters of polygamy, arranged marriages and dowry, inheritance patterns, adoption practices and such like are often identity related and figure as central features of a community's way of life. Put another way: not protecting these features would amount to forcing the community to assimilate and give up part of its cultural identity. But, on the other hand, these institutions, although upheld by local leaders, are usually not favoured by all community members, or at least introduce unfair treatment for some members. Inheritance institutions, for instance, usually favour men over women. Therefore, existing differences in status and wealth are maintained and consolidated through local law. Even if one fully acknowledges that liberal individualism cannot automatically be the yardstick with which to gauge the legitimacy of these practices, majority legal order has to address the plight of these dissenters and the marginalised. The marginalised already know of other more promising laws and procedures, and sometimes dare to go 'forum shopping', looking outside their own community for a court and a law that has a more favourable stance toward personal autonomy and rights. After all, usually they come to feel like citizens of two worlds, the one where they are rooted and the one defined by the larger political entity. People think of themselves not only in the sometimes more collectivist terms of their own community, but also in the often individualist terms of a politically liberal state. These feelings of being an autonomous person and having individual rights then feeds back into the local community. Discussions are going on in these communities concerning some local practices that imply restrictions of a person's autonomy. Obviously, local communities are not static, merely traditional social entities. There is fierce debate about features of their way of life to be preserved, and features to be changed. Sure enough, sometimes the internal debate is thwarted and repressed by local leaders, probably under the pretence of a common fight for social and cultural survival. But there are many reports about ongoing debates over, for example, the position of women in local indigenous politics or the practice of arranged marriages.

Co-Management of Natural Resources

In a professed multinational state, one of the most demanding areas calling for legal reconstruction concerns the management of natural resources.[14] Both in the experiences of state-led management of resources as in the policies adopted by such donors as the World Bank the participation of local user groups in the making and implementation of management policies is the key to possible success. However, the participation of local user groups may, according to a useful distinction made by Lund (1990), be of two different kinds: as a means for development purposes or as an ideal to empower local groups. In our case of the existence of distinct communities, however, participation acquires yet another connotation: to show respect for the collective right to be different.

The common form of participatory management, particularly in the field of natural resources, is a *co-management regime*.[15] This can be defined as *a set of material and procedural rules, principles and goals that require governmental agencies to share with local user groups decision-making powers concerning the control and regulation of a natural resource* (see also Osherenko (1993: 94)).

I define the phrase 'to control resources' as 'to be able to decide policy on the harvesting and control of resources, from subsistence through commercial use to conservation' – in other words, resource management. 'Regulation' is concerned with access to resources and their use. The best-known type of regulation is through communal tenure of land and other resources. In other words, it concerns resource use.

Having a co-management regime does not necessarily mean that the state agencies have to relinquish or transfer their legal jurisdiction or authority. Systems in which common consultation and deliberation is declared mandatory, but in which the ultimate decision-making power is vested in a federal or state minister could also qualify as co-management regimes. Of course, in actual practice, it remains to be seen to what degree and under what conditions local user groups' representatives effectively can and do influence the policy-making process. This is a matter of social evaluation, lessons from which show that the legal structure alone, although important, does not determine how the participatory scheme works out in practice.

Generally, authorities tend to shrink from co-management regimes beyond the rather modest type consisting of simply hiring local people to do maintenance work in local forests or rivers. As already suggested, the case for co-management schemes is far stronger in such pluralist societies as Canada, Colombia and Ethiopia. Cultural and social diversity, if it is here to stay, calls for political and legal means to express, to put forward and to implement the views of specific communities concerning what constitutes development and how to achieve it. One cannot take for granted the existence of but one way of viewing the world, and its natural resources, and of defining the way mankind relates and should relate to these resources. Normally, in local communities different, sometimes sharply contrasting, definitions of the relationship between man and nature and of the meaning of 'development' stand out compared with the one that informs state or federal policies and law. These views of nature and development are certainly identity related. This is why they deserve special protection, protection that is also provided for in international legal or paralegal instruments such as the ILO 169 treaty and the various declarations of indigenous peoples' rights pending before the UN and the OAS.

So, instituting co-management regimes not only might provide for effective management policies, but also serves as a vehicle for the institution of collective rights for distinct communities. Obviously, should these co-management regimes contain the seed of associative relations between the various (distinct) communities making up a society, relations here have to be based at least on an equally autonomous position of all the parties involved. Under the present conditions, indigenous peoples cannot boast much power to amend weak legal schemes or make such schemes live up to their promise. A turn of the tide may happen, however, under the pressure of 'green' interests (sustainable resource management). Such policies only promise long-term success on the basis of more or less equitable cooperation with local user groups, that is, on the basis of negotiating governance. This new insight strongly informs the present policymaking of such entities as the Asian Development Bank, the World Bank, and others. This possibly helps some peoples and minorities living in sensitive areas, but not the ones living elsewhere.

It is time now to analyse a bit more precisely how the structure of such co-management schemes and the conditions under which they work foster or prevent the development of an ethos of cooperation. In other words, are there changes promoting the case of associationalism through these co-management regimes?

Here, I restrict myself to two points: the scope and domain of the formal powers involved, and the accommodation of traditional knowledge. It is best to tackle these points in a concrete case of co-management, as laid down in the James Bay and Northern Quebec Agreement (JBNQA).

The James Bay and Northern Quebec Agreement

This is the agreement (the oldest of its kind) between the province (state) of Quebec and the Federal State of Canada, on the one hand, and three indigenous peoples who inhabit the vast territory of Northern Quebec, on the other. They are the Cree, the Inuit and the Naskapi (Innu). The most important aspect of the agreement is that for the first time, it confirms a type of co-management which presupposes and recognises the existence and social functioning of a local system of resource regulation. That is to say, there is a linkage between state regulation and self-regulation. Only on the basis of a respect for the local system of self-regulation can any effective co-management of the environment be achieved. Even more important, only on this basis can new, more egalitarian relationships spring up between the state and distinct communities.

The agreement arose from the struggle of the Cree tribes[16] against huge hydroelectric projects in the James Bay area developed around 1971. The Cree, fearing a complete loss of their subsistence resources, after a laborious process of self-organisation[17] which brought all their nine communities together for the first time in the new Grand Council of the Cree, opted for a huge barter. They accepted the eternal abolition of all their claims to rights of ownership or authority in the whole territory (a very large territory) in exchange for official rights which would allow them to safeguard their daily means of survival and obtain money in compensation as well as public powers offering an opportunity to be able to defend themselves against other threats in the future. The Cree and the rest of the peoples obtained rights to hunting and fishing in the whole territory. For some species they hold exclusive rights, and non-native hunters are banned. For other species, in a large part of the territory, they have to share the hunting with non-natives. The rights are conditional on the hunting being for traditional subsistence only. The authorities are not allowed to interfere with the regulation of native use except in emergencies, that is to say, for conservation under strict conditions. State regulation should guarantee that the Cree have maximum access to the animals which serve for their basic nutrition, while hunting by non-natives for these species should be restricted throughout the territory.

Quebec State regulations in the field of resource management, says the agreement, should be presented to a consultative coordination committee, half of which is formed by members of the indigenous peoples and the other half by state officials. The procedure is such that the minister cannot ignore the committee's recommendations.[18]

Evaluation

As to the first problem of the scope and domain of the formal powers involved, the JBNQA, being an early agreement, is very weak. The coordinating committee has only consultative powers (article 24.4.23). The minister of Quebec certainly has to respond to the committee, but there is no procedure to give special weight to the committee's suggestions. In some other co-management systems, a provision has been introduced such that if the official fails to respond within a given time period, the proposals of the committee become law. For example, The Yukon Fish and Wildlife Management Board includes this provision, called a 'disallowance procedure' (*Current Issues* 1996: 46). Without this provision the position of the committee is very weak. I do not want to suggest that as a result, a coordinating committee will be worthless. In situations where there are no major political interests involved, a genuine dialogue could spring up and consensual regulations could come forward and make it into binding law. In matters of parallel local and state interests, the agreement does work well, as Feit has commented (1989: 82, 83). But in a majority of cases interests clash, as is the case in matters referring to the position of non-native hunters. Then, the non-native hunters have it their way, because of their greater political power, even though this is in flagrant violation of the agreement (Feit 1989: 85).[19]

A major stumbling block for the development of partnership relations is the very restricted field of policy covered by the power-sharing arrangement. The agreement practically excludes the distinct communities from participation in the making of development plans, such as forestry concessions, not to mention the continuous enlargement of the gigantic plants of Hydro Quebec.[20] This amounts to a fundamental weakness of the system. Cree subsistence territory is being reduced further and further by the development policies of the Quebec authorities.

The second problem concerns the issue of frame reflection again, which here seems to be nearly a mission impossible. Even if formal powers are sufficient, the fact remains that the dominant society on the one hand, and the distinct communities on the other represent vastly different views of the relationship between man and nature and of ways to gain knowledge of the world. Their frames of reference, or the constitutive rules of their respective societies, differ enormously. Local communities, for instance, more often than not have specific sources and methods for obtaining knowledge, and different ways of storing and transferring such knowledge. In co-management schemes already in place, a fierce struggle is raging over whose knowledge will prevail, that is, whether it will be the knowledge produced in line with the canons of western-style science or that produced by the different culture.[21] In this respect, experiences in the JBNQA are not rosy either. First, the committee lacks the funds to carry out detailed studies on the state and health of animal populations and flora. But more importantly for my point, methods and concepts of western science generally dominate. It is rare for local experts to be involved as equal partners from the start of the design of research methods and goals. In the article 'Circumpolar aboriginal people and co-management practice' (*Current Issues* 1996: 10), we find, among many others, a report on the James Bay Committee which says about the Inuit, who are also partners in that committee: 'The non-aboriginal parties do not want to accept the traditional knowledge systems of the Inuit at a scientific level.'[22]

In contrast, the same publication and also Osherenko's report (1993) provide some examples of successful integration of western science and local knowledge, for example, in the case presented by Osherenko: the regime of co-management of the population of white whales (Beluga) in the extreme north of Quebec. This regime sprang up as a very informal one, precisely because of the malfunctioning of the JBNQA institutions, under which competence this territory falls. Because the agreement is so inflexible, the state authorities and the Inuit organisations bypassed the official system in order to create an *ad hoc* system which has been very successful in several aspects.

Nonetheless, this success story is the exception.[23] On one occasion, the Porcupine Management Board, a co-management system concerned with the population of an enormous herd of caribou, a wild animal important in the nutrition of several communities and peoples, made an appeal against both the state authorities and the other co-management unions, demanding that they better integrate traditional knowledge systems (*Current Issues* 1996: 92).[24] Clearly, there is an appalling scarcity of 'approaches for successful merging of indigenous forest-related knowledge with formal forest management', as the title of a recent report reads (Van Leeuwen 1999).[25]

This problem is exacerbated by a lack of genuine communication, as evaluation reports of the JBNQA regime make clear. Conditions for an open-minded dialogue are lacking. Confrontation dominates and an atmosphere of conflict and senseless legal jargon seems to prevail. The process is fully politicised, and this does not at all support the growth of mutual confidence. Even between the various indigenous representatives a lot of discordance makes itself felt.

Concluding Remarks

In these pages, I did not elaborate the problems of coordination and the exercise of higher authority connected with any thorough scheme of 'federative and plural organization of the state' (Hirst 1994: 170), including in my two (or three) examples of it. It stands to reason that such pluralisation, like the archipelago of reflexive platforms all over the field of public policymaking, raises crucial questions about steering and determining the overall direction of all the various and different outcomes of the platforms. Pluralisation, lacking a synthesis in terms of national interests and policies, could therefore lead to the fragmentation of national policymaking. But this topic is beyond the scope of my article.

I have dealt with some empirical tendencies that for various social backgrounds and conditions make for a far less centralised way of exercising state power. While these two cases of a renewal of citizenship and democracy are very different in social background and effects, they both point toward pervasive tendencies to pluralise state structures. State power is shared with non-state organisations and groups. Are there any lessons for associative democracy to be learned there? Yes, there are. First, such reflexive platforms as I described them could easily slide into closed structures like the ones characterising neo-corporatism, although the very nature of the problems to be dealt with 'forbids' such a closed shop and commands extensive and flexible communication. Regarding my other example, the sharing of state power with the governments of indigenous peoples and with the leadership of minorities, we have to be wary of the palpable risk of these reforms having a very restricted scope and force only. They might turn out to be only a token gesture within a project of neo-liberal reforms. This at least seems to be the case in some Latin American countries. The (obvious) lesson here is that not all that is decentralisation, participation and federalisation on paper has any real bearing on the institutions within which vital public policies are developed and implemented.

Second there are more concrete lessons to learn. The concept of associative democracy can build on formidable trends already well under way. Indeed, it is not utopian at all. But apart from doubts regarding the (restricted) scope of policy matters which are tackled by reflexive governance or by (in)direct consociationalist structures, the main element which casts doubt about the associative character of these trends is the non- or only half-voluntarily character of the 'associations' being empowered. Thinking of reflexive governance in highly developed states, the problem of disciplining the members of, say, citizens groups, asks for consideration. It is not Hirst's view that no constraint whatsoever has to be found in a fully associative democracy. So I feel that in some empirical instances of 'multiple cooperation networks' where citizens groups played a role at the platform table, associative democracy is in the making. At least our team of researchers on reflexive governance came across impressive examples in the Netherlands. It is true that the high tide for such structures seems to be changing. Interactive policymaking is charged with various crimes. I am not too worried about the charge that this structure takes over from representative parliamentary-style democratic institutions. It is widely felt that these institutions are in a crisis today, precisely for which reason Hirst started his associative odyssey anyway. The charge of being too slow and producing only weak compromises, although largely unfounded, is more serious as it may lead to attempts to discredit this form of governance and restore hierarchical ways of policymaking. One headline in a recent newspaper issue said that to be a successful policymaking device, interactive networks (or what the Dutch nowadays call the *poldermodel*) should have a tinge of Stalinism. This type of overall and unjustified criticism deflects serious attention from real problems toward confusion over phoney problems. I am thinking of the real problems of accountability of these new networks as well as the problem of inter-network coordination.

Notwithstanding this change of the tide, I feel fairly confident that interactive governance as an empirical trend will conquer the world of public policymaking. There is simply no alternative to tackle the complex problems of today under the conditions of broken consensus and the huge cognitive problems that go with it. It will therefore be a promising venture to do careful research into the conditions that make for what I like to call the most important element of the networks: the development of an ethos of reciprocity that prompts people to give up entrenched interest positions, engage in serious frame reflection and motivates people to act on the belief that investing trust in the other parties will pay in the long run.

The one and only important condition for this to happen is the independence that the partners have to win from their national organisations. Without such a daring posture, the network process recedes into old, fixed interest representation again and the participants tend to disregard non-represented third-party interests again. I offered empirical proof for the importance of this condition.

Optimism for the future of associative democracy is less warranted in the case of sharing state power with indigenous peoples, national minorities and immigrant communities. In themselves these are different cases, but I now mix them together for a moment. As a rule, the position of these distinct communities is far weaker, and the opportunity for the elite to ignore their claims and needs are far bigger. But for some ecologically sensitive areas the state can do without them. Nevertheless, as an observer of recent trends in state renewal on many continents one cannot help being struck by the massive upsurge of 'multicultural constitutionalism'. Yes, it is professed on constitutional paper only, but to some extent it pervades political and social life too. But the obstacles are bigger than in the case of reflexive governance.

The associative character of these tendencies to provide forms of self-rule to distinct communities is also compromised by the non-voluntary character of the self-governing entities. The various situations in the world show remarkable differences however. Communities of fate often do not isolate themselves from the surrounding world. Within these communities debates flourish as to their gender practices and other hot points. But the claim for self-rule inescapably produces the claim from any such community to exercise some form of internal sovereignty over its own members, even against the will of these members. The liberal exit option is not acceptable to these communities as the main yardstick with which to decide about the legal validity of the decision of their public authorities and courts. So, whatever internal debate is, or is not, going on, a crucial dilemma presents itself. This dilemma is born out clearly by the way the Colombian Constitutional Court tackles problems of balancing individual autonomy and group autonomy. It will not do to elevate human rights to an absolute position. But we should be wary of constructing absolute contradictions here as in many indigenous communities local leaders are in the process of adopting human rights as part of their own internal constitutive rules too. The Colombian Constitutional Court shows that the value of the human rights has to be balanced against the value to be assigned to the collective right to be different. I qualify this approach as a shrewd way to foster conditions for an intercultural dialogue. For, even under benevolent social conditions, the question of how to conduct frame reflection between widely different cultures is the key question.

Prospects here are bleak. Take the example of the need for integration of indigenous knowledge, or, in other words, 'the need for a conceptual pluralism in resource and ecosystem management' (Berkes 1998: 9). From evaluative reports on co-management schemes it transpires how little is won in this respect. Frame reflection seems to stop at the borders of western-style scientific knowledge and its methods. And this is not all, to the contrary, frame reflection has to address the almost insurmountable problem of how to come to terms with constitutive rules of societies that differ widely one from another. I fully endorse De Sousa Santos's observation (1997: 13): 'What are the possibilities for a cross-cultural dialogue when one of the cultures *in presence* has been itself molded by massive and long lasting violations of human rights perpetrated in the name of the other culture? ... The cultural dilemma is the following: since in the past the dominant culture rendered unpronounceable some of the aspirations of the subordinate culture to human dignity, is it now possible to pronounce them in the cross-cultural dialogue without thereby further justifying and even reinforcing their unpronounceability?'

Lastly, while it tends to fall outside the scope of concluding remarks, there is one theme I want to mention, and here I leave the empirical altogether. A possible deficiency of the concept of associative democracy would be to push it in the direction of a non-authoritarian dialogue between equally authentic citizens as was the ideal after the cultural revolution in the west during the late 1960s and early 1970s. Informal, respectful cooperative behaviour between people is a precious thing. But it needs formal structures to be kept transparent and accountable. It needs such structure to prevent the partners from drowning in a sea of fluid and open-for-debate concepts and cognitive questions. It needs formalities to prevent free-riders from wrecking the system and to ward off the influences of the weaknesses of the human condition and good will. It needs authority to make participation and bottom-up associative democracy viable.

NOTES

1. Terminology is a weak point here. Usually, I call these 'new' institutional arrangements 'negotiating government', but obviously this terminology introduces confusion with neo-corporatism, where negotiations between public and private actors are the heart of the matter too. Moreover, in reflexive arrangements, the relative importance of negotiation shrinks and that of reflection takes precedent. This point will be developed below, in the second section.

2. But they deal mainly with one variety, private-interest government, where private actors, such as companies or a standardisation agency, care for interests that are also public ones, such as safety and health matters, and act upon these in terms of forms of self-regulation. Although these self-regulatory schemes are manifold now, at least in the Netherlands, where they are elevated to official status particularly in the regulation of industry, they comprise only a fraction of a far wider phenomenon of interactive or reflexive policymaking.

3. This latter terminology comes from Hirst. I shall also use some of his expressions in what follows, without all the time giving the exact reference.

4. Reflexive governance, then, may be reconstructed as a mighty thrust toward a process of dispersion of state power among many private actors. After all, Hirst (1994: 99–100), in his paragraph 'associationalism as the supplement to modern economic governance' gives an account of the main elements of precisely the interactive forms of governance that I call reflexive governance.

5. A warning is at order here. Hirst uses 'mutuality' for the ethos inherent in free dialogues between self-ruling associations, which I tend to call 'reciprocity'.

6. This was tried in vain in the 135 countries' deliberations at the WTO in Seattle during December 1999.

7. The reference here is to my essay on the Dutch practice of condoning policies in the volume in honour of Professor Blankenburg (Hoekema 1998). Part of my current views stem from that article.

8. Very generous indeed. In the constitution, the various nations, nationalities and peoples have the right to secession, under a specific procedure. Eritrea took that way out, the price the Tigray Liberation Front had to pay for Eritrean help in the war against Menghistu.

9. We may therefore come across situations of empirical plus formal pluralism, empirical without formal pluralism and even formal legal pluralism without empirical pluralism (in the event of a constitution that still recognises distinct legal orders which, however, no longer exist).

10. Such a case is discussed in Assies (2000). First reports of it appeared in Gómez Rivera (1995).

11. Take the case of Indian peyote users in the USA (an external case by the way). In a famous US case, the sacramental use of the hallucinogenic drug peyote at a ceremony of the Native American Church was at stake, as this sacramental use had triggered a private employer (a drug rehabilitation centre) of two native Americans, devoted members of that church, to sack the two, whereupon the State of Oregon refused to pay unemployment compensation (State of Oregon 1990). Is this sacramental use identity related? (Tully 1975: 172; Tsosie 1997.) If so, does it fall under USA constitutional protection? The US Supreme Court case ended in not granting such protection, but the reasoning is, of course, most narrowly tied to specific US doctrine, among which is freedom of religion. So, I will leave aside the intricacies of this judgement.

12. As this is not an essay in jurisprudence, I skip the legal question of how the Colombian court manages to get away with the legal force of international human rights treaties to which the state of Colombia is a signatory.

13. These conflicts surface not only in courts. In administrative matters regarding family

problems (for example, when official agencies are involved in cases of the guardianship of minors, or of adoption), officials encounter the same problems. Once, in Colombia, a girl who was considered an adult was married off at a young age by her mother's brother (the normal practice in matrilineal societies) in exchange for a dowry (animals). This conforms to a principle of reciprocity that permeates that indigenous society. Spokespersons for the girl claimed that she had an individual right to continue her schooling, a right any citizen of Colombia has. The child-protection agency, the brother and a local arbitrator negotiated a deal in which the girl could continue her education, would not be treated as an adult by her community, and would have to renegotiate her status when she reached formal adulthood. This story shows how one could escape the quasi-inevitable sacrificing of either individual rights or collective rights. This case is analysed in Sánchez Botero (2000).

14. I elaborated this theme in Hoekema (1994).
15. The majority of land and freshwater or marine territories in the north of Canada and Alaska are under regimes of co-management of natural resources, with greater or lesser degrees of participation by governments and indigenous representatives (*Current Issues* 1996: 2).
16. I tell the story more from the point of view of the Cree and less from the Inuit point of view.
17. This process is described and analysed in La Rusic et al. (1979) and Feit (1985).
18. In addition, the Cree gained a stronger position to influence decisions about health, housing, education, social services, administration of their communities, and justice. Most importantly, they obtained considerable supplementary funding to subsidise families who wanted to maintain their traditional way of life, in other words, to spend six to eight months of the year in the open countryside, living in mobile camps in order to hunt and fish. For the Cree this offered an important opportunity to continue their traditional lifestyles, which are intimately connected with hunting. They were also offered a large amount of compensation money, both for the loss of their territory caused by the hydroelectric plants and for yielding all their other territorial claims.
19. Feit (1989: 83) also documents a lack of attention given the committee's suggestions and the patronising attitude of Quebec's officials. The state administration tends to prepare regulations and policies that are presented to the committee for consultation only at the end of the process. Clearly, this blocks co-production of policies.
20. This is a sore point all over the world where some form and degree of territorial rights and self-rule have been assigned to indigenous peoples. Take the case of an indigenous community, Awas Tingni, in Nicaragua (Acosta 2000) and many similar cases in Bolivia, where forestry concessions are granted to third parties without any consultation, even in territories where indigenous communities have legal powers to participate in such decisions (Assies & Hoekema 2000; Orellana 2000).
21. Nowadays, a documentary periodical deals with this form of knowledge: *The Indigenous Knowledge Monitor* (see the list of references for details).
22. Until now, according to Kuppe (1997), many officials and politicians have thought like this. Participation is praised, but resource management should be based on data gathered by scientific research, as a researcher said with reference to co-management systems (Berkes & Preston 1991: 25).
23. Terry Fenge (1995), discussing the Nunavut agreement in the extreme north of Canada (a very broad agreement which grants political autonomy to the Inuit of the north), is very optimistic about the potential of co-management systems in this agreement, which are very similar to those for James Bay. I think there is not sufficient cause for so much optimism. The Nunavut agreement was instituted in 1999.
24. As stated in the *Current Issues* report (1996: 43), 'Co-management must have co-research'.
25. For 'forest' read 'resources'.

REFERENCES

Acosta, M.L. 1998. 'Nicaragua. El Estado y la tierra indígena en las regiones autónomas. El caso de la comunidad mayagna Awas Tingni'. *Asuntos Indígenas, IWGIA, Copenhagen,* 4, 36–44
2000. 'The state and indigenous lands in the autonomous regions of Nicaragua: the case of the Mayagna community of Awas Tingni'. Assies et al. 2000a: 261–74.

Arnfred S. & A. Weiss-Betzon. 1990. *The Language of Development Studies. New Social Science Monographs.* Copenhagen: Institute of Organisation and Industrial Sociology, Copenhagen Business School.

Asch, M. & S. Smith. 1992. 'Consociation revisited: Nunavut, Denendeh and Canadian constitutional consciousness'. *Etudes/Inuit/Studies,* 162/1–2, 97–114.

Assies, W. 2000. 'Indigenous peoples and reform of the state in Latin America'. Assies et al. 2000a: 3–21.

Assies, W. & A.J. Hoekema, eds. 1994. *Idigenous Experiences with Self-government.* IWGIA, 76. Copenhagen and Amsterdam: Universiteit van Amsterdam.
2000. 'Managing resources: between autonomy and partnership'. Assies et al. 2000a: 245–60.

Assies, W., G. van der Haar & A.J. Hoekema, eds. 2000a. *The Challenge of Diversity. Indigenous Peoples and Reform of the State in Latin America.* Amsterdam: Thela Publishers.

Assies, W., G. van der Haar & A.J. Hoekema. 2000b. 'Diversity as a challenge: a note on the dilemmas of diversity'. Assies et al. 2000a: 296–315

Bayly, J. 1997. 'The Denendeh Conservation Board: an experiment in aboriginal resources and environmental management'. Benda-Beckmann & Hoekema 1997: 175–210.

Benda-Beckmann, F. von & A.J. Hoekema, eds. 1997. *Natural resources, Environment and Legal Pluralism.* The Hague, Boston, London: Martinus Nijhoff Publishers.

Berkes, F. 1998. 'Do resource users learn from management disasters? Indigenous management and social learning in James Bay'. Conference paper presented at the seventh IASCP Conference, International Association for the Study of Common Property. Vancouver, 10–14 June 1998.

Berkes, F., P. George & R. Preston. 1991. *Co-management: the Evolution of the Theory and Practice of Joint Administration of Living Resources,* research report, 2/1. Hamilton, Ontario, Canada: Programme for Technology Assessment in Subarctic Ontaria (TASO).

Brand, J. & D. Strempel. 1998. *Soziologie des Rechts. Festschrift für Erhard Blankenburg zum 60. Geburtstag.* Baden-Baden: Nomos Verlagsgesellschaft (Schriften der Vereinigung für Rechtssoziologie; Bd.24).

Brantenberg, T.J.H. & H. Minde. 1995. *Becoming Visible. Indigenous Politics and Self-Government.* Proceedings of the Conference on Indigenous Politics and Self-Government, Tromsf, 8–10 November 1993. Tromsf, Norway: The University of Tromsf, Centre for Sámi Studies.

Chapeskie, A.J. 1991. 'Indigenous law, state law, renewable resources and formal indigenous self-government in northern regions'. *Proceedings of the Sixth International Symposium,* 1. Ottawa, Canada: Commission on Folk Law and Legal Pluralism.

Chenaut, V. & M.T. Sierra. 1995. *Pueblos Indígenas ante el derecho.* México DF: CIESAS, CEMCA.

Cor Constitucional, Sistemas. Jurisprudencia de la corte constitucional I de febrero 1992 hasta mayo de 1998. (CD-Rom)

Current Issues. 1996. 'Circumpolar aboriginal people and co-management practice; current issues in co-management and environmental assessment'. Alberta: University of Calgary, Arctic Institute of North America and Joint Secretariat Inuvialuit Renewable Resource Committees.

Depew, R.C. 1994. *First Nations Organizations: An Analytic Framework.* Ottawa, Ontario:

Department of Indian Affairs and Northern Development.

Dyck, N. ed., 1985. *Indigenous Peoples and the Nation-State: 'Fourth World'. Politics in Canada, Australia and Norway*. St. John's, Newfoundland: Institute of Social and Economic Research, Memorial University of Newfoundland.

Feit, H.A. 1985. 'Legitimation and autonomy in James Bay Cree responses to hydro-electric development'. Dyck 1985: 27–66.

——— 1989. 'James Bay Cree self-governance and land management'. Wilmsen 1989: 68–98.

Fenge, T. 1995. 'The Nunavut Agreement and sustainable development in the Canadian arctic and circumpolar world'. Brantenberg 1995: 171–86.

Freeman, M.M.R. & L.M. Carbyn. 1993. *Traditional Knowledge and Renewable Resource Management in Northern Regions*, 2nd edn. Edmonton, Alberta: The Canadian Circumpolar Institute, The University of Alberta.

Gómez Rivera, M.M. 1995. 'Las cuentas pendientes de la diversidad jurídica. El caso de las expulsiones de indígenas por supuestos motivos religiosos en Chiapas, México'. Chenaut & Sierra 1995: 193–220.

Hirst, P. 1994. *Associative Democracy. New Forms of Economic and Social Governance*. Cambridge: Polity.

Hoekema, A.J. 1994. 'Do joint decision-making boards enhance chances for a new partnership between the state and indigenous peoples?' Assies & Hoekema 1994: 177–94.

——— 1998. 'Condoning policies: the Dutch legal policy to prohibit behaviour and yet permit it'. Brand & Strempel 1998: 405–20.

Indigenous Knowledge and Development Monitor. The Hague (PO Box 29777, 2502 LT): Nuffic/CIRAN.

Kooiman, J., ed. 1994. *Modern Governance. New Government-Society Interactions*. London: Sage.

Kuppe, R. 1997. *Derechos Indígenas y protección del ambiente. Dos estrategias en contradicción?* Ponencia preparada para las VII Jornadas Lascasianas. Durango, México.

La Rusic, Ignatius, S. Bouchard, A. Penn, T. Brelsford & J.G. Deschenes. 1979. *Negotiating a Way of Life: Initial Cree Experience with the Administrative Structure Arising from the James Bay Agreement*. Montreal: SSDCC for Department of Indian and Northern Affairs, Policy Research and Evaluation Group.

Leeuwen, L. van. 1999. *Approaches for Successful Merging of Indigenous Forest-Related Knowledge with Formal Forest Management: How can Modern Science and Traditions Join Hands for Sustainable Forest Management?* Werkdocument IKC-Natuur beheer No.165. Wageningen: National Reference Centre for Nature Management, PO Box 30, 6700 AA.

Lund, S. 1990. 'Efficiency or empowerment? A meta-theoretical analysis of the concept of participation'. Arnfred & Weiss-Betzon 1990: 163–94.

Lynch, O.J. & K. Talbott. 1995. *Balancing Acts: Community-Based Forest Management and National Law in Asia and the Pacific*. Baltimore: World Resource Institute.

Mayntz, R. 1998. *New Challenges to Governance Theory*, Jean Monnet Chair Papers, No.50. San Domenico, Italy: Robert Schuman Centre, European University Institute.

Metcalfe, L. 1994. 'Public management. From imitation to innovation'. Kooiman 1994: 173–89.

Orellana Halkyer, R. 2000. 'Municipalization and indigenous peoples in Bolivia: impacts and perspectives'. Assies et al. 2000a: 151–94.

Osherenko, G. 1993. 'Wildlife management in the North American arctic. The case of co-management'. Freeman & Carbyn 1993: 92–104.

Pessers, D.W.J.M. 1999. 'Liefde, solidariteit en recht: een interdisciplinair onderzoek naar het wederkerigheidsbeginsel'. Doctoral Thesis. Amsterdam: University of Amsterdam, Faculty of Law.

Rahmato, D. 1994. 'Land policy in Ethiopia at the crossroads'. Rahmato, ed. *Land Tenure and Land Policy in Ethiopia after the Derg. Proceedings of the Second Workshop of the Land Tenure Project*, 1–34. Trondheim: University of Trondheim, Centre for Environment and Development.

Sánchez Botero, E. 2000. 'The *tutela*-system as a means of transforming the relations between the state and the indigenous peoples of Colombia'. Assies et al. 2000a: 223–41.

Schön, D.A. & M. Rein. 1994. *Frame Reflection. Toward the Resolution of Intractable Policy Controversies*. New York: BasicBooks.

Sol, E. 2000. *Arbeidsvoorzieningsbeleid in Nederland. De rol van de overheid en de sociale partners*. Den Haag: SDU Uitgevers.

Sousa Santos, B. de. 1997. 'Toward a multicultural conception of human rights'. *Zeitschrift für Rechtssoziologie, Abhandlungen*, 1–15.

State of Oregon. 1990. *Oregon v. Smith*. Employment Division, Department Human Resources, 494, US, 872.

Streeck W. & P. Schmitter, eds. 1985. *Private Interest Government. Beyond Market and State*. London & Beverly Hills: Sage.

Tsosie, R. 1997. 'American Indians and the politics of recognition: Soifer on law, pluralism, and group identity'. *Law & Social Inquiry*, 22/2, 359–88.

Tully, J. 1995. *Strange Multiplicity, Constitutionalism in an Age of Cultural Diversity*. Cambridge: CUP.

Wilmsen, E.N., ed. 1989. *We Are Here. Politics of Aboriginal Land Tenure*. Berkeley, CA: University of California Press.

9

Associative Democracy and the Incorporation of Minorities: Critical Remarks on Paul Hirst's *Associative Democracy*

VEIT BADER

Institutional pluralism promises to solve problems of cultural diversity and political unity in a more fair and sensitive way compared with its main rivals in political theory: traditional *liberalism*, (neo-) *republicanism, communitarianism, civil society*, and *political pluralism* (Hirst 1994: 13f, 202). Associative democracy is one rightly and recently more prominent variety of institutional pluralism. Compared with *other versions of associative democracy* such as those of Cohen and Rogers, Streeck, Mathews, and the 'neo-corporatism' strand, Hirst's associative democracy has the merit of addressing the religious, ethnic and national aspects of cultural pluralism directly. Compared with the *other varieties of institutional pluralism* such as consociational democracy, federalism, and recent group-rights approaches, which have focused more traditionally and directly on ethno-national minorities,[1] Hirst's version is more open and flexible (see Vertovec 1999) and it self-consciously linked to the most advanced theories and research in recent sociology regarding work, organisation and public administration. Compared with *pre-modern* and with *older versions of institutional pluralism*, Hirst clearly states that associative democracy should not 'replace' representative democracy, but has to be understood as an 'extensive supplement' (1994: 19) within the confines of the 'liberal constitutional state with limited functions' (1994: 33): 'There is no point in pluralizing the state only to create totalitarianist potentialities and authoritarian practices at the level of associations.' (Hirst 1994: 68.) Lastly, compared with many *post-modernist* paeans of cultural diversity, Hirst clearly points out the moral limitations of permissible diversity of cultural practices, that is, there has to be a 'set of legal limits on the pluralism of values and practices' (1994: 57), and he tries to elaborate the institutional dimensions of pluralism completely neglected by post-modern political theory.

In all these regards, Hirst's associative democracy is perhaps the most promising approach in recent political theory to developing more productive institutions and policies for the incorporation of minorities. I share these general intuitions and this theoretical strategy. The intent of my critical remarks in this article is to point out open and controversial questions in order to stimulate further debate and research into problems and dilemmas deserving better and more elaborate answers than all of us are now able to give. As a political philosopher, I am attracted by the hope and trust Hirst puts in the principles and the general institutional model of associative democracy. My critical remarks are inspired by more sober sociological afterthoughts in order to achieve a better balance between seductive normative principles and models and historically and sociologically informed criticism. I will shortly discuss the following seven issues. (i) Is the thin public morality of associative democracy thin enough? (ii) Conversely, is it strong enough? (iii) Are the minimal rules of associational law set out by Hirst convincing? (iv) How does the voluntary character of all associations relate to ethno-national 'communities of fate'? (v) Is the weakness on inequality, characteristic of Hirst's associative democracy in general, not particularly pressing in the case of minorities? (vi) Is Hirst's hope that the fragmentising tendencies of associationalism can be met by his design plausible? (vii) Which institutions and policies would follow from his general outline of associative democracy for the incorporation of minorities?

Is the Public Morality of Associative Democracy Thin Enough?

Hirst hopes that the principles and institutional setting of associative democracy will stimulate the 'thin and procedural public morality' (1994: 56) required by extremely diversified societies and their divergent 'cultures' and 'conception[s] of the good life', specific to the cleavages of class, occupation, sex and gender, language, religion, ethnicity, and nationality, which cut across each other. Two questions, however, remain largely unaddressed. First, is this public morality really *thin enough*? Does Hirst make plausible that all remnants in the interpretation and application of seemingly universalist principles of 'human rights and constitutional standards' (1994: 56)[2] in favour of dominant (gender, linguistic, religious, ethnic, national, Eurocentric or 'western') majorities are critically challenged? And how this is done?[3] Second, how does the institutional setting of associative democracy contribute to such a critical scrutiny, for instance, not only by giving all minorities a voice, but also by empowering them and giving them institutional 'muscle'? The second question seems to be more critical given the fact that Hirst's associative democracy provides only limited opportunities to challenge deep-seated inequalities (see below).

Is the Thin Public Morality of Associative Democracy Strong Enough?

Hirst clearly hopes that the 'thin' public morality is also 'strong', that it is, as he puts it:

> capable of generalizing strong common support. As the glue that holds a voluntaristic society together, it need not be thick, just strong. People are capable of a strong common identification with human rights and constitutional standards, accepting that these are the core of a civilized society. The view that liberal or associationalist societies are weaker than those with a common and thickly prescriptive morality is largely unjustified. (1994: 56f.)

Most Rawlsian political liberals as well as most Habermasian procedural democrats would, I guess, also easily tend to agree. Three critical reservations should be discussed. First, from a moral perspective, it may be that this version of public morality is needlessly thin, based as it is on a 'hands-off' view of 'justice as fairness' which treats people 'abstractly, taking into account only generic human interests ... rather than particular identities and communities' (Carens 1997: 814). Universalist morality does not prohibit 'justice as evenhandedness' which assumes 'that to treat people fairly, we must regard them concretely, with as much knowledge as we can obtain about who they are and what they care about' (Carens 1997: 814f.).[4] Second, the contested issues of how much and which kind of social 'cohesion' or 'stability' are required in modern societies, as well as the question of how much and which kind of political unity is required in modern states with liberal-democratic constitutions are not addressed.[5] The project of associative democracy wins plausibility if common prejudices are criticised which assume too much stability and unity (and, of course, stability and unity of the wrong kind) in most situations. Third, Hirst does not discuss how much loyalty and commitment is required in which situations.[6] Generalised answers to the second and third questions may be impossible and more theoretical and empirical work is needed to achieve plausible indications for specific institutional contexts, conjunctures and policy aims. Particularly pressing is the problem that projects of more radical change, such as associative democracy or a more egalitarian redistribution, may need much more commitment and loyalty than 'politics as usual'. Hirst himself does not spell out how to create and develop enough commitment to get the project of associative democracy started and going.[7]

Minimal Rules of Associational Law: Liberal Congruence or Group Autonomy?

The state in associative democracy has to be thin, but also strong. Apart from peace-keeping, the guarantee of the rights of individuals and public finance, its main task is to provide a 'common framework of regulatory rules'. 'Framework legislation' has to achieve two aims: to preserve the freedoms of individuals inside associations and to prevent harm to others. Four (traditional liberal-democratic) minimal rules of associational law are designed to give an institutional translation to these normative goals: (i) right to exit; (ii) democratic self-government (one (wo)man, one vote); (iii) accountability (annual publication of audit accounts); and (iv) if associations want public finance, then stricter measures of public regulation and scrutiny can be applied (Hirst 1994: 56ff).

Four critical remarks need to be made here. First, Hirst hopes that a certain delegation of legislative sovereignty to associations in combination with consociational standard setting (1994: 176) will 'permit the *reduction* of the extent and *complexity of the laws* and regulations of the central power ... The result might be that laws might once again become almost comprehensible to the citizen, rather than filling kilometers of shelf-space.' (Hirst 1994: 67f.) Experience with 'deregulation' shows that, contrary to all promises, neo-liberal deregulation has not been accompanied by 'less' law and it is not directly plausible why associative deregulation would be different.

Second, *exit rights*, important as they are, have to be complemented by *actual exit options* and this is already difficult enough for (unskilled) workers and other disadvantaged groups in formally free organisations.[8] For many ascriptive groups there are no exit options available and exit from ethnic and national organisations is not only very costly, but greatly inhibited by social pressure (ostracism often means social death and voluntary exit amounts to rebirth).

Third, guaranteeing considerable *autonomy* to associations on the one hand, and requiring *internal democracy* and the guarantee of *individual rights inside associations* on the other hand, are claims which cannot be easily reconciled. The strain between sovereignty of states in their 'internal affairs' and democracy and human rights is well known. Hirst clearly recognises that individual autonomy and group autonomy are conflicting aims inside states as well. As Hirst himself states (1994: 201), 'Associationalism does raise some acute dilemmas in that the desire to allow the maximum democratic self-governance to associations, and the desire to preserve the rights of individuals, will often come into conflict.'[9] But he does not discuss the two obvious dangers implied in any necessary balance of 'pluralism' and 'freedom and equality': (i) a 'strict', 'modern', 'individualist' interpretation of core human rights and the requirement of internal democracy, proposed by defenders of 'liberal democratic congruency' (Rosenblum 1998: Ch.2), does not leave much from the praised autonomy of particularly those groups and associations whose core values and practices may deeply contradict such interpretations of individuality and autonomy; and (ii) stressing autonomy in internal affairs and paying only lip service to 'freedom and democracy' undermines the minimal moral core Hirst wants to see guaranteed. How a sensible, context- and group-specific balance might be achieved is not discussed by Hirst.[10]

Fourth, problems of effective *accountability* (and of more exacting, critical public scrutiny of associations by the state in cases of state funding) are not taken seriously enough by Hirst. Hotly debated examples from Muslim schools in the Netherlands show how demanding the task of educational inspection of minimal standards is in all cases where one cannot place trust upon cooperation and control inside associations. Theoretical considerations as well as empirical evidence (work or environmental inspection) demonstrate that effective external control, which is always either *ex ante* or *ex post facto* control, thrives on information, qualification and the time of insiders (control *in actu*).

Voluntary Associations and 'Communities of Fate'

Hirst's design of 'societal' associative democracy underlines the *voluntary* character of all associations and the crafting of associations *'from below'*. In his view, 'all associations should be communities of choice, not of fate' (Hirst 1994: 51, 201f). With regard to ascriptive groups and associations generally, and ethnic and national 'communities' in particular, this claim seems not realistic for two reasons. First, if one conceptualises ethnic and national groups in terms of a more or less encompassing 'societal culture',[11] it is plain that one cannot choose these contexts of choice. One is born into them and raised in them. Second, many ascriptive groups are 'existential communities' or 'communities of fate' (Hirst 1994: 52f). If one distinguishes more clearly between 'groups', 'communities' and 'associations',[12] it is evident that minorities which are negatively privileged on the basis of ascriptive criteria are, inevitably, 'exclusive groups' (Hirst 1994: 69). Even if individuals want to leave, it will be their experience that they are defined by others (external majorities, but also internal elites) as belonging to 'excluded' groups (Hirst 1994: 58; Bader 1995: 98ff; Eisenberg 1995: 20, 24, 171ff; Williams 1998: 15f). They may, however, resist joining or being free to leave 'associations'. Voluntariness and choice would then have to be clearly focused on 'associations' and organisations, not on 'groups' and 'communities'. But even the voluntariness of ethnic and national associations is ridden with paradoxes, as Hirst himself acknowledges:

> At the same time old and new foci of identity compete to bind individuals' choice of communities of association – religion, language, lifestyle, gender and ethnicity. For those left at the bottom, these foci of identity may appear as classes used to, as communities of fate and resistance. For others, however traditional and communitarian they may claim to be, old and new identities are re-shaped to be sources of social solidarity around *chosen* standards. (1994: 66.)

In situations of severe, structural inequalities and from a perspective of organisation and mobilisation of resources, the freedom for members of ethnic underclasses not to join or to leave ethnic or national organisations ironically contributes to strengthening the power of dominant majorities.[13]

Inequalities and Minorities

Contexts of inequality also limit voluntariness and choice in another regard. Generally, Hirst emphasises that associations in associative democracy should be built up 'from below' and criticises Cohen and

Rogers for the role the state has to play in the crafting of associations (Hirst 1994: 37ff; 1997). His project of associative democracy is, admittedly, less egalitarian than the version advocated by Cohen and Rogers. It is also less egalitarian than my own balancing of standards of rough, complex equality with requirements of diversity.[14] That Hirst is 'weak on equality' has particularly serious consequences for ethnic underclasses and oppressed and exploited national minorities. It is only fair to state that he recognises the general problem. As Hirst himself puts it, 'The resources to form and sustain associations are far from equally distributed' (1994: 39) and this includes the threat that:

> associationalism is actually a society that favours the self-interested, the rich and the resourceful. It will favour them because they can make most use of the principle of voluntary association, and in such a society the state will be far weaker than in a collectivistic one. This means that the ideas of a rich culture of associations, of evening up disparities in power and wealth through associations ... are just naive. (Hirst 1994: 61.)

Hirst has proposed the following remedies: (i) associationalism does not prevent altruistic efforts, 'but they do not prevent efforts to construct or to rebuild means of campaigning on behalf of the poor, the excluded and the unpopular causes' (1994: 39); (ii) if one does not trust to altruism, he assumes 'the taxation system and the system of public funding of associations ... is already in place' (1994: 61), evading all paradoxes of strategy and transformation; and (iii) his associationalist system 'will favour the well-educated middle classes with ... the skill to work the self-governing components of the system. The system would exclude the poor and unskilled by the complexity of choices required. Actually, by giving the power of exit, the system would empower the poor to a considerable degree, and one that did not require them to participate extensively in the democratic machinery of an association.' (1994: 196.) These few remedies, however, cannot convince. In particular, they do nothing to alleviate the plight of ethnic underclasses: they do not facilitate the building of their associations and organisations nor do they empower them in any conceivable way. One looks in vain for ethnic affirmative action measures and the crucial role of the state (among other collective actors).[15] Policies of egalitarian multiculturalism have to combine egalitarian policies with regard to economic, social, political and legal opportunities with pluralist policies regarding culture.

Associationalism and the Fragmentation of Polities

Hirst responds to the objection that associative democracy would inevitably fragment polities 'into competing existential communities' (1994: 53). Both liberals and republicans see 'rent-seeking conspiracies', 'antagonistic pluralism' (Hirst 1994: 63, 65) and, eventually, the 'Ottomanization of America' or the 'virtual recreation of the Millets system in the Ottoman Empire in which plural and semi-self-regulating communities co-existed side by side, with very different rules and standards' (Hirst 1994: 66). In the USA, 'associationalism is a cure that is worse than the disease, it just endorses an entirely negative pluralism and permits groups to opt out of a common political culture' (Hirst 1994: 67; Rosenblum 1998; Waldron 2000). In his 'answer to Ottomanization', Hirst tries, on the contrary, to present associationalism as 'the only clear way – in the absence of enforced common standards – to make such pluralism a going concern' (1994: 67). Because I share his hope that 'the combination of a reduction in powerlessness in the control of one's own affairs and the removal of the fear of being at the mercy of hostile moral legislators may well promote more widespread feelings of security on the part of citizens, and a consequent lessening of hostility toward others'[16] (Hirst 1994: 69), I want to raise four sobering questions.

First, contrary to Hirst, I think there are more morally permissible institutional options, including the option of a relationally neutral, unitary republic, and that the choice of options depends crucially on the given institutional context and the conjunctural situation.[17] Second, Hirst's version of associative democracy does not do enough to reduce the powerlessness of negatively privileged groups in general, and of ethnic underclasses and national minorities in particular, and if it was to, it would reactively stimulate the 'fears' of majorities. Third, his separation of 'egalitarian' policies from 'pluralist' policies of multiculturalism has its price: his version of associative democracy does nothing against the tendency, in these situations, for groups to get 'ethnicised', for the development of 'religious' fundamentalism to spill over into politics,[18] and for groups to get even more 'totalising' features. Fourth, his hope, shared by all traditional political pluralists, that 'overlapping' cleavages, loyalties, commitments and identities (Hirst 1994: 66ff) can offer effective remedies against the threatening particularisation of a common political culture is in all such cases completely illusionary.

Which Institutions and Policies?

More or less formalised integration of ethno-national associations and organisations into decision-making and implementation is the grain of institutional pluralism. It remains astonishing that Hirst has not much to say about this issue. Which associations and organisations of which religious, ethnic, and national minorities? In which policy fields? What types of multi-ethnic councils with which powers? What would be their relative influence and say in 'framework legislation', in 'consociational standard setting' or in implementation, inspection and control? Paul Hirst's associative democracy, like most other proposals, remains institutionally fatally underdetermined both in general and with regard to specific countries and policy fields.

In order to exemplify these problems, I want briefly to discuss in the space of five major points what associative democracy, according to Hirst, means in education. First, it is plain that the basic principles of Hirst's 'ethic of freedom', that is, *individual autonomy* and *freedom of choice*, in a non-trivial sense, are modern, non-neutral conceptions. Education to autonomy is not only a difficult endeavour in general (Flathman 1996), it also creates specific problems for associative democracy in all cases in which ethnic or religious communities, which should be granted wide autonomy and self-government, do not interpret or evaluate education and individual autonomy in the same or similar ways. Hirst clearly recognises how acute this problem is when suggesting that associative democracy differs from, as he expresses it:

> the passionate commitment by liberals, democratic republicans and socialists that there be a common educational system in which, as far as possible, all citizens participate, that it should be secular and that it should promote common citizenship. These are worthy aims and it would be wholly wrong to brush them aside. An associationalist system *must* be more culturally and socially pluralistic than this republican model would desire; it will allow explicitly religious and other value-centred forms of education to receive public money. It creates fundamental problems about the curriculum. Can Torah schools be permitted, where children receive only a traditional Jewish education? Should Christian fundamentalist sects be allowed to teach 'creation science' with public money? These are not easy questions, nor are they confined to an associationalist Commonwealth... Associationalism would sharpen them acutely, however, since it seeks democratization through social self-governance. (1994: 201.)

Two combined principles of associative democracy would, according to Hirst, provide 'a way out of this morass'. The first is that:

> associations are voluntary ... they must be communities of *choice*, not of fate. Citizens must be at least in principle able to be informed enough to choose for themselves between different options and individuated enough to be able to choose. Education in blind conformity to given community standards thus violates the first principle of an associationalist society, that its communities must be voluntary. They will have different values; they will make demands on the loyalty of their members, but ultimately they must let them go if their members choose. (Hirst 1994: 201f.)

As Hirst (1994: 202) states, the second:

> fundamental principle to which associationalists and liberals together must adhere is that adult citizens do not own their children, they do not own their future lives as social beings. The public power has no interests, either in preventing the formation of identity or in peddling a multicultural pluralist mush as a substitute for religion and culture, but it does have an interest in ensuring individuation. That means the public power has the right to determine elements of the core curriculum in schools, to insist that schools in receipt of public funds conform to certain standards, and, in the last instance, to remove children from their parents.[19]

Many examples from education by religious, ethnic or national minorities stimulate critical questions, among them the following.

1. They 'are' not really 'voluntary' communities of 'choice'. Neither children nor, normally, adults 'join' freely, and only for adults does it make sense to say that they are (in principle though not in practice) free to leave (see Eisenberg 1995).

2. How is it possible to convince the Amish or the members of the fundamentalist Presbyterian Church of America[20] of the relative neutrality and fairness of the interest of public power to ensure individuation?

3. Should public power in associative democracy enforce exactly the same length of schooling upon the Amish, who clearly think very differently about educating their kids?

4. What does it mean for the curriculum of Amish schools in associative democracy that their kids should be educated to be 'informed enough to choose for themselves between the different options and individuated enough to be able to choose'? Are the Amish and others included, and if so in what way, in consociational standard setting when it comes to determining the 'elements of the core curriculum'?

5. How is control to be exercised?

6. How will 'social stewardship' be institutionalised? (Should there be a '*Raad voor de kinderbescherming*'(governmental agency for the protection of children)? With what powers? How will this be controlled?)

Of course, there are no easy answers to these questions. Obviously, it remains open how Hirst would respond to them. To me it is clear that they cannot be answered in a general way and context-sensitive answers depend on the history and specific cultural and educational practices of the communities in question, on the degree of their incorporation, on the specificities of the institutional arrangements of the educational system of a state, and so on.

The second major point is that the general weakness regarding equality of Hirst's associative democracy can also clearly be seen in education. Hirst's associational educational design either reproduces existing *inequalities* of resources, organisation and mobilisation between groups in the associational schools or would even strengthen them. I cannot see any institutional mechanism or policy proposal in order to reduce them. Associative democracy is vulnerable to traditional and republican challenges against all sorts of 'private' schools and falls far short even compared with existing practices in most European states who all try, one way or the other, to address inequalities in the educational system as well as the structural inequalities of educational outcomes.[21]

Third, the crucial question of how effectively to *control* minimal standards to which all schools (whether publicly funded or not) have to conform is not even mentioned. Fourth, concerns about *thresholds* (Hirst 1994: 196f)[22] and about the *practicability* of his flexible and fluctuating system of service provision (based on 'consumer choice' and a voucher system) are mentioned, but Hirst does not do much to alleviate the serious doubts of opponents of such a design.

Fifth, I guess that educational state policy (on different levels) would mainly consist in minimal standard setting, in public funding and in public inspection and control. It remains unclear what role, if any, the different (secular, religious, ethnic and national) 'communities' could and should play. Should there be some sort of educational advisory commission composed of the different groups according to their relative strength in the system of providing education? With what powers? It remains unclear how public standard setting would relate to 'relative autonomous' consociational standard setting in the field. It remains unclear what role, if any, existing or new representative boards of education would play in collective decision-making about the distribution of the state budget in the educational field or among different policy fields. In short, the design of educational institutions above the level of the schools as direct providers is seriously underdetermined. If Hirst expects all the advantages of cooperative competition in this regard, one would want to know how this could work. Two sobering experiences make these questions more pressing. Different forms of neo-liberal 'marketisation' stimulate the following questions: why we should be able to avoid them in associative democracy and, if so, how? At the same time, experiences with institutionally pluralist systems of education, such as the Dutch pillarised system, show that they are a mixed blessing reproducing their own rigidities and irrationalities.

Conclusion

Sober sociological criticism should remind us (that is, political philosophers and 'designers' of institutional alternatives) to study the realistic limitations more seriously instead of repeating our normative hopes.[23] Hirst's design of associative democracy, evaluated from the perspective of ethnic and national minorities, particularly from the perspective of entrenched underclasses, lacks any effective institutional mechanism or policy to challenge structural inequalities across the board. Instead of a sensible balance between rough, complex equality and pluralism, it discounts equality. Seen from the perspective of 'deeply different' cultures, it shows some uncritical remnants of 'unreconstructed liberalism'.

Hirst praises his version of associative democracy as a fairly general and 'coherent model to guide reform initiatives across specific organizations and localities' (1997: 17) and fields. It is difficult to find an appropriate level of generality and specification of institutional detail, an appropriate degree of institutional concreteness, in order to prevent two dangers: the danger of institutionally underdetermined principles and the danger of detailed blueprints (Mathews 1989: 14; Wright 1995: xi–xii; Cooke & Morgan 1998: 16f, 212). My evaluation of his proposals to incorporate minorities shows that his associative democracy suffers from both problems. Associative democracy would gain from a more detailed, critical discussion of basic principles such as individual autonomy, freedom of choice, and, obviously, from more detailed institutional and policy proposals. If it turns out to be impossible to give more detailed accounts of what associative democracy means for the educational system in general, we should choose the strategy that spells that out for specific cases. If a broader set of institutional options is morally permissible,[24] we can fill the gap of prudential and realist arguments only if we include detailed information about institutional histories and contexts, about specific groups and specific situations in political deliberation. In order to convince specific publics of the superiority of principles and designs of associative democracy we need more cases.

NOTES

1. From now on I speak of 'minorities', dropping the adjectives 'religious', 'ethnic' and 'national'.
2. See my critical remarks on Habermas in Bader (1997: 803f). See Hoekema in this volume.
3. See Bader (1997). Hirst often refers to 'certain common core standards' (1994: 67, 68) as if they would be unproblematically given without clearly explicating these standards. For criticism of this, see Bielefeldt (1998) and Carens (2000). Which 'human rights'? Which interpretations of these rights? How are they to be interpreted, given the fact that they themselves often conflict and that there is much strain between recognising crucial civil rights, democratic political rights and, at the same time, as wide an autonomy for culturally diverse groups as possible (see below)?
4. See more extensively the 'Introduction' and the chapter on Michael Walzer in Carens (1999). See Bader (2001).
5. See Bader (1999d) and also Nancy Rosenblum (1998: 19, 36).
6. See Bader (1999e).
7. See Bader in this volume for transformational and strategic paradoxes. Hirst's emphasis on democratic incrementalism, sympathetic as it is, does not solve the problem. In my view, more than just a minimalist liberal state and associationalism as a kind of 'ferry boat' (the metaphor used by Hirst during the Amsterdam workshop) for all possible interests and causes is needed, otherwise existing Dutch associationalism, for instance, would already live up to his concept. Too much 'liberal-democratic expectancy' may loom in the background.
8. See Iris Young, Melissa Williams, Ayelet Shachar and others for feminist criticism of the myopic libertarian focus on exit rights only, instead of real exit options. Paul Hirst seems to expect that 'exit' is more effective and has to do more work than 'voice' and 'participation' emphasised by republican and radical democracy

(workshop in Amsterdam). Real exit options, then, would become even more important.

9. Hirst also recognises that this dilemma faced by liberalism in general is sharpened acutely by associationalism (1994: 201). Obviously, this dilemma is even harder in cases of theocratic associations (see Swaine (1999) and Stoltenberg (1993)) and explicitly anti-liberal associations (see, for many examples, Rosenblum (1998)). First nations, indigenous peoples or aboriginals are clearly the hardest cases (see Hoekema in this volume). Though the basic tension in all these cases may be the same, the solutions may be very different.

10. See many good examples in Carens (2000). See also Bader (1997; 1998b: 200–202; 1999f). See Saharso (1998) for a sensible treatment of individual autonomy in the case of Hindustani women. See Ayelet Shachar (1998) and Oonagh Reitman (1998). Hirst seems to join sides with more 'unreconstructed liberals' such as Richards and liberal feminists such as Suzan Okin and Martha Nussbaum.

11. See Kymlicka (1995; 1997); see critical remarks by Carens (2000: Ch.3). See Bader (1999g) and more generally Bader (1995: 52–62).

12. See Rosenbaum's critical remarks (1998: 343ff).

13. For my treatment of this problem in the women's movement, see Bader (1984; 1991: 125ff). For similar strategic dilemmas in the case of religious and ethnic minorities, see Bader (1999f; 1999g) Horowitz (1985: 298, 324ff, 344, 353f).

14. See Bader (1998b: 189–92).

15. See Bader (1998a) and Williams (1998). Cohen and Rogers take this problem more seriously.

16. 'That way is to reduce inter-group antagonism by the acceptance of a substantial measure of self-regulation, at the price of mutual tolerance. No group could impose its vision on all, most groups could regulate themselves.' (Hirst 1994: 67.)

17. See Bader (1998b: 205 (Figure 2)) and Walzer (1997). See in more detail: Bader (2001a).

18. See Bader (1999f).

19. See Hirst (1994: 58): 'Children are, until some point in their lives, both highly impressionable and not fully capable of making an informed choice. If the principle of choice is to have any force then, children must be educated to be informed that choices are possible, and they cannot be forced to commit themselves to some course of action that will bind them for life – parents and the communities they join do not own their children, they have a conditional social stewardship of them and this gives the public power the right to set minimum educational standards, to enforce certain items on the curriculum, to prevent physical and mental abuse, and to remove children from their parents if needs be.'

20. See Stoltenberg (1993) for the famous case of *Mozert v. Hawkins County Board of Education*.

21. See Fase (1994) and, for a short summary, Bader (1998b: 195ff). All western European states have developed affirmative action programmes with a focus on improving the competencies of students and schools to reduce ethnic inequalities. Hirst could easily do something similar, for example, by adding an additional percentage to the vouchers for ethnic minority students, but he does not even consider that.

22. Compare recent discussions in the Netherlands about different methods to calculate minimal thresholds for allowances to open an Islamic 'secondary school' in Rotterdam, and for it to receive the usual public funding.

23. The words 'should', 'must' and 'cannot' are to be found too often in Hirst's treatment. For instance, see Hirst (1994: 201f).

24. This is the common core of all 'contextualised theories of morality'.

REFERENCES

Bader, V.M. 1984. 'Vrouwelijkheid, vrouwenonderdrukking en "vertooganalyses"'. *Tijdschrift voor Vrouwenstudies 20*, 5/4, 471–88.

1991. *Kollektives Handeln*. Opladen: Leske + Budrich.

1995. *Rassismus, Ethnizität, Bürgerschaft*. Münster: Westfälisches Dampfboot.

1997. 'The cultural conditions of trans-national citizenship'. *Political Theory*, 25/6, December, 771–813.

1998a. 'Dilemmas of ethnic affirmative action. Benign state-neutrality or relational ethnic neutrality'. *Citizenship Studies*, 2/3, 435–73.

1998b. 'Egalitarian multiculturalism: institutional separation and cultural pluralism'. Bauböck & Rundell 1998: Ch.7, 185–222.

1999a. 'For love of country'. *Political Theory*, 27/3, June, 379–97.

1999b. 'Religious pluralism. Secularism or priority for democracy?' *Political Theory*, 27/5, October, 597–633.

1999c. 'Citizenship of the European Union. Human rights, rights of citizens of the union and of member states'. *Ratio Juris*, 12/2, June, 153–81.

1999d. 'Unity and stability in modern societies and in recent political philosophy'. Harskamp & Musschenga 1999.

1999e. 'Institutions, culture and identity of trans-national citizenship: how much integration and "communal spirit" is needed?' Crouch & Eder 1999.

1999f. 'How to institutionalize religious pluralism?' Unpublished manuscript.

1999g. 'Culture, community, identity. Contesting constructivism'. Unpublished manuscript.

2001. 'Immigration'. (forthcoming) Caney, S. & P. Lehning, *International Distributive Justice*. London: RKP.

2001a. 'Democratic institutional pluralism and cultural diversity'. (forthcoming) Juteau, D. & C. Harzig, eds. *The Social Construction of Diversity*. Oxford: Berghahn.

Bauböck, R. & J. Rundell, eds. 1998. *Blurred Boundaries*. Aldershot: Ashgate.

Bielefeldt, H. 1998. *Philosophie der Menschenrechte. Grundlagen eines weltweiten Freiheitsethos*. Darmstadt: Wissenschaftliche Buchgesellschaft.

Carens, J. 1997. 'Two conceptions of fairness: a response to Veit Bader'. *Political Theory*, 25/6, 814–20.

2000. *Culture, Citizenship, and Community*. Oxford: OUP.

Cooke, P. & K. Morgan. 1998. *The Associational Economy*. Oxford: OUP.

Crouch, C. & K. Eder, eds. 1999. *Citizenship, Markets, and the State*. Oxford: OUP.

Eisenberg, A. 1995. *Reconstructing Political Pluralism*. Albany: State University of New York Press.

Fase, W. 1994. *Ethnic Divisions in Western European Education*. Münster, New York: Waxmann.

Flathman, R. 1996. 'Liberal versus civic, republican, democratic, and other vocational educations'. *Political Theory*, 24/1, 4–32.

Harskamp, A. v. & A.A. Musschenga, eds. 1999. *The Many Faces of Individualism*. Leuven: Peeters.

Hirst, P. 1994. *Associative Democracy*. London: Polity Press.

1997. *From Statism to Pluralism*. London: UCL Press.

Horowitz, D. 1985. *Ethnic Groups in Conflict*. Berkeley: University of California Press..

Kymlicka, W. 1995. *Multicultural Citizenship*. Oxford: OUP.

1997. *States, Nations, and Cultures*. Assen: van Gorcum.

Norman W., eds. 1998. *Citizenship in Diverse Societies*. Oxford: OUP.

Mathews, J. 1989. *The Age of Democracy*. Oxford: OUP.

Nussbaum, M. 1997. 'Religion and women's rights'. Weithman 1998: 93–137.

Okin, S. 1997. 'Is multiculturalism bad for women?' *Boston Review*, winter 1997.

Reitman, O. 1998. *Cultural Accommodation in Family Law*. ECPR paper. Warwick.

Richards, D.A. 1986. *Toleration and the Constitution*. New York, Oxford: OUP.

Rosenblum, N. 1998. *Membership and Morality*. Princeton: Princeton University Press.

Saharso, S. 1998. 'Female autonomy and cultural imperative: two hearts beating together'. Kymlicka & Norman 1998.

Shachar, A. 1998. 'Group identity and women's rights in family law'. *Journal of Political Philosophy*, 6/3, 285–305.

Stoltenberg, N. 1993. 'He drew a circle that shut me out'. *Harvard Law Review*, 106, 581–667.

Swaine, L. 1999. 'How ought liberal democracies to treat theocratic communities?' Unpublished manuscript.

Vertovec, S. 1999. 'Minority associations, networks and public policies'. *Journal of Ethnic and Migration Studies*, 25/1, 21–42.

Waldron, J. 2000. 'Cultural identity and civic responsibility'. Unpublished manuscript.

Walzer, M. 1997. *On Toleration*. New Haven, London: Yale University Press.

Weithman, P., ed. 1997. *Religion and Contemporary Liberalism*. Notre Dame, IN: University of Notre Dame Press.

Williams, M. 1998. *Voice, Trust, and Memory. Marginalized Groups and the Failings of Liberal Representation*. Princeton: Princeton University Press.

Wright, E.O. 1995. 'Introduction'. *Associations and Democracy*. London, New York: Verso.

Abstracts

Can Associationalism Come Back?
PAUL HIRST

Associationalism developed as a third way between collectivist socialism and capitalistic individualism. After a period of political popularity in the first decades of the last century it virtually disappeared, but re-emerged in response to changed conditions in the 1980s. Can this new revival provide a new doctrine of social reform and democratic accountability? Conventional institutions of representative democracy now find it harder to regulate social life and to scrutinise public services. The reason for this is that both the public and the private sectors have ceased to be effectively controlled by hierarchical management. Activities have become complex, practices differentiated and flexible, and change both rapid and multi-directional. This makes standardised and remote control mechanisms unable to cope. The result is a complex organisational society that is impossible to control democratically without the extensive decentralisation of accountability. This can best be promoted through the control of services by self-governing voluntary associations. Examples of such governance and the need for it are given in such areas as pensions provision and welfare services.

Problems and Prospects of Associative Democracy:
Cohen and Rogers Revisited
VEIT BADER

This essay tries to re-open the lively debate of the early 1990s about Cohen and Roger's variety of associative democracy pointing out that most controversial issues have not been adequately addressed by Cohen and Rogers themselves nor by other advocates of associative democracy. Associative democracy can be defended against generalised moral challenges that it undermines the sovereignty of the people, that the system of organised interest-representation is undemocratic, that it is weak on political equality and even weaker on distributive equality and that it would be prone to the mischief of faction. Such a defence requires fair evaluations instead of the widespread comparison of ideal models with actual muddle. It should, however, not make advocates of associative democracy self-confident and blind towards the largely unresolved theoretical and practical problems, the many difficult trade-offs and the difficult arts of balancing and designing institutions and policies. This perhaps is even more true regarding the many prudential and realist objections. To work out realist utopias for different countries or societal fields is still the major challenge confronting political theorists.

Associo-Deliberative Democracy and Qualitative Participation
PIOTR PERCZYNSKI

We can distinguish two forms of democratic citizen participation, one qualitative, which steers into competent decision-making, and one quantitative, which values a high-turn out on simple 'yes' or 'no' voting. In this context, two democratic models compatible with the modern representative (parliamentary, territorial, etc.) democracy are presented and analysed: associative democracy and deliberative democracy. These two models can coexist particularly well, when the former is understood as a system that provides the democratic structure, without describing what decision procedures or mechanisms should be applied, while the latter is perceived as a democratic mechanism without a fixed system to which to apply it. It is shown how deliberative democracy and associative democracy can strengthen each other, especially inside groups. In addition, a possible starting point is suggested for the use of deliberation on a higher, inter-associational level.

Association and Deliberation in Risk Society:
Two Faces of Ecological Democracy
WOUTER ACHTERBERG

In this article I argue that central tendencies in late modern society, conceived as a risk society (Beck), make it desirable to extend and enhance democracy beyond the level reached in present-day liberal democracies. Particularly the environmental problematic and the effort to achieve sustainable development as the (nationally and internationally) accepted way to reduce and contain it, make it unavoidable, prudentially and morally, to aim at what Beck has called 'ecological democracy'. Two models that seem appropriate to flesh out the desired shift to ecological democracy are discussed. These are the proposal to give secondary associations a substantial part in economic and social government (associative democracy) and the proposal to extend the possibilities for public deliberation in formal and informal political contexts (deliberative democracy). Having argued that there are reasons to enhance and broaden liberal democracy by associative and deliberative means, the question of their interrelationship naturally arises. In answer to this question I try to make plausible the presumption that both extensions of liberal democracy are needed because they cannot, in isolation from each other, deliver the goods.

Associationalism for 150 Years and Still Alive and Kicking:
Some Reflections on Danish Civil Society
LARS BO KASPERSEN and LAILA OTTESEN

The purpose of the article is twofold: first we shall demonstrate that associationalism is not an old fashioned idea or pure utopia. Associationalism is a model of governance with a long tradition in Danish society. It contributes to a strengthening of the democratic aspect in education, social and cultural life and other welfare areas. The second purpose concerns the state-civil society relationship. By examining some associational features of the Danish society we seek to point out that civil society did not emerge from nothing. Civil society is not an autonomous sphere clearly separated from the state, on the contrary, it is a sphere of social life dependent on the state. The state is the precondition of the development of civil society.

Globalisation and Multilevel Governance in Europe: Realist Criteria for Institutional Design, or How Pessimistic Should One Be?
EWALD ENGELEN

Although a myth, globalisation has proven to be an effective one. With this ideological construct economic and political elites have wrestled far-ranging concessions from labour movements, social democratic parties and other left-wing organisations. Critics of globalisation come in two shapes. According to the first it is business as usual. According to the second the social, political and economic condition has indeed changed beyond recognition. However this does not imply that each and every mode of economic governance has become obsolete. In this article I discuss three approaches to economic governance in the context of the European Union, those of Paul Hirst and Grahame Thompson, Wolfgang Streeck and Fritz Scharpf respectively. Lacking a description of the institutional logic to be able to identify constraints as well as possibilities Hirst and Thompson ultimately resort to a rather naive voluntarism. Streeck's and Scharpf's analysis, on the other hand, seem to introduce a certain degree of institutional determinism. The case of the European Work Councils as reconstructed by Wolfgang Streeck does fit into the deterministic mould. Scharpf's examples of multi-level problem-solving within a European setting, on the other hand, reveal that the logic inherent in the institutions of European decision-making is much more indeterminate than Streeck presupposes. The aim of this discussion is to come up with a set of realist criteria for institutional design in order to infuse Hirst and Thompson's moral cheerfulness with a healthy dose of sociological pessimism and *vice versa*.

Reflexive Governance and Indigenous Self-Rule: Lessons in Associative Democracy?
ANDRÉ J. HOEKEMA

Public-private inter-organisational networks in western public administration and new partnership relations between a state and the governments of indigenous peoples living on that state's territory, at first glance seem to be institutions of a vastly different nature. Moreover, they are emerging from widely different social backgrounds. Nevertheless, in this article they are discussed as cases of associative democracy in the making. They both tend towards empowerment of voluntary, or not so voluntary, associations, towards a sharing of power between states and elements of civil society. Although public-private partnership arrangements (also called: negotiating government) typically spring from functional problems (how to solve implementation and legitimation problems in western public administration) while forms of indigenous self-government spring answer the desire of a people (an encompassing community) to exert a form of (internal) sovereignty, problems of the conditions for the growth of a morale of trust to foster 'frame reflection' and serious dialogue can and will be discussed comparatively.

Associative Democracy and the Incorporation of Minorities: Critical Remarks on Paul Hirst's *Associative Democracy*
VEIT BADER

This article starts from the assumption that democratic institutional pluralism in general, associative democracy in particular, provides the best chances for morally legitimate and realistically feasible incorporation of religious, ethnic and national minorities. In order to achieve better answers to the many dilemmas confronting incorporation policies, Bader focuses on the following questions: Is the thin public morality of associative democracy strong enough to stimulate loyalty and commitment needed for political projects aiming at fairly radical societal and political transformations? Conversely, is it thin enough in a radically culturally diverse setting? How does Hirst try to resolve the tension inherent in all varieties of institutional pluralism between individual and collective autonomy? How does the voluntariness of associations, so much stressed by Hirst, relate to ethno-national communities of fate? Is the fact that Hirst's version of associative democracy is comparatively 'weak on equality' not particularly disturbing in the case of ethno-national under-classes? Is his hope that the fragmentating tendencies of associationalism could be met by his design plausible? Which institutions and policies follow from the general outline of associative democracy for the incorporation of minorities in the case of education? Finding convincing answers to these questions requires both theoretical clarification of policy dilemmas and comparative studies of different cases of pluralist incorporation.

Notes on Contributors

Wouter Achterberg is Senior Lecturer in the Department of Philosophy, Faculty of Humanities, at the University of Amsterdam. He also holds the chair of Humanistic Philosophy at Wageningen University. He specialises in ethics, political philosophy and environmental philosophy (particularly the ethical and political aspects). His most recent paper is entitled 'Environmental Justice and Global Democracy' (2001).

Veit Bader is Professor of Sociology and Social and Political Philosophy at the University of Amsterdam. In recent years his research has focused on inequalities and collective action, on varieties of capitalism and on normative issues of migration, particularly on first admission and on incorporation of ethno/religious and national minorities. He is the author of, among other works, *Kollektives Handein* (1991), *Rassismus, Ethnizität und Bürgerschaft* (1995) and *Citizenship and Exclusion* (1997).

Ewald Engelen is Post-doctoral Research Fellow at the Faculty of Humanities of the University of Amsterdam. He has published on economic sociology, neoliberalism, socialism, corporate governance, markets, democratic theory and citizenship. His current research project is on affirmative action, immigrant entrepreneurship and the labour market.

Paul Hirst is Professor of Social Theory at Birkbeck College, University of London and Academic Director of the London Consortium Graduate Programme in Humanities and Cultural Studies. He is the author of, among other works, *The Pluralist Theory of the State;*

Selected Writings of G.D.H. Cole, J.N. Figgis and H.J. Laski (1989), *Associative Democracy* (1994) and *From Statism to Pluralism* (1997).

André J. Hoekema is Professor of Sociology and Anthropology of Law at the Law Faculty of the University of Amsterdam. Together with Peter Oud, he is supervising a project called 'Images of Self-Rule', in which the experiences of indigenous peoples with systems of self-government are shown and compared. He co-organised (with Willem Assies) a workshop with Latin American experts *The Challenge of Diversity. Indigenous Peoples and the Reform of the State in Latin America* and co-edited (also with Willem Assies) the IWGIA Document No. 76, *Indigenous Peoples Experiences with Self-Government*. He supervised a series of empirical and conceptual multidisciplinary studies on negotiating governance in economically highly developed states.

Lars Bo Kaspersen is Associate Professor in the Department of Sociology at the University of Copenhagen where he teaches sociology, history and politics. He is currently working on the origin, development and transformation of the Danish welfare state, and on state formation in early modern Europe.

Laila Ottesen is Associate Research Professor in the Institute of Exercise and Sport Sciences at the University of Copenhagen where she teaches sociology and ethnology.

Piotr Perczynski is a post-doctoral researcher at the Department of Political Science, Leiden University and Assistant Professor at the Institute of Political Studies, Polish Academy of Sciences. He has published on liberalism, political pluralism, functionalism and citizenship, and is currently working on a research project on pluralistic citizenship and democracy in uniting Europe.

Index

CHESTER COLLEGE LIBRARY